home run

hank aaron

with dick schaap

foreword   ted williams

special essay   jerome holtzman

afterword   lonnie wheeler

with commemorative

observations by notable friends

TOTAL
SPORTS

new york

project editor   kenneth shouler

book designer   barbara marks

pictorial archivist   mark rucker

my life in pictures

Permissions appear on page 221.

A conscientious attempt has been made to contact proprietors of the rights in every image used in the book. If through inadvertence the publisher has failed to identify any holder of rights, forgiveness is requested and corrected information will be entered in future printings.

Total Sports is a trademark of Total Ltd. Petra

Published by Total Sports.
Distributed by Publishers Group West
Corporate Office
1700 Fourth Street
Berkeley, CA 94710

BOOK DESIGN BY BARBARA MARKS

Library of Congress Catalog Card Number:
99-60142

ISBN 1-892129-05-1

Printed in the United States of America

10 9 8 7 6 5 4 3 2 1

a load of people, enough to fill four team rosters, must be thanked for contributing to *Home Run: My Life in Pictures* by Hank Aaron. The book, published by Total Sports, commemorates the twenty-fifth anniversary of Aaron's 715th home run and joins in Major League Baseball's year-long celebration of that historic event.

First off, 80 celebrated individuals consented to give their personal views of their friend, Hank Aaron. They offered thoughtful, incisive, warm recollections about Hank's life, his career, and his mission. The reason for the easy, conversational tone of the book is that the interviews were conducted on the fly, without a scripted query-and-response format, and then transcribed. Many of the players, commissioners, owners, general managers, broadcasters—and one former President—thought that Hank Aaron has been vastly underappreciated, that his achievements in baseball have not been given due credit. To that end, we hope this book not only provides a thoughtful arrangement of their views but goes a long way toward enhancing this generation's perspective on Aaron's stellar career.

As the project's editor, I interviewed 75 of those whose opinions are expressed here and will always remember one 24-hour period in November, when I was fortunate enough to speak with Johnny Bench, Willie Mays, Joe Morgan, Ted Williams, and Frank Robinson. Forget interviews, I thought, why not start a Dream Team? Let's see, Morgan could lead off. Robby second, Ted third, Mays cleanup, Bench fifth . . . yeah, I'll take my chances with that top of the lineup. Of so many memorable observations, one keeps coming to mind. I can hear Denzel Washington saying, "Hank's career wasn't a sprint; it was a marathon. In 1954, who would have thought that Hank would be the one to break the record? Who knew? I tell you what, they know now."

Dick Schaap and Jerome Holtzman contributed sinew to the book, Ted Williams added class, and Lonnie Wheeler provided a final note of grace—telling us why Hank Aaron was the right one to break the record. In fact, grace—often under pressure—is what best describes the team that brought this sprawling raw manuscript, improbably, to its final form.

The classy design of the book's interior is as important to telling Hank's story as the text or the images, and for that, all credit to Barbara Marks, a consummate professional. Todd Radom gave us a truly memorable jacket design.

Donna Harris coordinated the entire project, handling with daily equanimity what would have broken a mere mortal. Alicia Berns contacted many of the players and celebrities and scheduled the interviews. Without her incredible diligence and proficiency early on, this book could not have been half as good as it is. John Thorn polished the copy and helped to push the project forward.

Major League Baseball, especially Don Hintze, Bill Henneberry, Kathleen Francis and Shirley Edwards, was unfailingly cooperative and inventive, and not only in the areas of marketing and sponsorship—they made the book better, too.

Baseball archivist Mark Rucker dug deep into his own formidable collection at Transcendental Graphics, and secured prizes from other outstanding collections. The National Baseball Library likewise opened their photo files to turn up many treasures for us; all our old friends there were as helpful as ever: Pat Kelly, Milo Stewart, Bill Burdick, Greg Harris, Bruce Markusen, Dan Bennett, Scott Mondore.

Photographer Stephen Green gave us a glorious portfolio of images showing Hank as he is today, just past his 65th birthday. Photographer Chris Hamilton's craft is on display as well. And of course Hank and Billye Aaron shared with us their personal scrapbooks. Susan Bailey was extraordinarily helpful on our visits to Atlanta.

A great team needs great strength in reserve, and our bench players each took star turns—Connie Neuhauser, Herb Fagen, Peter Haugen, Tom Dyja, F-stop Fitzgerald, David Pietrusza, Peggy Goddard, Chad Lawrence, Ann Sullivan, Bob Hueber, and Jed Thorn. So did our friends at Coral Graphics Services, Gene Stuttman and Jimmy Biedrzycki, who created the digital images and produced the jacket; and at World Color Book Services, Mike Linville, Kevin Rafferty, and Michelle Rothfarb, who printed the book.

And finally, a tip of the cap to Hank, whose book this truly is.

—KENNETH SHOULER

contents

foreword

by ted williams

Well, what do you think about when you say Hank Aaron? Seven hundred and fifty-five homers. Better than the Babe! More RBIs than Ruth too. More RBIs than *anyone*. More total bases than *anyone*. How did he do it? He HIT! When Henry Aaron got his pitch he *hit* it. He didn't foul it off. He didn't watch it go by. He hit it. Henry Aaron—*hitter*! My kind of guy.

Where do you start with Hank? I know where *I* started. I had just come back from Korea. I was playing in spring training in Sarasota, and because I was an older, more experienced player, I got to play the first three innings and then BOOM! they take me out. I went in and showered and came on out because I wanted to watch the rest of the game. In Sarasota there was a nice little field, and you had to go through a little dugout door and then sit on the bench. So I went out and just as I dove through the door, I hear WHACK!, and then the roar of the crowd—it was a small crowd but it was a helluva roar anyway—and one of my teammates said, "Did you see that guy hit that ball?" I didn't know who in the hell they were talking about—never heard of Hank Aaron before, I don't think—and he was rounding second. Boy did he hit that ball.

Aaron really wasn't very big then. He's a big guy now, but he was thin then and still growing, I guess. He looked great for sure, but he hadn't hit any home runs and nobody knew too much about him. Years later I became manager of the Washington Senators and we had a couple of young pitchers on our club. One of them—Joe Coleman—was starting and he had good stuff, but I had to tell him, in some situations stuff is not enough.

So anyway, Joe's starting this spring-training game and Hank Aaron is in the Braves' starting lineup. So I took Coleman aside and I said, "You know today you're going to pitch against a great hitter." And I said, "Here's the way I want you to pitch to him. I want you to throw a curveball, another curveball, another curveball, another curveball." Aaron finally grounded out to shortstop. Then I took him aside and said, "Now, the next time he gets up, you throw curveball, curveball." He did and he got two strikes real fast. And I had said, "When you get two strikes, I want you to throw the hardest, fastest, high fastball you can throw." And he did. The first one Aaron had seen. First time he had ever seen this guy. But he hit a ball that's still going on a line out of the ballpark. Boy, did he *hit* it! So we were convinced of one thing, he could hit a fastball, that's for damn sure. But he was a great hitter, period, and an all-around great player. No question about it.

He was more of a line drive hitter and if he got a ball 20 to 23 feet in the air and hit it good, he'd get it out. A lot of my home runs were big fly balls. Greenberg's homers were big high flies. So were Ruth's. Hank was more of a *line drive* home run hitter, but a great hitter all around, I think one of the greatest. The technique he had, and *all* great hitters have, is that they can hit a fastball high or low. You know, some pitchers get by with high fastballs, but the really outstanding hitters don't get beat on the high fastball. They might miss it one time, but when they hit it, it

Hank was more of a *line drive* home run hitter, but a great hitter all around, I think one of the greatest.

—Ted Williams

The young Hank Aaron, here wearing number 5, impressed Ted Williams with his hitting. Williams' homers were neck-craning fly balls. Aaron's were line drives.

was goodbye Charlie. That was my feeling about Joe DiMaggio, too.

How was Hank as a runner and fielder? He did everything great. He was plenty fast, a good baserunner, good defensive outfielder—a helluva ballplayer. I'd like someday to talk a little more hitting with him. No question about it, my admiration and respect for him are as high as you can get.

And you know something—he's *stayed* in the game. Now, I suspect a fellow with 755 home runs might not have to do that. Might be able to take it easy. Play a little golf. Hit some long ones with those wrists of his. But Hank Aaron has *stayed in the game,* kept working at it. He keeps giving *back to it.*

And he gives back to the community. Community, that's a two-dollar word for *people.* Hank Aaron cares about kids and people and cares about doing what he thinks is right. Maybe the average person doesn't know that about him. But it's true. You see, Hank Aaron works for people and causes just the way he played baseball—without a lot of noise. Then, before you know it, there's Hank stepping across home plate. Making a difference. Standing up for what he believes in.

Like I said before—Hank Aaron, he's my kind of a guy. And *Home Run* is my kind of book. ⚾

—TED WILLIAMS

by hank aaron with dick schaap

i just hit baseballs

> It is a little strange to me that the name "Hank Aaron" and the phrase "home run" should be linked together . . . I did not think of myself as a home-run hitter.

i am in awe of the great home-run hitters, the ones who are no longer with us. The Reverend Dr. Martin Luther King, for one. Jackie Robinson, for another.

Forget about Babe Ruth and Roger Maris. Forget about Mark McGwire, Sammy Sosa and Ken Griffey Jr. Forget about Hank Aaron.

King and Robinson. They're the real home-run hitters.

I know. I rode in the back of the buses in Birmingham in my home state of Alabama. And I remember my father telling me, when I was just ten or eleven years old, and in love with baseball, to forget about being a big-league player, there was no such thing as a colored big-league ballplayer.

Dr. King and Jackie Robinson, they changed my life. They helped me turn my dreams into reality. They helped millions of African-Americans turn their dreams into reality. Their courage and their wisdom were enormous. They were giants. They hit tape-measure home runs.

I just hit baseballs.

it is a little strange to me that the name "Hank Aaron" and the phrase "home run" should be linked together, as they are in the title of this book and in the minds of so many baseball fans, because for much of my career as a baseball player, I did not think of myself as a home-run hitter. I thought of myself, and my teammates thought of me, as a line-drive hitter, a contact hitter, a solid hitter, a man who was more likely to bat .400 than to hit a record-breaking number of

home runs, a man who was more likely to catch up to Ted Williams than to Babe Ruth.

For the first thirteen seasons of my major-league career, I was not the leading home-run hitter on my team, the Milwaukee Braves and then the Atlanta Braves. All through those thirteen years, our third baseman, Eddie Mathews, was ahead of me in home runs. In fact, a lot of people thought if anyone was going to break Babe Ruth's career record for home runs, it was going to be him. Eddie was two years and a few months older than me, and he had reached the big leagues two years ahead of me—two years in which he hit 72 home runs—but still, in our first twelve seasons as teammates, head to head, Eddie hit more home runs than I did. Not until 1966, our final season together, our first season in Atlanta, did I cut the margin between us to fewer than 72 home runs. Not until 1969, the year after Eddie wrapped up his Hall of Fame career in Detroit, did my lifetime major-league home-run total surpass his.

For thirteen years Eddie Mathews, sometimes batting behind me and sometimes in front of me in the Braves' order, took the pressure off me. Because of his power, I didn't feel that I *had* to hit home runs. Still, I did hit my share. In those thirteen years, Eddie and I hit 863 home runs, 442 for me, 421 for him, a record for a pair of teammates. In comparison, in the twelve seasons Babe Ruth and Lou Gehrig both wore Yankee uniforms, they hit 859 home runs between them. To be fair, Gehrig hardly played the first two years, and certainly, if he and the Babe had played a thirteenth season

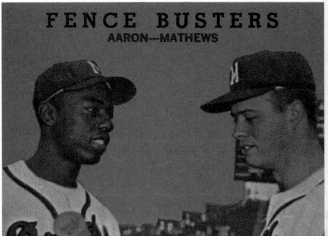

FENCE BUSTERS
AARON—MATHEWS

Hitting home runs like a metronome in the televised contest *Home Run Derby,* Aaron walked off with $30,000, nearly double his $17,000 salary in 1959.

together, Eddie and I would not have matched their total.

(In the National League, Willie Mays and Willie McCovey, both Hall of Famers, were teammates on the San Francisco Giants for thirteen seasons, the same as Eddie and me, and during that span combined for precisely 800 home runs. Another pair of Hall of Famers, Ernie Banks and Billy Williams, were teammates on the Chicago Cubs also for thirteen seasons, and during their years together produced 648 home runs. For their full careers, Banks and Williams wound up with 938, Mays and McCovey with 1181, Ruth and Gehrig with 1207, and Eddie and I with 1267. I'm kind of proud that among that eight-man Murderers Row, four of us were born in Alabama— Mays, McCovey, Williams and I—and each of the four except Mays grew up in Mobile. I guess that makes Mobile the undisputed home-run capital of the world.)

When Eddie Mathews left the Braves before the 1967 season—and even earlier, when his power was per-

ceptibly diminishing—I decided I had to become more of a power hitter, a home-run hitter. I consciously changed my swing. I concentrated on pulling the ball to left field. Until then, I was more of a straightaway hitter and a good percentage of my home runs, especially in my early years, went to right field. Of course, the move from Milwaukee's County Stadium to Atlanta Stadium, a much cozier park for home-run hitters, particularly right-handed home-run hitters, didn't hurt me, either.

(In a sense, I suppose I started thinking about concentrating on home runs back at the start of the 1960s, after I competed in a television event called *Home Run Derby.* In each installment of the show, two players went head-to-head to see which one would hit the most home runs in nine innings, before making twenty-seven outs. Any ball that went over the fence was a home run; any ball that didn't was an out. The loser was eliminated; the winner

For the first thirteen years of my major league career Eddie Mathews was ahead of me in home runs . . . a lot of people thought if anyone was going to break Babe Ruth's career record for home runs, it was going to be him.

I asked the Cincinnati front office to offer a moment of silence in memory of Dr. King. They didn't do it, but at least I tried to make the point that the legacy of Dr. King was every bit as important to me as the legacy of Babe Ruth.

defended his title in the next show. I hit more home runs and won more money than anyone else. I earned about $30,000, which was, at the time, roughly double my annual salary. I figured out pretty quickly that you didn't get paid that well for hitting singles.)

In my first thirteen seasons, playing with Eddie, I averaged 34 home runs a year. In the next seven seasons, I averaged 39 home runs a year. I seemed to grow stronger as I grew older. The last five years I was in my thirties, I averaged better than 40 home runs a season. I was, finally, a true slugger, a late-blooming slugger, a consistent slugger.

I never hit 50 home runs in a season, never more than 47, and the idea of hitting 70 never even occurred to me. Still, for twenty straight seasons, I never hit fewer than 20 home runs. Neither Babe Ruth nor Willie Mays nor anyone else had a streak even close to mine; Ruth hit 20 or more for sixteen consecutive years, and Mays fifteen.

By the time I turned forty, on February 5, 1974, I had hit 713 home runs. I

ALLTIME HOME RUN LEADERS

714

673

654

was one short of tying Babe Ruth's career record, two short of setting a new record.

a s I threatened Ruth's record, I was threatened, too, deluged with mail filled with hatred, with warnings that I would be killed and that my children would be kidnapped. I wished I had hit two more home runs in 1973. I wished I had gotten the record and the pressure out of the way. But I didn't (even though I hit 40 home runs and batted over .300), and I had to wait anxiously for six months till the start of the next season.

The manager of the Braves in the spring of 1974 was my old teammate, Eddie Mathews, the man who had himself once been considered the leading candidate to break Ruth's record. Eddie had averaged 37 home runs a year for the first nine years of his career and had hit more than 20 in each of his first fourteen years. But Eddie lived hard, and punished his body, and his playing career ended before he was 37 years old. Mine lasted beyond my 42nd birthday. One of the things I'm most proud of is that I never abused the talent that God gave me to play the game. Instead, I used it to the maximum.

Eddie could not have been more helpful, more supportive. We had always pulled for each other and pushed each other, and now he was clearly rooting for me to break the record he had once set his sights on. Many fans were rooting for me, too. I was getting thousands of letters a day, and most of them were positive. Some, however, were ugly.

Dear Nigger,

Everybody loved Babe Ruth. You will be the most hated man in this country if you break his career home run record.

Dear Nigger,

You black animal, I hope you never live long enough to hit more home runs than the great Babe Ruth.

Dear Henry Aaron,

I hope you get it between the eyes.

I had a bodyguard assigned to protect me during the spring of 1974, a man named Calvin Wardlaw, and I also had an army around me, an army of reporters, many of them from Latin America and from Japan. The Braves, at first, wanted me to sit out the season-opening series in Cincinnati, to save the record-tying and -breaking home runs for a homestand in Atlanta, but after a sanctimonious uproar from a flock of sportswriters who were self-proclaimed baseball purists, the Commissioner of Baseball, Bowie Kuhn, ordered the Braves to play me, whether I felt like it or not, in at least two of the three games against the Reds.

The opening game, the first of the major-league season, was on a Thursday—all the other openers were on Friday—and it happened to be the sixth anniversary of the assassination of Martin Luther King. I asked the Cincinnati front office to offer a moment of silence in memory of Dr. King. They didn't do it, but at least I tried to make the point that the legacy of Dr. King was every bit as important to me as the legacy of Babe Ruth. More important, really.

Opening Day was cold and damp, and Jack Billingham was the pitcher for

Several of Aaron's greatest home run hitters: Martin Luther King, Jackie Robinson and Frank Robinson, who in 1975 became baseball's first black manager.

the Reds. I came to bat in the first inning, with two men on and one out, and I knew Billingham would throw me sinking fast balls, trying to get me to hit into a double play. I was always a guess hitter, but, like most of my guesses, this one was an informed guess, based on my own history, and

Seven hundred and fifteen. And one of the very few that I actually saw go over the fence. I guess it caught my attention, too.

based on the pitcher's. I decided to wait for the sinker. I took the first four pitches, three balls and one strike. The next pitch came in low and fast and sinking, and with my first swing of the 1974 season, I hit the 714th home run of my career, just high enough and far enough to clear the fence.

I had caught up to Babe Ruth. I ran around the bases, not quite a sprint, but more than my usual trot. I touched home plate and was touched in turn by the reaction of the Cincinnati catcher, Johnny Bench, and all my teammates who had rushed out of the dugout to greet me. Everyone congratulated me. Everyone was happy. Gerald Ford, then the Vice President of the United States, came out on the field and shook my hand, and so did Commissioner Kuhn. Whether either or both of them was drawn to the park by the possibility of my hitting a home run or two, or by the traditional pageantry of the season's opening game, I was never certain.

After the game—I didn't hit another home run—I held a news conference, which gave me an opportunity to pay tribute again to Dr. King. Eddie Mathews had his own message for the media. He announced he was not going to play me in the next two games, on Saturday and Sunday. In response, the Commissioner announced the Braves had to play me in one of the two games. I knew Eddie didn't like the idea of anyone dictating his lineup to him, but I also believe he liked creating a little controversy, a distraction to take some of the spotlight, and some of the pressure, off me.

I sat out the second game, but Eddie, threatened with suspension, was forced to play me on Sunday.

I batted three times, struck out twice and grounded out. By then, we were comfortably ahead, and the Commissioner could not stop Eddie from taking me out of the game. Some people wondered if I had deliberately not hit a home run, which was both stupid and insulting. I had too much pride in my ability and too much respect for the integrity of the game to make an out on purpose. In retrospect, I'm glad I didn't break the record on the road, but it wasn't for any lack of effort.

We came home to play the Dodgers on Monday, April 8, 1974. It was Hank Aaron Night, and almost 54,000 people, a record crowd in Atlanta, turned out for the game. (Not every game during my march toward the record drew a capacity crowd. When I hit my 711th, in Atlanta, late in the 1973 season, only 1,362 people were in the stands. But the final game of that season attracted almost 40,000 spectators, and even though I failed to hit my 714th home run, when I trotted out to left field for the ninth inning, the fans rose and gave me a standing ovation that lasted five minutes.)

The crowd on Henry Aaron Night included Pearl Bailey, who had asked to sing "The Star-Spangled Banner"; Sammy Davis Jr., who didn't want to miss the moment; and Jimmy Carter, who was then the governor of Georgia. The Commissioner of Baseball was conspicuously absent. Bowie Kuhn was giving a speech to something called the Wahoo Club in Cleveland. I suppose he wouldn't exactly have gotten a standing ovation in Atlanta, not after demanding that I play the opening series in Cincinnati. The Commissioner sent Monte Irvin, the former New York

> I love baseball, always did and always will. I love the essence of the game, the contest between the pitcher and the hitter. I love the variety of skills that the game demands, arm strength and leg strength, the ability to run and throw and hit and think.

Giant who had once been a star in the Negro Leagues, to represent him.

My father threw out the first ball, and then, in the bottom of the fourth inning, with two outs and a runner on first base, with a count of one ball and no strikes, with the Dodgers leading, 3-1, a solid veteran pitcher named Al Downing threw a slider low and down the middle, and I swung and connected and hit a line drive that shot over the shortstop's head and kept rising and kept going and cleared the left-field fence and landed in the bullpen in the glove of Tom House, one of our relief pitchers.

Seven hundred and fifteen.

And one of the very few that I actually saw go over the fence. I guess it caught my attention, too.

The crowd went wild. My teammates went wild. Eddie Mathews hugged me. My mother fought her way to home plate and hugged me. Tom House got to me and gave me the baseball. The game stopped, for this moment, and a microphone was set up, and I said to the crowd and to a national television audience, "Thank God it's over."

Then it started to rain. The game was only in the fourth inning. It was not yet official. I was not yet officially the home-run king. The rain quickly stopped, and the game was completed, and the record was mine. I have the feeling that only if the rain had broken the record set when Noah launched his ark would the umpires have called off the game before the 715th home run became official.

When I came to bat again, my teammate Ralph Garr shouted to me, "Come on, Supe"—a good-natured nickname that was short for

Superstar—"break Hank Aaron's record!"

Eventually, of course, I did. But not that night. There were millions of kind words spoken and written about me after the historic home run, but none meant more than the words of my manager and my friend, Eddie Mathews. "All the sportswriters were mad at me that night," Eddie later recalled, "because they wanted to get to Hank after the game and I closed the clubhouse to everyone but the team and families. At that point, I didn't give a damn about the sportswriters, the way they had treated Hank and me and the Braves in Cincinnati. I cared about Hank. I stood up on a table and said what I thought about Hank, which was that he was the best ballplayer I ever saw in my life. Then we had champagne and everybody toasted him."

I finished that season in Atlanta with 733 home runs, then, recruited by Bud Selig, returned to Milwaukee, played two seasons with Bud's Brewers, broke Hank Aaron's record twenty-two more times and wound up my career with 755 home runs. I also had 2297 runs batted in, which was another record.

After my retirement, Ted Turner, the new owner of the Braves, brought me back to Atlanta with a job as director of player development. I have worked with, and for, Ted Turner ever since, in a variety of capacities—most of my work now is for his television network, CNN—and I have thoroughly enjoyed my post-baseball years.

Some people think that I did not enjoy my baseball years, that I am bitter about the experience. I am not bitter. I have no regrets about the life I've lived. There is no one in the

world I would rather be than Henry Louis Aaron. But I am a realist. I have eyes and ears to see and hear what is wrong, and I have a mouth to express my feelings about what is wrong.

People called me terrible names when I played in the minor leagues and in the majors. I was refused service in restaurants and rooms in hotels. I was threatened because I had the nerve—and the skill—to challenge the record set by Babe Ruth. I was portrayed as slow—of thought and deed—by sportswriters who knew me no more

than superficially. The Commissioner of Baseball did not come to the game when I broke the career home-run record. I was not besieged by offers of endorsements and commercials during my career. These are not complaints. These are facts.

But none of these facts dilutes this truth: I love baseball, always did and always will. I love the essence of the game, the contest between the pitcher and the hitter. I love the variety of skills that the game demands, arm strength and leg strength, the ability to run and

While Aaron thought himself "less spectacular" than Mays, he also knew that he could do everything there was to be done on a baseball field.

Roger Maris set the record with 61 home runs in 1961, when Mickey Mantle dropped off the chase in September with an injury. The duo's record of 115 home runs in a season still stands.

throw and hit and think. I know I owe everything I have to the game of baseball, and when baseball's appeal appeared to be declining in recent years, especially when I realized that black youngsters were no longer drawn to the game and thrilled by it as I had been, I was saddened.

Then, in the spring and summer of 1998, as Mark McGwire and Sammy Sosa mounted their attack upon the all-time single-season home run record, as interest in their achievements grew, and people came back to the game, I was absolutely delighted. I followed McGwire's and Sosa's pursuit of 60 and 61 just as everyone did, and I rooted for both of them. It was the greatest thing that had happened to baseball in a long, long time.

Baseball needed McGwire and Sosa so badly. Maybe the country, wounded by the Presidential scandal, needed them, too. The work stoppage that had wiped out the World Series in 1994 also

wiped out a lot of fans. They stopped coming to the ballpark, stopped watching on TV and, worst of all, stopped caring. McGwire and Sosa made them care again.

One of the things I noticed right away was that both McGwire and Sosa were having fun. Oh, maybe Mark got a little irritated by all the attention and all the questions and all the pressure in the middle of the season, but if you've ever spent a July or an August day in the heat and humidity of St. Louis, you know it's pretty easy to get irritated. And McGwire got over it so quickly, started smiling and kidding and enjoying the chase. Sosa helped. He seemed to enjoy every minute of the season, except maybe the end, except when he and his team were eliminated from the playoffs.

The good feeling, the joy, the camaraderie between them and the mutual admiration, that's what made their pursuit of Roger Maris and Babe Ruth so different from my pursuit of Ruth a quarter of a century earlier. I didn't have fun. How could I? I had people threatening to kill me and kidnap my children if I broke Ruth's record, people calling me vile names. Some of them hated seeing a black man challenging Ruth. Some of them hated seeing a black man playing in the major leagues. Some of them hated seeing a black man making a living—or just seeing a black man living. There was so much hatred, it stained the whole thing.

Roger Maris didn't have much fun, either, when he was going after Babe Ruth's 60, and in his case, obviously, it didn't have anything to do with color. There were people who hated him just because he wasn't Mickey Mantle, because he hadn't grown up in the Yan-

You're supposed to root for the home team, the home "man." Just the way Brooklyn Dodger fans, black and white, were united by their appreciation for Jackie Robinson half a century ago, Cub fans, black and white, were brought together by pulling for Sammy Sosa, no matter what color he was. Baseball can have that effect on a town, on a team's fans; it's one of the great things about the game.

I rooted for Sosa and McGwire, but I identified more with Sosa, whom, incidentally, as surprising as it might sound, I have never met. Sosa was six feet tall, my height exactly, and he weighed only a few pounds more than I weighed during my playing days. He played right field, as I did, and he was batting above .300, as I usually did, and he could steal bases, as I did.

kees' farm system, because he wasn't *entitled* to break the Babe's mark. Maris suffered during 1961, lost some of his hair and lost patience with the media. I was playing with the Braves, and I read and heard about what Maris was going through. I never suspected then that I would go through worse more than a decade later.

But in 1998 there was so much love around McGwire and Sosa, love of the chase, love of their talent. When McGwire and Sosa began threatening to hit 60 home runs, I didn't hear one person say, "Well, I want McGwire to win because he's white," or, "I want Sosa to win because he's black." This is a country of black and white, and, of course, everyone could see that McGwire was white and Sosa was black, but that wasn't what defined them, that wasn't what mattered. Sure, Dominicans and

other people of Hispanic heritage were delighted to see Sosa doing so well, but they didn't hate McGwire because he was white. Those people know baseball too well not to appreciate what McGwire was doing. They just wanted to see Sosa do it better. You're supposed to root for the home team, the home "man." Just the way Brooklyn Dodger fans, black and white, were united by their appreciation for Jackie Robinson half a century ago, Cub fans, black and white, were brought together by pulling for Sammy Sosa, no matter what color he was. Baseball can have that effect on a town, on a team's fans; it's one of the great things about the game.

I rooted for Sosa and McGwire, but I identified more with Sosa, whom, incidentally, as surprising as it might sound, I have never met. (I met

aaron, like most everyone in America, was caught up in the home run race between Mark McGwire and Sammy Sosa.

i was as excited by the deadlock as everyone else in America, and like many, I would not have been upset by a tie. Neither man deserved to be anything less than a winner.

McGwire when he was playing for Oakland, but I haven't had an opportunity to talk to him since he came to the National League.) Sosa was six feet tall, my height exactly, and he weighed only a few pounds more than I weighed during my playing days. He played right field, as I did, and he was batting above .300, as I usually did, and he could steal bases, as I did. The funny thing is that most home-run hitters are Sammy's size, and mine. Roger Maris, Mickey Mantle, Reggie Jackson, in their prime, were all around six feet tall, none over 200 pounds. In fact, Babe Ruth, even though he was big for his day at six-foot-two and 215 pounds, was closer to our size than to Mark McGwire's.

Mark is six-foot-five and weighs 250 pounds. How could I identify with him? He plays first base—extremely

well—and rarely tries to steal a base. How could I identify with that? And, most significantly, he hits baseballs 500 feet, 550 feet, almost into orbit. I hit home runs 340 feet, 350, barely clearing walls and fences, occasionally exploding with a 400-footer. The only one of McGwire's home runs I could truly identify with was the 62nd one, the one that broke the record, a bunt by his standards, a 341-foot home run, his shortest of the season.

As McGwire and Sosa began to close in on Ruth's 60 and Maris's 61, baseball started to prepare for the moment the record would be broken. The newly anointed Commissioner of Baseball, my old Milwaukee friend Bud Selig—we used to watch Green Bay Packer games together—invited me to be part of the celebration. He asked me to come to St. Louis for the series

Ken Griffey Jr. Sammy Sosa. Mark McGwire. Roger Maris. Babe Ruth. Sadaharu Oh. We're all part of sort of a fraternity of home-run hitters. We all know what it's like to hit a ball so right, so perfectly, that you realize you don't have to run fast or hard to first base because you know the ball is going out of the park. It's a terrific feeling, all over your body, even if you don't hit the ball as far as McGwire or Sosa hit it.

between McGwire's Cardinals and Sosa's Cubs on September 7th and 8th. He also invited Roger Maris's widow and the Marises' children.

The Marises accepted, as they should have. They were certainly an integral part of the occasion. It was their husband's, their father's record that was about to fall. They were a link in the history that was about to be made. I declined. I appreciated the invitation, appreciated the fact that baseball had a Commissioner who understood my role in the game's history, but this was not my record, this was not my moment, and I did not want to take anything away from those two guys, from McGwire or Sosa. They had earned the spotlight.

McGwire came into the series with 60 home runs, even with Ruth, one behind Maris, two ahead of Sosa. The suspense did not last long. I saw it on television, which is the way I prefer to watch baseball games these days. In the first inning of the first game of the series, McGwire hit his 61st, tying Maris's mark, and, through word and gesture, with upraised fist and blown kisses, he shared his exultation with the Marises, who were sitting near home plate; with his friend and rival, Sammy Sosa, who was standing in right field; with his parents, who were celebrating his father's 61st birthday; with his ten-year-old son, who was serving as a batboy; and with his manager and coaches and teammates. He certainly didn't need me there, but I still felt represented, by the Hall of Fame Cardinal, Stan Musial, my opponent, my friend and for several weeks, during a State Department tour of the Far East, my roommate. Musial stood

and applauded McGwire for all of us who had played before.

The next night, the same appropriate group was on hand to see McGwire erase Maris's record, to hit his 62nd home run, the one that just managed to clear the fence by inches. I watched it once again on television. I silently welcomed Mark to a very small club. He had broken a home-run record that had lasted 37 years. I had broken one that had lasted thirty-nine.

And just as I went on to put some distance between myself and Ruth's record, McGwire went on to put some distance between himself and Maris. He put miles between him and Maris. So did Sosa. In the following weeks, Sammy actually caught up to Mark at 62 home runs, and again at 63, and 65. Two days before the end of the season, Sosa moved in front of McGwire: He hit his 66th home run forty-five minutes before McGwire hit his. I was as excited by the deadlock as everyone else in America, and like many, I would not have been upset by a tie. Neither man deserved to be anything less than a winner.

On the final two days, Sosa went homerless, and McGwire went crazy. He hit two each day, lifted his record to 70. Seventy home runs. It sounded so strange, so unbelievable. He hadn't broken Maris's mark. He had shattered it. For that matter, so had Sammy. They both merited the attention, the cheers, the financial rewards, the love that they reaped. I was delighted, and I was jealous. I wish my chase had been so joyous, so fulfilling.

Will the record ever be broken? I would think so. But I don't think it will happen soon. McGwire and Sosa are both hitters who have come a long way in recent years. McGwire is a much more selective hitter than he once was; it may be, as some pitchers say, that the way to pitch Mark is high and tight, but if you pitch him high and tight, he's not going to swing, not any more, and, with today's strike zone, it's not going to be called a strike. Sammy was not a disciplined hitter in his early seasons in the major leagues. You threw him any kind of breaking ball, even outside the strike zone, and he would swing at it. He's learned to be selective, too. I'd like to have either of them on my team.

I think they're both going to have big years in 1999, and Sosa, who is only 30, five years younger than McGwire, should have many more big years. But I think everything came together in 1998 to produce 70 home runs—they both stayed remarkably fit, physically and mentally— and even though the pressure on McGwire is probably less now that he owns the record, I doubt the record will be seriously challenged.

Eventually it will fall, and it could fall to the player I consider the one most likely to surpass my record, Ken Griffey Jr. Junior hit 56 home runs last year for the second season in a row; like McGwire, he managed to stay focused on his task even though his team, the Seattle Mariners, was out of the pennant race. He is, at 29, a year younger than

Sosa, and he has hit 350 home runs in his career, 77 more than Sosa and 52 more than I had hit when I turned 29. (McGwire is a long shot; at 457, he has to average 60 a year for five years to pass me. Of course, he *has* averaged 60 a year for the past three seasons.)

I think Junior will hit more than 755 home runs *if* . . . if he stays healthy and if he stays focused. These days, it's probably harder to stay focused than to stay healthy. I stayed focused because I was hungry for a long time, for maybe the first fifteen, sixteen years of my career, constantly trying to prove and to improve myself, on the field and off. I don't mean I wasn't making good money, but it wasn't the kind of money they make today, nowhere close. This

Will the record ever be broken? I would think so. But I don't think it will happen soon. Eventually it will fall, and it could fall to the player I consider the one most likely to surpass my record, Ken Griffey Jr.

Ken Griffey Jr. is young enough and strong enough to catch Hank Aaron. But the question remains: will he play long enough to do it?

kid makes more each year than I made in my career. He doesn't have any idea what hungry is, and hunger makes you concentrate.

Yet Junior still goes about his business the way he's supposed to, with grace, with enthusiasm, with commitment. That's what I like about him. I think he showed that he's growing up when he changed his mind and agreed to take part in the home-run hitting contest at the All-Star Game. He's not a kid any more. He's at the age where he can get serious about himself, serious

about what he wants to accomplish before his career is over. Until you approach thirty, it's hard to conceive that your career is ever going to be over. But now he's got to decide what he wants to leave behind him. I knew his father well, and I know Junior a little, and I think he's going to be a little different from now on, a little more dedicated. He's going to concentrate, tell himself, "I know what I've got to do." If he does that, and avoids major injury, he'll break my record before he turns forty. All he has to do is average

37 home runs a season for eleven seasons.

Ken Griffey Jr. Sammy Sosa. Mark McGwire. Roger Maris. Babe Ruth. Sadaharu Oh. We're all part of sort of a fraternity of home-run hitters. We all know what it's like to hit a ball so right, so perfectly, that you realize you don't have to run fast or hard to first base because you know the ball is going out of the park. It's a terrific feeling, all over your body, even if you don't hit the ball as far as McGwire or Sosa hit it.

It's great, but, still, it's only baseball, it's only a game. The real sluggers, as I said before, are the ones who hit home runs off the playing field. Malcolm X was a home-run hitter. He was a magnificent speaker, a leader, an inspiration. When I was growing up in Alabama, when prejudice and discrimination demeaned and impoverished African-Americans, black people were made to feel ashamed of being black. Malcolm made us proud to be black.

Jesse Jackson is a home-run hitter, too; he and I have worked together many times. We met with the Commissioner of Baseball after Alex Campanis put his foot in his mouth on *Nightline,* with his remark about blacks not having the necessities to manage in the major leagues. Andrew Young. Julian Bond. Ted Turner. Jimmy Carter. These are people I know who've made a difference in society. They've changed people's ideas and changed people's lives.

The greatest home-run hitter in baseball history was Jackie Robinson. He swung the strongest bat. If he had failed, if he had not been the player he was and the man he was, if he had not been able to intimidate pitchers with his skills and if he had not

refused to be intimidated by words and threats, I would have failed, too. I would not have gotten to the major leagues in 1954.

I am so proud that I knew Jackie, that I hung around him whenever I could, that I listened to his words and followed his example as much as I could. We didn't agree on everything—Jackie campaigned for Richard Nixon in 1960, I campaigned for John F. Kennedy, and I won that one—but he was my hero from the day I first heard his name, the day he signed with the Brooklyn Dodgers, till the day he died too young, less than thirty years later. It bothers me, really bothers me, when I meet young black baseball players who have little, or no, idea of who Jackie Robinson was. I am proud that I know his widow, Rachel. With her beauty, her intelligence, her dreams, she is also a home-run hitter.

I have tried to be a home-run hitter off the field, too. I may not have hit the huge home runs that Jackie Robinson hit, or that Martin Luther King and Jesse Jackson hit, but at least I'm hitting line drives, and maybe some of them will clear the fences.

My first concern is trying to help children. Through the years, I've put money and energy and hopes into my Chasing the Dream Foundation in Atlanta and the Henry Aaron Scholarship Program in Milwaukee. Through Chasing the Dream, we've encouraged youngsters to take chances, to explore opportunities, to try to become the

beginning his baseball career seven years after Jackie Robinson, Aaron has tried to follow Robinson's off-field model of leadership.

greatest pianist in the world or the greatest schoolteacher or the greatest accountant. For some kids, the dream may be beyond their reach, but the fact that they have the spirit and the courage to try, that's what important. Everybody who is successful has failed sometime. That's one of the beautiful lessons of baseball. It doesn't matter how great a hitter you are; two out of three times you're going to fail. A lot of people never understand that it's all right to fail—as long as you make the attempt.

Through the Henry Aaron Scholarship Program, which Bud Selig helped start in Milwaukee, we've raised millions of dollars to send young people to college. A wonderful thing happened to me a few years ago when I was playing in a golf tournament in Milwaukee, a tournament conducted to raise money for our scholarship program. A young woman came up to me and told me that our program had helped her attend Marquette University, and now she was a researcher working in a laboratory in Chicago, and she had come back to work as a volunteer at the tournament as a way of showing her appreciation. It makes me feel terrific that I've been able to have a positive influence on at least one life, and possibly more.

Right now, we're combining the Chasing the Dream Foundation and the Aaron Scholarship Program so that we can share the funds to help kids pursue educational and vocational and avocational dreams. We're starting off with 44 kids—44 was my uniform number—and, eventually, we hope to expand the program to 755 youngsters. (I don't know where we got that number from.) We want to help kids all over

the world. Sadaharu Oh and I have worked together on a program in Japan that brings together children from dozens of countries. They learn baseball, but, more important, they learn to get along with people from all parts of the world.

I know that most people, when they think of me, think of home runs or, if they really know the game, think of 755. But what I would like them to remember about me is not the home runs, or the hits or the runs batted in, but that I was concerned about the well-being of other people.

In a certain sense, I always had that concern. It was passed down to me by my mother, whose life revolved around the church, and by my father, who was a good man. I was a boy scout when I was a child, and in a way, I've always lived by the boy scout motto—trying to be kind, loyal, brave, clean, obedient, all those simple virtues.

My concern has been nurtured by many people—my wife Billye, for one, who has always been an advocate of civil and human rights, and Jackie Robinson, of course, who influenced me in so many ways. Jackie once said, "Life owes me nothing. Baseball owes me nothing. But I cannot as an individual rejoice in the good things I have been permitted to work for and earn while the humblest of my brothers is down in the deep hole hollering for help and not being heard." I wish I were as comfortable with words as Jackie was, but I agree with him entirely. I guess the way I'd say it is: You have to reach out and you have to speak out.

I was a Big Brother for many years, and one of the children I was teamed up with was a boy about twelve years old who lived in the projects with his grandmother. They had to take him away from his mother and put him with his grandmother because his mother was a drug addict, and her boyfriend was a drug dealer. The child had seen the boyfriend flashing big rolls of bills, and when I got together with him, he was starting to hang around with kids that I could tell were going to be trouble, for themselves and for him.

I tried to show him there were other paths he could follow. For instance, I took him to one of the local television stations once to watch them prepare and deliver the evening news. I wanted him to understand that the news, of Atlanta and of the country and of the world, was something he could relate to. Other times, we'd just go for a hamburger and talk, not about anything special, just about the things in his life, and once in a while, I'd tell him how important education was, how you've got to be able to communicate, to express yourself, if you want to be successful. I was his Big Brother for a few years, and then he and his grandmother moved out of the district, and I didn't see him any more, but every now and then, I'd write him a letter, and he'd write back, telling me how he was doing.

After I'd gone about two years without seeing him, I heard from his grandmother, and she told me, "Mr. Aaron, you don't know what a tremendous influence you had on this boy. He's making all A's in school, he's planning on going to college, he's thinking about doing something with his life." I felt just like I had hit a home run. Maybe not a big Mark McGwire home run. But a nice solid timely Hank Aaron home run.

I own seventeen fast-food restaurants, most of them in Georgia, some in Milwaukee, mainly in minority neighborhoods, and the kids we try to employ are the kind of kids who really need to work, who want to work. I know these young people have more opportunities than I had when I was a child. I know they're not frightened by Ku Klux Klan marches, like I was. But I also know they need a financial hand, and if the jobs we provide can help some of these kids lift themselves to the next level, go on to college or a business of their own, then I feel I'm contributing something.

I am 65 years old now. My wife and I have a more than comfortable home on the southwest side of Atlanta. My five children have all gone to college. I even have a grandchild in college. I love being who I am. I love what I've accomplished and I still look forward to accomplishing more, to continuing my campaigns to give African-Americans

I have tried to be a home-run hitter off the field, too. I may not have hit the huge home runs that Jackie Robinson hit, or that Martin Luther King and Jesse Jackson hit, but at least I'm hitting line drives, and maybe some of them will clear the fences.

L TO R: 1st Row: ___y, W. (p), Goryl, J. (3b), Brown, R. (p), Jordan, D. (p), Subbiondo, J. (of)
2nd Row: Aaron, H. (__ Auten, D. (c), Doehler, R (of), Adair, B. (Mgr.), Blaney, L (of), Kornack, G. (p), Bowers, W. (c)
3rd Row: Morgan, c. (of), Engquist (1b), Toth, E. (p), Roach, G. (p), Covington, J. (of), MacConnell, R. (2b), Reitmejer, K. (p)

The 1952 Eau Claire Bears

Hank Aaron first signed with the Braves in 1952, playing for the Eau Claire Bears of the Northern League. His life later intersected with another Claire, Mrs. Claire Ruth, who knows that Hank is just behind her and the Babe.

equal opportunities in baseball and outside of baseball. (As a man who remembers clearly when African-Americans were not welcome in Organized Baseball, I know how far we've come; when I look at the number of black executives and field managers today, I also know how far we have to go.)

I'm secure in my job with the Atlanta Braves. My title is senior vice president, but my work mostly involves going around and selling the CNN network to airports. We're in about seventy-five to a hundred airports now, and we keep growing. Every now and then, I stop in to see John Schuerholz, the general manager of the Braves, and we talk about players on our team and on others. I offer my thoughts and my opinions, but I don't make trades or sign free agents or get actively involved in the day-to-day baseball operations. The window of my office looks out on Turner Field, and if I wanted to, I could watch games

i always took hitting very seriously. I gave it a lot of thought. I still can remember almost every home run I ever hit. Maybe not 755 of them. But ,more than 500 of them, I bet.

from my desk. The only thing I wouldn't be able to see very well, ironically, would be home runs clearing the left-field fence. If I go to a game, there are always autographs to sign, and people to talk to, so I'd rather go home and sit down in my chair and watch the games on television.

Of course my mind wanders back to my playing days, all the way back to the Negro Leagues, to going off with the Indianapolis Clowns in 1952, when I was only eighteen years old, scared to death of being on my own and uncertain whether I was good enough to earn a living playing ball. It was, in a way, the best experience of my life, being with the Clowns, a learning experience on the field and off. The hotels we stayed in, the restaurants we ate in, the buses we traveled in—all of that made me appreciate not just life in the major leagues, but life in the minor leagues of Organized Baseball. When I played for Eau Claire, my first stop in the Braves' farm system, we stayed in hotels that were far from fancy, but they were the Waldorf Astoria compared to the hotels in the Negro Leagues. It helps me appreciate everything I have today.

When I traveled around the country with the Clowns, I batted crosshanded. In other words, instead of having my right hand above my left when I gripped the bat, I had the left hand on top. Why? I don't know. I just had always held the bat that way, the wrong way. Then one day we were playing in Buffalo, and a scout for the Braves was at the game, and he told me he wanted me to try batting with my right hand above my left. I said I'd give it a try. I didn't think it felt comfortable at first, but I hit three home runs that day, and by the time the third one went over the fence, I was feeling very comfortable. I never went back to my old way.

One of my few regrets in baseball—the other, I suppose, was that I never won the Triple Crown, though I did lead the league in both home runs *and* runs batted in three different times—was that I never became a switch-hitter. When you bat lefthanded, you do put your left hand above your right, and I had a head start doing that. I tried learning to switch-hit when I was at Eau Claire, but once, when I was taking batting practice hitting left-handed, the bat flew out of my hands and sailed into a teammate and broke his nose, and I was so upset I never again swung lefthanded.

I always took hitting very seriously. I gave it a lot of thought. I still can remember almost every home run I ever hit. Maybe not 755 of them. But more than 500 of them, I bet. It used to be that at the end of each season, I

the real danger with a curveball was that it could frighten you, back you off the plate. I wasn't afraid to stand in to a curveball. As a matter of fact, I wasn't afraid to stand up to a fastball, either. I had no fear of any pitch or any pitcher.

would remember every home run I hit, who the pitcher was, what pitch I hit, what pitches he threw trying to set me up, what his fastball did, what his breaking ball did. I was a breaking-ball hitter. I liked to be thrown a breaking ball rather than a fastball. A pitcher was more likely to make a mistake with a curveball, get it a little too high, or a little too fat, too close to the heart of the plate, and he was less likely to get away with the mistake. If a fastball was slightly off target, it still might overpower you. But you could jump on a breaking ball that came into your zone. I'm pretty sure that if you go over their 136 home runs in 1998, Mark McGwire and Sammy Sosa hit most of them off breaking balls.

The real danger with a curveball was that it could frighten you, back you off the plate. I wasn't afraid to stand in to a curveball. As a matter of fact, I wasn't afraid to stand up to a fastball, either. I had no fear of any pitch or any pitcher. I wasn't afraid of Bob Gibson. I wasn't afraid of Sandy Koufax. I wasn't even afraid of Don Drysdale, though he was the closest thing to an intimidating sight, so tall and coming in sidearm. I didn't have

Great pitchers, like Sandy Koufax, had their plans for how to handle Hank; Hank had his plans, too.

that kind of fear in me. The only thing I was afraid of was failing.

I loved facing the good pitchers. Maybe the challenge made me concentrate more. If I were playing today, I'd love facing Greg Maddux, and I've told him this. If I were facing him, I'd have a game plan, and he'd have a game plan, and sometimes he'd win, and sometimes I would. He'd come after me, no question about that, and I always loved that. You know, when Tom Seaver came into the league, and he was as smart a pitcher as there was, the first time I faced him, he got me to hit into a double play. He told me later that I was his hero when he was a youngster, and he had watched me play so many times and had dreamed of facing me, that even the first time we went one on one, he had a plan. The next time I came up, I hit a home run off him. I told him I always had a plan, too.

It makes me feel good to know that Seaver admired me, and it makes me feel even better to know that the reason he admired me, he said, was my consistency, my ability to perform night after night, year after year. I was never a really spectacular player, but I might beat you with a home run one day, and a good catch the next, with a stolen base or with a strong throw. (Willie Mays always had a reputation for being exceptionally fast; I did not. But did you know that during the decade when we were in our thirties, I stole more bases than Willie did, a lot more? Of course he stole more when we were in our twenties, and the year we were forty, Willie stole twenty-three bases, and I stole only one. I admit he was faster than me, but not that much. Add lifetime home runs and lifetime stolen bases together, and Willie beats me just by a nose, 998 to 995.)

In all my twenty-three seasons in the major leagues, I never got comfortable enough to feel that I was as good as some people said I was. I always felt, even in my best seasons, that I could have gotten a little more out of my ability. Mark McGwire, after he broke the home-run record, said, without bragging, "I'm awed by myself." I never was awed by myself. Then again, I never hit 70 home runs, either.

Mark McGwire is a hero today. So is Sammy Sosa. Which means they are role models, whether they want to be or not. In their cases, unlike some other ballplayers, too many of whom care only about themselves, I think McGwire and Sosa accept that role—and try to live up to it. They both obviously care about other human beings. Mark has contributed time and money and energy to helping children in need. Similarly, Sammy has tried to improve the quality of life, especially the quality of education, for young people in the Dominican Republic. I applaud them both.

Perhaps that's why I would feel better if Mark McGwire were to stop using something like androstenedione, the legal over-the-counter drug which he took regularly during his record-breaking season. "Andro" did not give Mark extra power. He would have hit his 70 home runs without the drug, too. Maybe it did help him shake off some of the customary aches and pains of a long baseball season. Maybe not. But kids are going to follow in Mark's footsteps, are going to do whatever he does, and while androstenedione may not be a harmful drug, all the evidence, over a long period of usage, is not yet

in. I don't think young people should take the chance of using "andro." I don't think Mark McGwire should take the chance of promoting its use.

a m I a hero? I suppose I am, to some people. If I am, I hope it's not only for my home runs, for my physical accomplishments on the baseball field. I hope it's also for my beliefs, my stands, my opinions. Still, I'm not at ease being a hero. Heroes, I feel, should be people you see on an everyday basis. Your parents. Your teachers.

My pastor, William Guy, is one of my heroes. I enjoy going to church and hearing his sermons. With his manner and with his words, he brings everything to life. One of my earliest heroes was an English teacher I had when I was a teenager. I used to walk past her house every day on my way home from school, and I'd stop and we'd talk, and she'd tell me what I had to do to be successful in life. She had a pecan orchard by her house, and I'd pick them and fill two or three buckets for her, and she'd fill me with dreams.

So many of my dreams have come true, and for that, I am deeply grateful.

But the world is not yet perfect, far from it, and in the words of one of my heroes, "I have a dream . . ."

Wow! I wish I'd hit one like that. ⚾

So many of my dreams have come true, and for that, I am deeply grateful.

1934	February 5	Estella and Herbert Aaron give birth to Henry in Mobile, Alabama.
1947	April 15	Aaron is 13 as Jackie Robinson plays first game for Brooklyn Dodgers.
1950		A shortstop, Aaron signs for $10 a game to play for the Mobile Black Bears.
1952		Aaron plays his first game for the Indianapolis Clowns of the Negro Leagues. He is paid $200 per month and $2 per day meal money. A reporter in the *Chicago Defender* writes, "Aaron is the best Negro-League prospect since Willie Mays."
1952		Dewey Griggs of the Boston Braves scouts Aaron and offers him $100 more per month than the Giants offered, ultimately keeping Willie Mays and Aaron from playing in the same outfield. Aaron's signing bonus is a cardboard suitcase. Aaron plays for the Braves' Northern League team in Eau Claire, Wisconsin. He is named outstanding rookie for the 1952 season.
1953		Hank Aaron, along with Horace Gorner and Felix Mantilla, becomes the first black player to integrate the Sally League.
1953		After Milwaukee Brewers (the Braves' top farm) manager Tommy Holmes sees Aaron in spring training, he says "He'll never play Major League baseball; he can't pull the ball."
1953		Jacksonville (Sally League) manager Ben Geraghty moves Aaron from shortstop to second base; Aaron later calls Geraghty "the best manager I ever had." Aaron makes 36 errors at second base but leads the league in batting (.362) and RBI (125) and wins the league MVP award.
1953	October 13	Marries Barbara Lucas of Jacksonville, Florida.
1953	Winter	Playing for the Caguas of the Puerto Rican League, Aaron is converted to an outfielder.
1954	Spring	Not expected to make the team, Aaron becomes the Braves' regular left fielder when Bobby Thomson breaks his ankle while sliding in spring training.
1954	April 23	Aaron hits his first homer off Vic Raschi.
1954	September 5	Aaron breaks ankle while sliding into third, costing him any chance for Rookie of the Year honors.
1955		Earning $17,000 a year, Aaron knocks in 100 runs and scores 100 and changes his uniform number from 5 to 44. Braves public relations man Donald Davidson protests, "You're too skinny to carry two digits on your back."
1956		Aaron wins his first NL batting title with .326 mark but Braves surrender first place to Dodgers in final series of season, losing two of three games to Cardinals.
1957	August 15	Aaron hits his 100th home run off Don Gross in Cincinnati.
1957	September 23	Aaron is carried off the field by his teammates after belting an 11th-inning homer against St. Louis pitcher Billy Muffett to give Milwaukee the NL pennant. He leads league with 44 homers, 132 RBI, and finishes third in batting behind only Musial and Mays.
1957	October	Braves win World Series over New York Yankees in seven games as Aaron hits three homers, knocks in seven and bats .393.
1957	November	Named the National League's MVP, Aaron would later say "1957 was the best year of my baseball life."
1958		Aaron hits three homers in a game for only time in his career, against Giants in Seals Stadium in San Francisco.
1958	October	The Braves win another pennant but lose Series in seven games to Yankees.
1959		Aaron wins his second batting title with a .355 average.
1959	Post-season	Aaron wins more home run contests on the television show *Home Run Derby* than any other competitor. He wins $30,000 in prizes, nearly two years worth of salaries. "The show changed me," he says. "I realized that home run hitters made the money."

1960	July 3	Aaron hits his 200th homer off Ron Kline in St. Louis.
1962		Aaron makes $50,000 a year.
1962		Aaron hits "the longest ball I ever hit" off Jay Hook of the Mets. The ball, which traveled about 470 feet, landed in the center-field bleachers.
1962	April 10	Brother Tommie Aaron joins Braves, becomes Hank's roomate.
1963	Spring training	Braves' manager Bobby Bragan tells Hank, "Mays makes $125,000 and you make $75,000 and the only difference is, he runs. You have the green light to run any time you want." Aaron steals 31 bases in 36 attempts and makes a six-figure salary the following season.
1963	April 19	Aaron hits 300th homer off the Mets' Roger Craig in Milwaukee.
1965		Aaron and Eddie Mathews break the National League record of homers by teammates, previously held by Duke Snider and Gil Hodges who totaled 745. Babe Ruth and Lou Gehrig hit 859 between them, but Aaron and Mathews finish with 863 as teammates.
1965		*Sport Magazine* article quotes Aaron on the issue of black managers. Aaron claims that Jackie Robinson and Bill White are the best candidates, but also mentions Bill Bruton, Junior Gilliam, Ernie Banks, Willie Mays and himself.
1966		The Braves move to Atlanta; Aaron leads the league with 44 homers.
1966	April 20	Aaron hits his 400th homer off Bo Belinsky in Philadelphia.
1967		*Jet Magazine* cover story claims, "Aaron Blasts Racism in Baseball."
1960		Aaron wins his fourth NL homer title.
1968	July 4	Aaron hits his 500th homer.
1970	May 17	Aaron collects his 3,000th hit.
1970	December	Aaron divorced from Barbara Lucas.
1971	April 27	Aaron smacks his 600th homer off the Giants' Gaylord Perry in Atlanta.
1973	July 21	Aaron hits his 700th homer off Philadelphia's Ken Brett in Atlanta.
1973	November 12	Marries Billye Williams of Atlanta.
1974	April 4	Hits his 714th homer off Jack Billingham of Cincinnati.
1974	April 8	Hits his 715th homer off Al Downing, setting a new major-league home-run record.
1974	November 2	Traded to Milwaukee Brewers.
1976	July 20	Hits his 755th homer off Dick Drago.
1976		Retires after the season, his 23rd.
1976	December	Joins the Braves to work in the organization's farm system.
1982	August 1	Aaron inducted into the Baseball Hall of Fame.
1984	August 16	Tommie Aaron, who played for the Milwaukee and Atlanta Braves during his seven-year career, dies of leukemia at age 45.
1987		The Atlanta Braves become the first team in baseball with a fair-share agreement — a contract stipulating that the organization will grant minorities a fair share of everything, from executive positions to professional services. The NAACP pushed for the agreement. Aaron's work for the NAACP began in the late 1950s.
Recent Years		While continuing as an executive with the Braves, Aaron has served on committees for leukemia and cancer research and executive boards for PUSH and Big Brothers/Big Sisters. He also began The Hank Aaron Chasing the Dream Foundation, which helps youngters reach their artistic and educational goals.

chronology

a line drive hitter

Real baseball people understand that the best thing you can have in a sport with a long season is consistency. Henry Aaron, by that measure, is the greatest baseball player ever, period, end of discussion.

—George F. Will

When I think of Henry Aaron I think of understatement. He was like Joe DiMaggio. He was too good at making the difficult things look too easy and that probably hurt his reputation. Aaron's career is a bit like the 1998 Yankees: Look at the Yankees and you say, where are the stars? Look at Henry Aaron and you say, where are the really gaudy numbers? Aaron's cumulative number of 755 home runs is enough to knock your socks off, but when you go to his year-by-year totals you say, where is the 50 or 55 home-run season? But then, you have to take a step back from the record books. Real baseball people understand that the best thing you can have in a sport with a long season is consistency. Henry Aaron, by that measure, is the greatest baseball player ever, period, end of discussion.

Real baseball fans, when they look at a professional's career, ask particular questions. How was he going from first to third? Could he throw the ball?

Could you count on him in August, in Cincinnati, in a day game? Ask that about Henry Aaron, and the single answer to all these questions is simple: This is a guy who showed up to play every day. I am not one of those people who gets misty-eyed over Mickey Mantle because we just know too much about his approach to the game. Aaron was playing at a time difficult for black people. Nowadays, when three of the most popular Americans are named Oprah Winfrey, Michael Jordan and Colin Powell, it's quite a different country from the one Aaron thrived in during the 1960s.

The chase to break Babe Ruth's all-time home run record did not interest me much in 1974 for two reasons. First, Aaron's great years were behind him. I grew up in Champaign, Illinois, and Aaron will always be a Milwaukee guy to me, playing for those great, fabulous teams of the fifties. Second, though I wanted him to get the record, the chase spanned over two seasons and the result was too foreseeable. Yet, for many baseball fans the home run

While Ruth (opposite) dominated play between the World Wars, Mays, Mantle and Aaron were the dominant players of the next generation.

TOPS IN NL

HANK AARON • WILLIE MAYS

record is the only noticeable feature of Aaron's twenty-three year career.

Ruth, even minus the home run title, does hold a mythic place in the history of American sports that no one else has ever had. The person who has come closest to his stature is Michael Jordan. And Jordan plays a sport where one man can take control of a game in the final two minutes. Baseball is not like that. In his niche, Ruth is different, in part because he played in the twenties, when we first began to have superstars. Mature sports fans are able to stand back and observe that Ruth and Aaron had very different kinds of baseball careers. And frankly, I will take Aaron's.

Most fans will try to compare Aaron's career with that of the Giants' Willie Mays, but these were vastly different ballplayers and men. First of all, Mays' personality came through on the baseball field in ways that Aaron's did not. Aaron was a man of reserve while Mays was more flamboyant. They played according to their disposition. Bob Addie of *The Sporting News* once described Aaron as "the quiet, soft-spoken fellow that department stores put in complaint departments." Also, Mays not only had the advantage of just playing center field, but a huge center field to showcase his talent when he was making his first reputation. Imagine if Aaron had played in Yankee Stadium eighty-one times a year.

Aaron's greatest attributes were his craftsmanship and workmanlike approach to the game. Milwaukee pitcher Lew Burdette once picked up a bat to show that the marks where Aaron's bat made contact with the ball were within the size of a quarter. Just unbelievable consistency. And, with

the emergence of high-caliber relief pitching, I think it was harder to hit at all in Aaron's day. I have always wanted to know what Ty Cobb batted in his fourth at bats of a game. I bet it was around .600. By the eighth or ninth inning, Cobb had the luxury of batting against the same tired pitcher that he had seen three times before. Now, by the third at bat you are facing some flamethrower whose job is to get to the next flamethrower.

The modern puzzle for people evaluating baseball records is that we live in an age of the extended career. What do you do with players like Aaron or Don Sutton? My view is that they played baseball for twenty or more seasons and you do not disparage what they did because they took care of themselves and sports medicine enabled them to play an extra year or two. Keep in mind, not too many ballplayers—no matter what position they played—could bat .301 and hit 40 home runs . . . at age 39. I regret the designated hitter rule, in part because it puts an invisible asterisk over Aaron's last years. That's one good reason for getting rid of the rule. Henry Aaron was just too good of a ballplayer and is too good of a man for his legend to be tainted.

Out of 755, how many home runs did Aaron see leave the ballpark before he touched first base? Zero. "Looking at the ball going over the fence isn't going to help," he explained. Remember Aaron's understatement the next time you see one of today's stars pausing at home plate to watch a home run. Based on his consistency and craftsmanship, Henry Aaron is the greatest baseball player in the history of Major League Baseball.

If Aaron was afraid of the inside pitch, he didn't show it. He hit 15 home runs off Hall of Famer and noted brushback artist Don Drysdale.

Hank was the kind of guy I knew had great talent when I first saw him play. In fact, he had unusual talent. I remember a couple of plays that he made as an outfielder and he had great instincts, and when I saw him hit, he used the whole field to hit in and he had great power to right-center field at that time. I thought that Hank would be a guy who would hit .400 in his career. As time went on, I think he tried to excel over Willie Mays and Eddie Mathews. So Hank started to pull the ball more and more until he became the fantastic home-run hitter that he became. He also became more susceptible to the ball away from him—instead of hitting line drives and using the whole field, he started to pull more and more. I still think he could hit .400, he was that great a hitter. He adapted to various kinds of pitching. I only saw Hank leave his feet one time from a ball thrown at him or inside. He was that quick.

—Warren Spahn

i first saw Hank his first year with the Indianapolis Clowns. Over in Montgomery, Alabama, that's where I first saw him. I'm looking over the lineup and I see this Aaron in there, and Aaron was hitting in the third spot. And I said, "Buster [Haywood, Clowns manager], who is this kid you got, Aaron?" He said, "Buck, you've got to see him. He can really swing that bat." They had him playing shortstop. The first time up, I've got a big right-hander pitching, good fastball. He threw him a first-pitch fastball on the outside. Aaron hit it up against the right field fence. Well, anybody hits one there every once in a while. The next time he comes up, I've got a left-hander, Gene Collins, good curveball, good fastball. I say, "I tell you what you do, Gene, kind of push him back and then throw a good fastball outside and see what he'll do with it." He did, he moved him back off the plate, and the next pitch, he hit it up against the center field wall. Now, I got my ace, Hilton Smith, good curveball pitcher. I say, "Hilton, when this kid hits these balls, Buster is over there looking at me laughing." Next time up, I say "Hilton, move him off and throw him that good overhand curveball, see what he'll do with it." He threw it, and he hit it over the left field fence. I said, "Damn." And then now, after the game, Buster and I were eating together and I say, "Buster, I won't have to worry about this kid when we get to Kansas City." He said, "What do you mean you won't have to worry about him?" I said, "Somebody is going to sign him soon." And they did. Man, he could swing that bat.

—Buck O'Neil

Chicago Cubs coach Buck O'Neil, here standing with his former Kansas City Monarchs protégé, Ernie Banks (far left), saw the eighteen year-old Aaron play shortstop for the Indianapolis Clowns in 1952. Two years later, when Aaron debuted with the Milwaukee Braves, the Clowns (right) relied upon such gate attractions as manager Oscar Charleston, pantomimist "King Tut" (Richard King) and second basewoman Connie Morgan.

I saw Hank play in Puerto Rico in 1953 when I was a 16-year-old kid in San Juan. He came to play for the Caguas that winter as a 19-year-old second baseman. The day he was going to get released he suddenly went 4-for-4 and went on to lead the league in hitting. You could see back then how well he swung the bat. Then when I came to the big leagues myself in 1958 and the Braves came to San Francisco on their first road trip in May, Hank was batting over .400. He amazed me.

—Orlando Cepeda

While Aaron was playing for the Caguas team of the Puerto Rican League in 1953 (above), manager Mickey Owen moved him from second base to the outfield. Aaron won the MVP of the All-Star Game that winter. With Cleon Jones, Tommie Agee, Willie McCovey and Aaron, Billy Williams (below) made Mobile, Alabama, the grooming ground of baseball stars.

I first saw Henry Aaron play baseball with the Mobile Black Bears. He played second base. My brother was a pitcher on that ball club. I followed my brother down to Mitchell Field and I got a chance to see Hank play. I didn't see any kind of talent there. Maybe I saw some talent, but I saw a lot more in other players. I wasn't focused on Henry Aaron, but I do remember that he was on that ball club playing second base.

—Billy Williams

hank was on his way to Jacksonville. The Braves were going to send him back to Jacksonville as a second baseman, but Bobby Thomson broke his ankle sliding into second base in spring training. And I happened to be in the shower at the time when Charlie Grimm came into the clubhouse and started talking over with the coaches who they were going to keep. And they decided they were going to keep Hank and make an outfielder out of him. Then Hank just went on from there.

—Lew Burdette

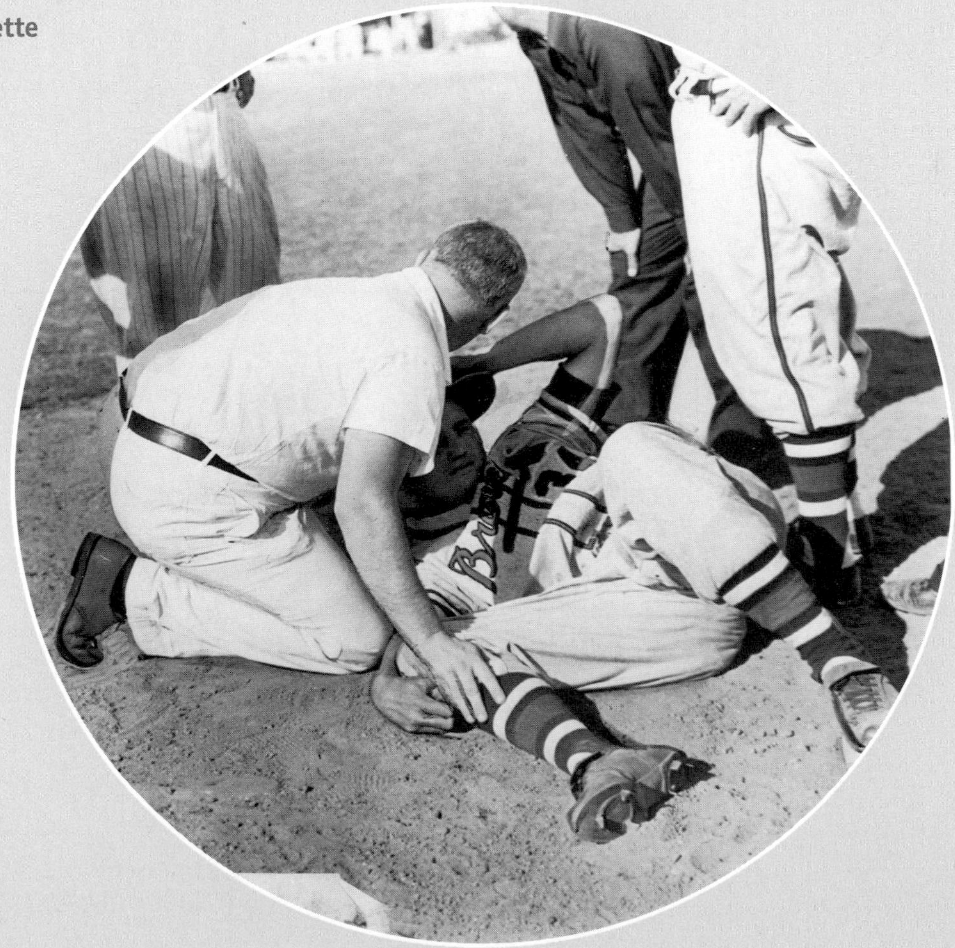

Indianapolis CLOWNS Negro

We go way back. When he first signed with the Boston Braves, before they became Milwaukee, back when he first went up to the majors, I followed him. He was with the Indianapolis Clowns, I was with the Memphis Red Sox. I was a pitcher and outfielder. When he went to the majors, I also played against him, because all the Negroes in the majors at

merican League Champions

The *Chicago Defender* called Hank Aaron "the best prospect seen in the Negro Leagues since Willie Mays." Aaron might have played in the same outfield as Mays, but the Braves were offering $350 a month for his minor league services, while the Giants were offering $250. Aaron also thought that his chances to make the Braves were better.

that time would come down and play us. They were called the Willie Mays All Stars. They'd come down and play us, the best out of the Negro Leagues, after the World Series.

We tooled all through the South—North Carolina, Alabama, Mississippi, and Texas, that sort of thing.

—Charlie Pride

Jack knew of Hank and his talents early on. He also saw Willie Mays play on a barnstorming trip through the South before he came into the majors. He had great expectations of both men, and somehow lived vicariously through them. That was a trait that I admired in Jack. In those years, he was especially excited and proud of achievements and triumphs of others, particularly those of members of our race or his teammates.

—Rachel Robinson

The Braves Bashers—
Aaron, Adcock, and
Mathews—hit a combined
1,603 home runs.

Well, it's pretty hard to put Hank's career in a nutshell. I knew Hank and saw him play in the beginning days of his career when he came up with Milwaukee. And at that time he was basically a player that had come out of the Negro Leagues and wasn't really considered to be a home-run-type hitter. They had other players on that club like Eddie Mathews and Joe Adcock who really got your attention. Hank was an opposite-field hitter and a singles and doubles hitter, a line-drive-type hitter. As his career lengthened, and he learned a little more about hitting, he started to become a power-type hitter.

—Ralph Kiner

he was a good hitter. He could hit to all fields. The 1957 World Series was the first time we ever faced him. And then at spring training a little bit. He certainly could hit the ball to right field and up the middle.

—Yogi Berra

Aaron (above) hit three homers, batted .393 and slugged .786 as Milwaukee won the 1957 World Series in seven games. Aaron was shocked that when Jackie Robinson (far left with his wife, Rachel) walked into the Oakland locker room during the 1972 World Series, none of the players came up to talk to him. Supported by a cane and worn down by diabetes, Robinson went back to his Cincinnati hotel room. He died nine days later.

i feared Hank more than anybody, because he upset defensive patterns. You pitch away and he hits it over the right field fence. Hank was virtually impossible to defense. When the game was on the line, of all the greats I played against, I feared Hank the most.

—Bobby Bonds

I first remember seeing Hank in the 1957 World Series. Because the Dodgers didn't win that year, I made sure I rooted against the Yankees.

—Kareem Abdul-Jabbar

Left fielder Wes Covington's great catch off Gil McDougald was the defensive gem of the 1957 World Series. The grab helped preserve Lew Burdette's 1-0 victory over Whitey Ford in Game Five.

He was a sound outfielder and a very difficult person to get out at the plate. They never struck Hank out very often. He always hit for percentage, even if he didn't hit a lot of homers. His fielding was sound, too, but no flash. At that time I didn't take note of that because there was a center fielder in Manhattan named Willie Mays, who outshone everyone.

—Kareem Abdul-Jabbar

Aaron (hitting number 714 against Jack Billingham above) and Willie Mays (right) were tops in the National League for most of their careers. For many fans, astounding plays like his catch of Vic Wertz's drive in Game One of the 1954 World Series placed Mays in a category all by himself.

HENRY AARON

Henry L. Aaron

O
h yes. I followed him. I'm a baseball fanatic, more than a fan. And when I was stationed as a young Marine at Great Lakes, Illinois, in 1955 and 1956, I would catch the train and go to Milwaukee and watch those

The Braves' lineup in 1955 (including, from left to right, Billy Bruton, Danny O'Connell, Eddie Mathews, Andy Pafko, Hank Aaron, Joe Adcock, Johnny Logan and Del Crandall) had as much power as any club, except Brooklyn. The Dodgers won the pennant by 13 games and went on to win their first World Series.

Milwaukee Braves—back when Hank was in right field, and Joe Adcock was on first. Del Crandall was behind the plate, Billy Bruton in the outfield and all that crowd.

—**Zell Miller,** Governor of Georgia

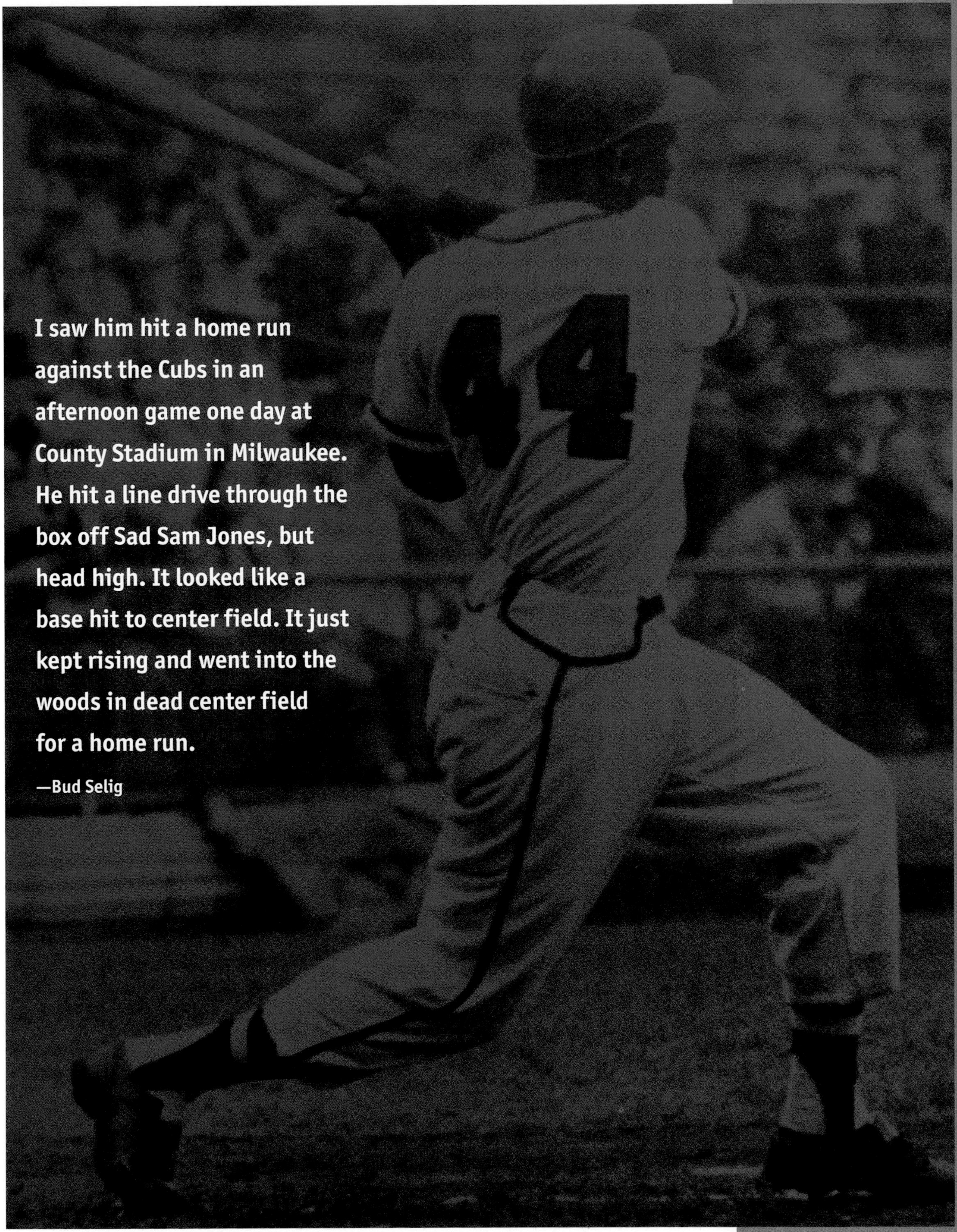

I saw him hit a home run against the Cubs in an afternoon game one day at County Stadium in Milwaukee. He hit a line drive through the box off Sad Sam Jones, but head high. It looked like a base hit to center field. It just kept rising and went into the woods in dead center field for a home run.

—Bud Selig

When Henry Aaron first came around in 1954, I had just left the National League as a player to manage in the minor leagues. When I came back in 1956 to manage the New York Giants, the Milwaukee Braves were just starting to put that great team together. And boy, did Hank ever fit! For a fellow who was rather slight, I don't think we ever saw a better

pair of hands swinging a bat. What impressed me—and what others focused on—was that Henry very rarely swung at a bad ball. He had good discipline at the plate. One thing about Hank: When you heard the noise you didn't have to look where the ball was going, because you knew you had to buy a ticket to find it. I heard that noise enough. I know that.

—Bill Rigney

With his consistent, ever-balanced swing, it didn't seem to matter what kind of pitcher Aaron was facing. Here he takes one deep off Philadelphia's ace, Robin Roberts.

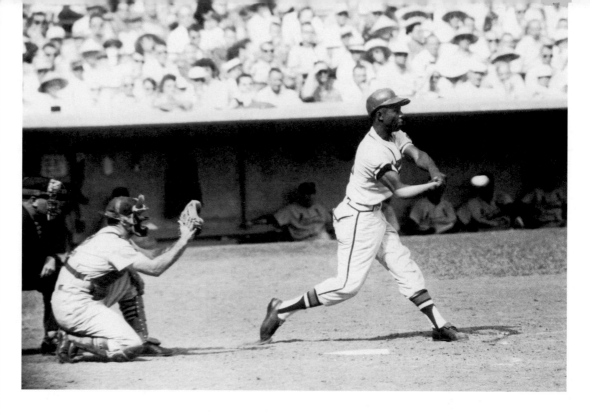

What I admire most about Hank Aaron was that he always came to play. Truly, he was a real professional, and that is a very important word for me. He had a job to do and he did it well each and every day he put on his uniform. I recall driving from Cleveland to Milwaukee after the 1958 season to see the Yankees and Braves play in the World Series. I watched Hank on the ball field and was greatly impressed. He played what I call a natural game. He had tremendous natural ability, but he didn't try to make himself look sensational. I believe he felt it was his obligation and duty to give it his best each time he stepped to the plate or took to the field. This is the type of player I respect. Year after year he was one of the best on the baseball diamond. And he did his job with dignity and without any big public relations campaign.

—Minnie Minoso

He was wiry. He was strong looking, but not big. Most of the home run hitters then, Ernie Banks and guys like that, they weren't big. They weren't huge, lumbering guys. They could run, steal some bases, hit the ball out of the ballpark. Hank was built, but you wouldn't know just by looking at him how he could hit the ball that far, that hard, and that often.

—Frank Robinson

I got called up in 1959 with the Cubs. There were people hollering "Hank"; that's what they used to call him, "Hank" Aaron. I remember, it seems like it was yesterday, he was standing outside Wrigley Field and I came out and I said, "Henry." That's what we called him when he played down in Mobile. He immediately spun around because he recognized somebody was there that knew him well.

—Billy Williams

he was one of the great hitters and great players.
But Henry gives me credit for making him a complete
ballplayer. In my first meeting with him down in spring
training, I said, "Hank, Willie Mays is making $125,000 and
you're making $75,000. The only thing he does that you
don't do is run. You got the green light." He stole 38 bases,
38 out of 43.

—Bobby Bragan

the groove

I don't think I ever saw Hank Aaron hit a ball 500 feet. I'm sure he did, but I don't think I ever saw it. He just hit home runs.

—Joe Morgan

by joe morgan

m

When you watched Hank Aaron, his hat didn't fall off.

y first impression of Hank was that everything seemed to look easy to him. He made it look easy I should say. Mays you could tell was always working hard, Frank Robinson too. With Hank it just seemed like, "Hey, I can do what I want to do." And I think that's one of the problems he's always had—people have always thought that he probably just took things in stride, and that he wasn't as focused as Mays and those guys. You'd be watching Mays run from under his hat and all those things. When you watched Hank Aaron, his hat didn't fall off. He just seemed to get there, make the play in right center and catch the ball. He always hit the cutoff man. He always hit home runs, but his home runs were not monster blasts. I saw Mays hit balls 500 feet. I don't think I ever saw Hank Aaron hit a ball 500 feet. I'm sure he did, but I don't think I ever saw it. He just hit home runs.

As Willie Mays used to say, "I'm out there performing; I'm on stage." I don't think Hank ever thought of baseball as a stage. I think he was playing a game that he loved and he just played.

When I think of home runs, I just think of Hank Aaron. Like I said, I don't think of Mark McGwire and these guys hitting to the upper reaches. Willie Stargell, Willie McCovey and guys like that were the long, long ball hitters. Aaron was just a home run hitter. He was *the* home run hitter I should say. I think he was a lot stronger than people gave him credit for. He had very strong hands and wrists, but more than anything else, it was his timing and bat speed. The few home runs I hit were because of bat speed, not being overly strong. Hank was the same way. I think the thing that amazed me the most about him as a hitter was that he could

The debates about who was better, Aaron or Mays, only began later in their careers. Aaron always used Mays as a standard against which to measure his own performance.

take that inside fastball four to five inches off the plate and keep it fair down the left field line. Most hitters can't take that ball off the plate inside and keep it fair. But he could, and he hit a lot of home runs right down the line because of that.

When I think of 715 home runs, I think of it just the way Hank Aaron did. When he got to 715 it didn't mean *anything* to him. I shouldn't say it didn't mean anything, but he wasn't finished. And he felt like that was a number that he reached and he just kept going until he finally stopped at 755. When we were playing, I always thought that Mays and Aaron had a chance to reach 715. I think Mays was hurt because he never played in a great ballpark—a hitter's ballpark—plus he spent time in the Army. So I think those things hurt him.

Mays was a different kind of a hitter. He relied upon strength in his home run hitting. Aaron was more about timing. And that was going to last longer as he got up in age. He was kind of like Ted Williams, who was able to hit home runs even after he was 40. It's a matter of timing and the swing that he developed all those years. He never lost it.

Hank was just so consistent. He never hit 50 home runs, but he was just so consistent that as he got closer— actually, when he got to about 550, I just assumed that he was going to do it. Barring a major injury, nothing was going to stop him from reaching 715.

I don't compare Hank to the guys today, like Mark McGwire and Sammy Sosa. It's a different game now. It was a lot more difficult to hit home runs when Hank Aaron played. First and foremost, the parks were usually bigger overall. The ball wasn't juiced. And the pitching was better. That's why you have so many guys hitting 50 home runs in one year. That's why you have more guys than ever before hitting 40 in one year. That's why you have forty-something guys driving in 100 runs. It's a different game now. I try not to compare these guys to Hank Aaron or Willie Mays, or all the great players that I saw, because the game is different. I'm not taking anything away from these guys today, they're doing their thing in their era, and that's the way I separate it.

I find that Hank is a happier person than he's ever been. I was at a Player's Choice Award ceremony the other day and he was just unbelievable. Not only humility—but just his giving credit to McGwire and these young guys. I think all the negative stuff took a toll on him for a while. He was very suspicious of people, which is natural. He got a lot of hate mail and all those things affected him. And, whether he says it or not, I don't think baseball ever gave him his due for what he did. The commissioner wasn't even there the day he broke the record. Little things like that can bother you. It's not big things that bother you. You deal with big things. All the little things that you have to deal with on a daily basis add up to making you kind of cynical toward the game. He's happy now with his place in history. ⚾

It's a matter of timing and the swing that he developed all those years. He never lost it. Hank was just so consistent.

t he thing about it is, he hit 15 home runs off Don Drysdale. And Drysdale and Early Wynn and Sal Maglie were headhunters. They didn't believe in pitching a little inside, they believed in pitching about a foot inside. It didn't intimidate Hank at all. . . . In one game I was coaching for the Dodgers, Alston told Drysdale to put this guy on and he hit him. Alston came out and said "I wanted you to walk this guy." Drysdale said "You wanted him over there, he's over there." Now

Aaron could hit all kinds of pitches, except maybe this sort. Hank wasn't fazed by brushbacks: eventually, he knew, the pitcher would have to leave a ball where he could reach it.

it's a Federal case when someone gets knocked down. But with Hank, he'd just roll his head back and let the ball go through. Or move it forward and let it go behind him. There wasn't a big ol' confrontation.

—Bobby Bragan

With Aaron, some of the most dangerous hitters in the National League (clockwise from top left)— Willie Mays, Willie McCovey, Frank Robinson and Ernie Banks—became members of the 500 home run club in the 1960s.

there were about five individuals in the National League that I had total respect for: Willie Mays, Willie McCovey, Hank, Frank Robinson, and a teammate of mine, Ernie Banks.

—Ferguson Jenkins

He did something that wasn't customary for the old-style home run hitters—Babe Ruth, Jimmie Foxx and the others. Hank was a front-foot type hitter. He had his weight on his front foot, somewhat like Stan Musial. They both hit with their back foot off the ground, basically the opposite of what the hitters did in the early days, which was swing hard, follow through and twist around and fall back. But Hank was the type of hitter that got his weight all onto his front foot and snapped with his wrists.

—Ralph Kiner

Aaron's weight shift to the front foot replicated Stan Musial's style at the plate (left) but was in stark contrast to that of Mel Ott, the five-foot-nine, left-handed slugger of the New York Giants (below) who needed to pivot off his rear foot for maximum power.

he hit like he was half asleep. But throw something in there and he strikes like a cobra.

—Willie Stargell

The first time I saw Hank Aaron was 1962, at the end of spring training. We were in Fort Myers and I was sent up to Daytona Beach and on my way I was driving through Bradenton, so I decided to stop and watch the game. At the time, before they reconstructed McKechnie Field, straight-away center was about 433 feet and there was a wall about 50 feet or more. It just seemed like a fifty-dollar cab ride from home. He hit two home runs over that wall that day. I was feeling that I had done well enough to make the major-league ball club. Then I thought if he hit balls like that, maybe I need to go to Daytona.

—Willie Stargell

Aaron's steady, no-nonsense approach to the game inspired many young players, including a Pittsburgh rookie in 1962, Willie Stargell (right). Teammate Phil Niekro believes Sammy Sosa and Mark McGwire are much stronger than Aaron. But he thinks Aaron was quicker.

To do what Hank did, you must be very consistent until late in your career. I was ahead of his pace in hitting home runs early in my career. But he hit a lot of home runs late in his career. That's difficult to do. You're supposed to be on the decline then.

—Frank Robinson

I hit like the majority of hitters—off the back foot, with the follow-through. Hank hit off the front foot, without a big follow-through. The bat stayed out in front or to his left side rather than following through over the left shoulder.

—Frank Robinson

Aaron excelled across three decades and hit an astounding 245 home runs after his 35th birthday. Of the 15 members of the 500-homer club, only Aaron, Ruth and Mays finished above 600. It wasn't unusual for Aaron, here hitting off Pittsburgh's Bob Friend (right), to lose balls in the center field trees in Milwaukee.

He had one of the quickest swings that you'd ever want to see. He had the ability to wait back and then swing quickly at the ball. We call him a front-foot hitter, but I always thought that that's what you're supposed to do, hit against your front leg.
—Harmon Killebrew

Davey Lopes is a good friend of mine. He'd let me hang out in the Dodgers locker room. I remember the pitchers talking about how to pitch opposing hitters, but when they got to Hank they'd just skip him. There was no pitch he couldn't handle and there was no use talking about it.
—Kareem Abdul-Jabbar

Nolan Ryan, who threw the ball harder longer than anyone, had to go to other pitches besides the fastball to get Hank Aaron out.

I remember he hit two home runs off me— one in each league, I believe. And he broke up a no-hitter of mine, I think in the eighth inning, when he was with the Milwaukee Brewers. He was always an extremely tough out because he didn't chase bad pitches; he hit the ball where it was pitched. He'd go with the ball away or he could pull the ball. He was disciplined, very conscious of the strike zone.

—Nolan Ryan

he wasn't a home run hitter. He didn't think home run.

Aaron connects for number 714 off Jack Billingham of the Cincinnati Reds. Bench congratulated him (right) as soon as the touched the plate, Aaron recalls, then retreated as the swarm of Braves pushed Bench away from home.

He thought of going up and getting good contact, hitting .300, hitting the ball where it was pitched. Hank always was one guy who played within himself, even on 715. It was

just the top hand rolling over, those great wrists, fly ball to left field, just creeped over into the bullpen. But that's the way they seemed like they all were.

—Johnny Bench

i think we were both the same. I think he was about 187 pounds like I was. I remember he was a right-center-field hitter. He didn't start pulling the ball until later on in life. He was right-center, left-center. But he hit the ball out to all fields.

—Willie Mays

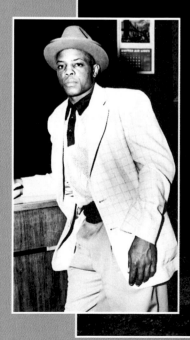

While hitting .477 for the Minneapolis Millers, Willie Mays received a contract from the New York Giants and hopped a bus headed for New York City.

they talk about Willie Mays as a five-tool player, and certainly he was that. But Henry was at least as much a five-tool player as Willie. Because Henry was consumed—and rightfully so—with breaking the home run record toward the end of his career, I think the other parts of his game were overlooked because of his prowess as a home run hitter.

—Tim McCarver

i saw Hank play in 1967 in spring training when I was traded to the Yankees. I can remember in batting practice, his first at bat, it was like, you know, somebody else got in there. There was a difference. The rings to the bat were different. When he hit the ball, it sounded like metal or iron hitting the ball, it really did.

—Bobby Cox

In the penultimate game of the 1973 season, Aaron became the last of three Braves, after third baseman Darrell Evans and second baseman Davey Johnson, to reach 40 home runs for the season. It was the only time that three players on one team have hit 40 homers. Playing his first year in Atlanta, Johnson hit 43 after never hitting more than 18. Evans' previous high was 19.

I learned a lot watching him play and hit.

I learned more from Hank Aaron than I did from any other player in the game. Rarely did he take batting practice, but when he did it was an absolute joy to watch. He put on a show all by himself and I forgot where I was or who I was, or what I was doing at the time. He is the greatest hitter I ever saw. Hank Aaron could do whatever he wanted to do at the plate. He wrote his own script and what an author he was.

—Davey Johnson

the only way you can be named greatest home run hitter is to beat Hank Aaron's record. Hitting 70 homers isn't that record. The greatest ever is Hank Aaron. He hit 755, didn't he? That is the greatest, and that's quite a few years down the road for me.

—Mark McGwire

Hank was a better hitter for a longer time than I was. Hank hit with pronounced wrist and top hand action. He hit line drive home runs, not towering fly balls like Mark McGwire.

—Mike Schmidt

h**e's not a** real big guy, but he had incredible hands and wrists. He generated a lot of bat speed with those two tools. He kind of reminds you of, well, Eric Davis—that kind of frame—though as he got older of course he gained size. It was just amazing to see, on the tapes of him hitting, that an inside pitch was never really an inside pitch because he could always get the head of the bat to the ball. He was a gifted person, who persevered. He really liked to speak his piece about what he thought and what he felt, which was good for us.

—Cecil Fielder

d**o you realize what happened in 1963? We** both ended up with 44 home runs. We both wore number 44. We were both from Mobile. Over all these years, nobody even seemed to notice, how much a coincidence that was. We tied for the league home run crown. I really kind of enjoyed that year more than my MVP year because of the coincidence.

—Willie McCovey

t his is going to sound funny, talking about a person who accomplished the things he did and hit 755 home runs, but to me the worst thing that happened to Hank Aaron was County Stadium. I was under the impression that Hank could hit .400 or close to it every year, if he hadn't gotten to the point where he discovered home runs. They were always talking about nobody will ever hit .400. I thought Hank would do it several times. But then he developed the home run stroke and naturally that's going to take from your average. County Stadium was a home-run-friendly stadium, so I just personally think that's the worst thing that could have happened to him.

—Willie McCovey

Ron Lewis painted this in 1989, when the living members of the 500 home run club were (from left to right) Ted Williams, Frank Robinson, Harmon Killebrew, Reggie Jackson, Mickey Mantle, Willie Mays, Hank Aaron, Mike Schmidt, Ernie Banks, Eddie Mathews, and Willie McCovey.

because of the amount of time you have to react and how hard pitchers throw, you can't overpower the ball necessarily, you have to be quick to the ball. I think Hank's had a big influence in the teaching of hitting and how good hitters are able to hit .330 and .340 and still hit their home runs. Griffey is a great example. Griffey has such a compact swing, a pretty swing to watch. But the other thing about the home run record is here is someone who has to be good, and be great, and hit home runs for a long period of time. Anyone that has any idea of math, you can start doing the numbers in your head and go, 20 years and 30 home runs a year still only gets you 600. Then you start thinking, how does that happen?

—Cal Ripken Jr.

As great as Ken Griffey Jr., Mark McGwire, and Barry Bonds have been in recent years, they still have a hefty climb up the mountain to see eye-to-eye with Aaron and Mays.

hitting 755 home runs without ever hitting 50 in a season can't be done unless you have amazing consistency.

—Albert Belle

It's remarkable how he packed so much power in such a short, compact swing. I think that he became, as he rightfully should have, the model power hitter. You don't have to be a real giant of a man like McGwire. And even a giant like McGwire, he still possesses a quick bat, similar to Hank. I think Hank really showed everyone what power there was in the flick of the wrist and hand power, hand speed. I think a lot of people model their swing, a short quick swing, on Henry.

—Cal Ripken Jr.

There is a tendency to focus on Henry's 700-plus home runs. Maybe that can be done through sheer ability. But Henry was a thoughtful hitter too. He knew what he was doing. He evolved from a right field hitter to a dead pull hitter when he had to.

—Tony Kubek

h is swing was smooth and grooved. He had a grooved swing like DiMaggio's—the swing was always the same. Willie Mays' swing varied, I think my swing varied, I even think Mantle's swing varied. Ted Williams had a grooved swing, Musial had a grooved swing. Aaron's style was a smooth, catlike, very consistent, grooved swing— the way you try to groove a golf swing.

—Reggie Jackson

Joe DiMaggio lines a hit in his 56th straight game, July 16, 1941.

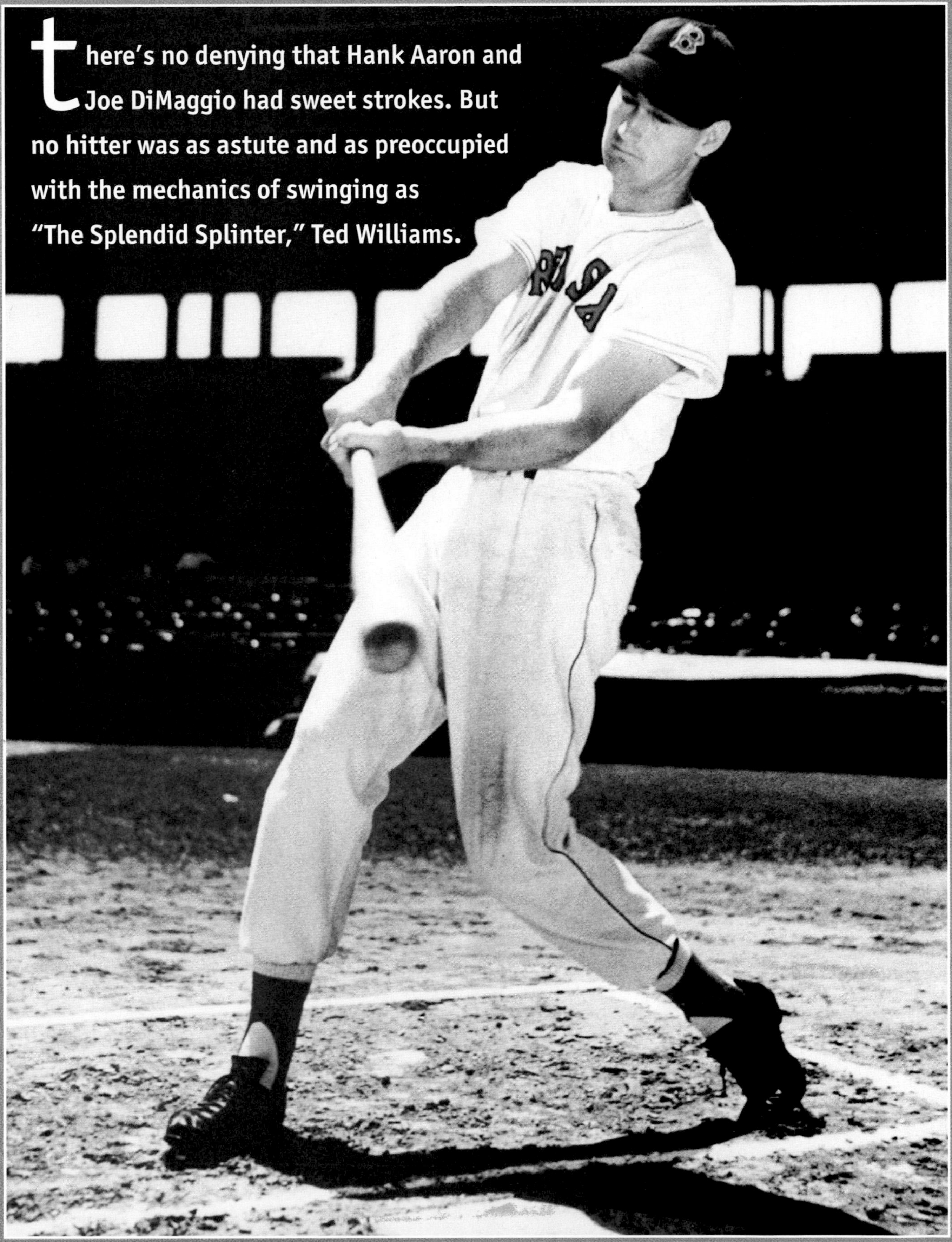

there's no denying that Hank Aaron and Joe DiMaggio had sweet strokes. But no hitter was as astute and as preoccupied with the mechanics of swinging as "The Splendid Splinter," Ted Williams.

the view from the mound

The swing was just right there, smooth, and that bat came around. When Henry hit a baseball, you knew it was gone.

—Phil Niekro

by phil niekro

> I think he had a great feeling for the strike zone. He really did. You didn't make Henry look bad too much. You never fooled him . . .

hank never came out of his shoes to hit a baseball, you know what I mean? He just never took an ungodly cut like he wanted to hit it out of the ballpark. The swing was just right there, smooth, and that bat came around. When Henry hit a baseball, you knew it was gone.

I think he had a great feeling for the strike zone. He really did. You didn't make Henry look bad too much. You never fooled him; you very seldom got those check swings or half swings. When he started that bat going, it came through all the way. I think everybody would agree that his wrists were his greatest asset, and his eyes. He's been known to hit balls "out of the catcher's mitts," as they say. He had the quickness; how quick he turned his bat over to hit the ball long, especially to the power alleys and the left field line! Strong, I don't know, not when you compare him to a Mark McGwire or a Sammy Sosa, as far as brutal strength. But those guys, they just don't have the quickness of that bat, the wrists that Henry had.

I never pitched against him because we were always teammates. I couldn't even pitch against him in batting practice in spring training. He wouldn't let me because of the knuckleball. I can't ever remember him hitting off me. Maybe once when I first came up or something. When I went out there I always wanted to throw a few knuckleballs at batting practice in spring training and kind of get the feel for the batter and the strike zone. Henry didn't want me to do that. He just didn't see any knuckleball pitchers around then, not in the National League, so he didn't want to take the time to try and hit them.

Speaking as a pitcher, you wanted Henry as your right fielder. You wanted that line drive to come to him in right field, with a man on second. A lot of people forget or don't realize how good of an arm he had, and accurate, and what a great outfielder he was. The same quiet way, what a great base runner he was. He did everything so fluidly. He wasn't a showoff. He hit a home run, he circled the bases. High fives weren't in then.

He just didn't spotlight everything he did. That wasn't Henry's style. He'd come in, he knew what his job was. He'd put his uniform on, he went through his daily exercise and his programs and his routines, the game started, and he went out there and played exceptionally well as everyone knows. He was consistent. It was day after day after day after day. You'd think sometimes, "Geez, when is this guy going to break down?"

He was quiet. I don't know about shyness; I don't think he was shy. When he wanted to say something he said it, and it had a meaning to it. I always thought to some point that Henry was maybe too quiet in the clubhouse. I thought maybe he could have led by speaking. When he did speak to players it was basically one-on-one at their lockers, sitting down. But he very seldom took charge in a team meeting or really said, "Okay you guys, here's the way we're going to do it." I think what he thought was, "Watch how I play, guys, and you won't have any problems in this game." He mostly led by example. We didn't really run a lot off the field together. He was a pretty private man off the field.

When he was chasing number 715, everyone knew the pressure was there, it was certainly in the clubhouse. The toughest part of it was probably away from the clubhouse—trying to find someplace to have breakfast, or lunch, or dinner, how to be out in the public without just being absolutely pounded by fans and autograph seekers.

You know, he had to have a bodyguard. I know he had some death threats at one time. He never talked about it. I think a lot of the people, we didn't even know that was going on until it was all over and the story came out. I know when we'd go on the road, no one would see Henry until it was time to go to the ballpark and dress. He was probably staying in a different hotel, checking in one hotel in his name and staying privately someplace else. I'm sure that happened at times. He had to have special ways to get to the ballpark, special ways to get out of that ballpark. He always had someone watching him, there with him. A nightmare is what it

was. But he wouldn't let it bother the ball club.

Press conferences—he would have them someplace outside the room. He would come in and get dressed and the locker room would just be full, reporters everywhere. The guys could walk around in the clubhouse and then Hank would go off someplace, or set a time, or go in the back room.

When he finally reached 715, I think everyone was glad it was over. Especially Henry. I think maybe the Braves would have liked to see it go on a little bit more because we were packing the ballparks.

The 755 record is going to stay there. With the way baseball is today, with injuries and the disabled list and everything like that, the record is just going to last. I don't know if anybody can stay that consistent, stay as healthy as he did. He didn't get too high or too low. He was even, right on the board, right down Main Street. With the salaries and the problems players are having today, I just don't see anyone passing him. ⊙

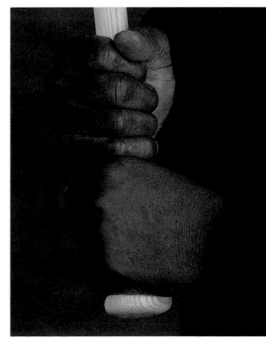

Note the difference in wrist and hand size in the grips of Ted Williams and Hank Aaron.

even if you had him 0-2, you never knew the difference between that and the time you had him 3-0. He never showed any facial expressions that would let you know otherwise.

—Al Downing

he was never off balance. When you have balance, you have longevity because you won't put undue stress on your body. It was like a heavyweight fighter always in position to hit you with that right. But in case you make him miss, he could hit you with a left. That's the way he batted. That's pure balance; he's never going to get a bad swing. That enables you to hit the ball hard, even if you read the pitch wrong. Take for instance, if he was up there looking for a fastball and you hit him with a curveball, he might have been a little bit out in front of the pitch, but instead of hitting that line drive off the wall that he was anticipating hitting with the fastball, he'd probably hit the ball four rows up in the seats off a curveball.

—Al Downing

How did I pitch to Hank Aaron? I was careful. Leo Durocher was one of my first managers and he said, "Never let the good hitters beat you." And Hank was in that particular class, so you had to give him total respect.

—Ferguson Jenkins

A pitcher in the mold of Catfish Hunter and Robin Roberts, who allowed few walks and more than their share of home runs, Jenkins was a bit more careful with his location while pitching to Aaron.

i only pitched to Hank a few times and I think he actually hit right-handed pitchers better than he did left-handed pitchers. I think Hank liked the ball out away from him, so— I don't know how successful I would have been—I would have pitched in on him and I would have changed speeds more than I saw other pitchers do against him. Of course it's easy to say, but Hank looked so calm and relaxed at the plate and then when he saw the ball he was so quick to address it. He had quick hands and though Hank wasn't a very big guy, he got the bat through the strike zone so quickly that he was a definite threat on a ball pitched anywhere.

—Warren Spahn

a t the beginning he hit the ball from a "line drive down" and used the whole field to hit in. As time went on he tried to pull the ball more and more, so instead of hitting the ball from the line drive down, he was hitting it from the line drive up. I remember one particular time that he hit a home run in Milwaukee, that the shortstop literally jumped for it, and it just went out of the park about 20 rows up in the bleachers.

—Warren Spahn

I faced Hank in the 1970 All-Star Game, my first. He didn't know what I threw. That was probably the best method. Of course, in that particular lineup I think Mays led off, Rose second,

Aaron, McCovey, Bench. You know, it was such a good lineup I think Dick Allen hit seventh or eighth. I was scared to death. It's the only migraine headache I ever had. That's when I knew Earl Weaver didn't like me because he made me start that All-Star Game. When I woke up that morning I had a massive headache, I never get headaches, and I think that was from looking at that lineup. In an All-Star Game, if you have your stuff there's a distinct advantage that you only have to face a hitter like Hank Aaron one time and he doesn't know you. You're working on adrenaline, and it's not like he can adjust because by the time he's due to face you the second time, you're sitting on the bench.

—Jim Palmer

Aaron made what he called his "first substantial contribution to black society" when he staged a 1972 bowling tournament to benefit Sickle Cell Anemia. Willie Stargell and Jim Palmer were among those invited, along with Reggie Jackson, Tom Seaver, Eddie Mathews, Gale Sayers, Lew Burdette, Frank Robinson, Ernie Banks and more.

hank was a great hitter. I tried to mix it up on him, in and out. You know, we both hit our first home runs off the same pitcher—Vic Raschi.

—Whitey Ford

I didn't get a chance to pitch against him too much, until about 1965. You know, they just said try to keep the ball in the ballpark. They said he didn't like the side-arm too much so . . . he only hit doubles when you side-armed him. So I tried to side-arm him a lot. But I mostly pitched around him because he seemed to be such a better hitter with men in scoring position. I only gave up I think two home runs in ten years, plus a home run in the All-Star Game. But he got many, many key base hits with men in scoring position.

—Gaylord Perry

the first time I faced Hank Aaron, I didn't know how to pitch him because I was only 19 years old and I was pretty intimidated because I grew up being a Henry Aaron fan as a teenager when he was back with the Milwaukee Braves. So it was pretty overwhelming facing, at 19, one of your childhood idols. So all I was trying to do was make good pitches, keep the ball down and hope that he didn't hit a home run off of me. I threw fastballs because in those days I didn't have very good command of my curveball. And he had never seen me before and I was basically a fastball pitcher. He popped up foul to the first baseman.

my attitude about him was, and I think it was true with great hitters, that you didn't fall into any certain pattern with them. I tried to give them a little different look every at bat because I felt like

those guys were very good at making adjustments so I tried to throw Aaron—because of his power—I tried to throw pitches that would lessen his chances of hitting me out of the ballpark. So if I missed with a curve, I wanted to miss down with it. I tried to stay pretty much out of the middle of the plate with him. I felt like he hit more home runs to left field than anywhere else, so I felt like low and away I had a better chance of staying in the ballpark with him.

i tell you what, he's an amazing hitter. For the number of home runs he hit, look at the average that he made contact. Strikeouts were few and far between. I would prefer to face a power hitter that had a big swing. You made a mistake, you knew you were going to get hurt. But if you made your pitch, you knew that you had a pretty good chance of getting him out.

—Nolan Ryan

Admiring his Hall of Fame plaque in 1982, Hank could afford to smile. Aaron was elected nine votes short of unanimous. At that time, only Ty Cobb had received a higher percentage of votes than Aaron.

Well, as he got older and when I say older I'm talking toward the end of his career, he became more of a pull hitter. He used to be able to take an outside pitch, one out over the plate, and hit it out of the park in right field. But as he got older he lost a little of that strength, he couldn't hit it out over there. He pulled the ball, he started hitting the inside pitch for home runs.

—Bob Gibson

i've got a funny story. Aaron had reached first base somehow. He was going to steal second on me and I went into my stretch. A lot of guys tried to time me, I'd go into my stretch and they'd take off. Well, I went into my stretch and I looked over my shoulder and he started running. I turned around and chased him. I got within about four feet from him and he was standing there facing me and I was facing him. We both were standing still. He would fake to the left, and I'd fake to the left. He'd fake to

Gibson's statement that "You couldn't throw a fastball by Hank Aaron" was borne out by the facts. The Hall of Fame strikeout artist, who was routinely murder on right-handed hitters, surrendered eight home runs to Aaron.

the right and I'd fake to the right. I started grinning and I said, "I got you now." And he started laughing, then he just fell on the ground and I touched him.

—Bob Gibson

One incident I remember, when I was going for my 3,000th strikeout, Hank was a little on in his career. He was playing down in Atlanta and I was trying to strike him out. I had two strikes and one ball or something like that. I kept throwing the ball a foot outside, but he didn't want to be that 3,000th strikeout. Finally he hit the ball to second base and as he ran past the mound he kind of grinned at me and said, "I wasn't going to be it."

—Bob Gibson

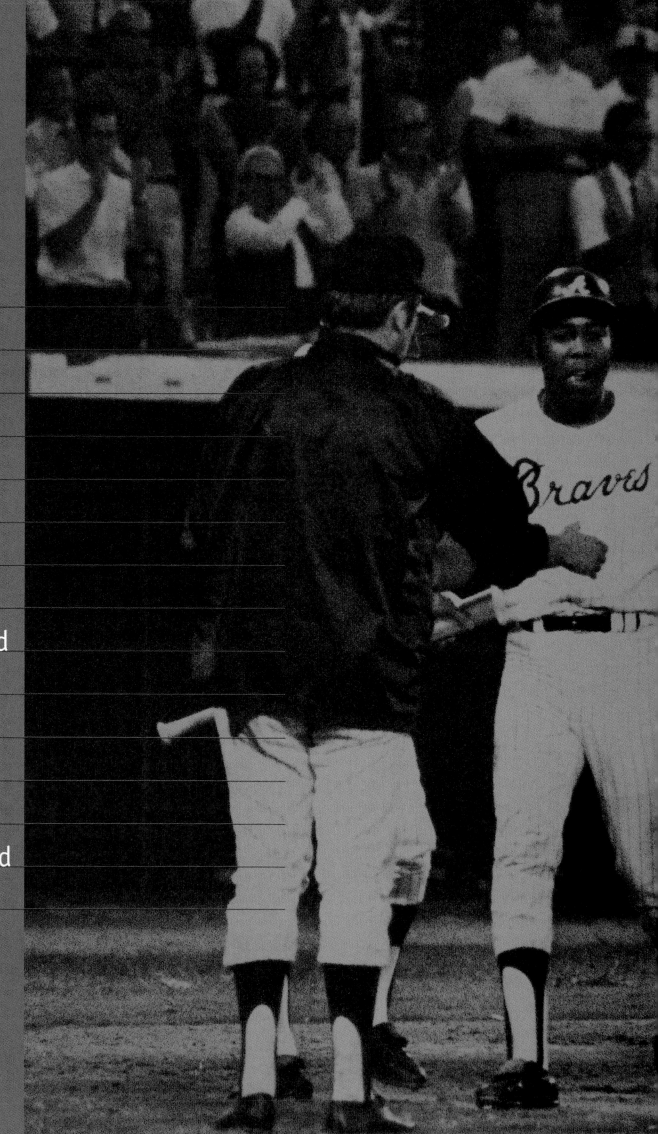

What comes to mind when I think of Hank Aaron? Consistent excellence. That's what I think about, absolutely. And the wrists—watching his hands, his wrists. The way he snapped the bat.
—Peter Gammons

persistence

by peter gammons

W

hen I was in college at the University of North Carolina, I used to occasionally drive down when the Braves were in Atlanta. I would drive down there to see him play, so it was a great trip. It was only a four-hour drive. We'd go down there and see good teams come into Atlanta. Of course, Joe Torre was on the Braves, but it was mainly Henry. You went down there to see him play and see him hit. Having been from Boston, I was too young when he was coming along, but he did come up the year after the Braves moved out of Boston. So it was kind of a shame that we were robbed of having Henry Aaron play here.

The first time I covered Hank was when I was going back down to Atlanta in 1971 to do a story when the Giants were in the pennant race. I did a kind of comparison story because Bobby Bonds was having the year of his life. He was having a breakthrough year, but what did he dream of being? He dreamt of being Henry Aaron. And yet trying to be that consistent is something that's almost impossible to do.

Hank was almost like a metronome. He was there with very similar numbers every year. So he never hit 58 home runs, because he was always banging 44 or whatever. To me, that's greater. I'm not at all taking away from McGwire, because he's done it three straight years, Griffey has done it several years; it's phenomenal. But to be able to play at that level every single year is what's so great. That first time I was writing about Aaron versus Bobby Bonds, people were saying Bobby Bonds is the greatest this, he's the greatest that. The whole point was, let's see if he can have Aaron's kind of consistency.

What comes to mind when I think of Hank Aaron? Consistent excellence. That's what I think about, absolutely. And the wrists—watching his hands, his wrists. The way he snapped the bat. I think that was the first thing that ever struck me, the first time I ever saw him play, which was the All-Star Game of 1960. I was also amazed how small he was in person. He wasn't ripped like Sammy Sosa or something. The incredible athletic ability that he had for someone that small amazed me. Watching him hit, the power he generated with those wrists, was just astounding to me. And there was a real grace to him. Other than the bat speed, the acceleration, there was nothing flashy about him. But there was a style to the way he hit.

I think he was really hurt in the comparisons with Mays. I have to admit, my favorite player was Willie Mays. And why is that? Well, I was in Boston, but he came along in New York, and he made the memorable play in the 1954 World Series, actually a couple of memorable plays in that first game, the catch off Vic Wertz and the stolen base in the tenth inning. Willie played center field, which is more glamorous. He was flashier, he'd make the bucket catches and things like that. I can't judge one way or another who was better. I didn't see them enough. I have to go on what others say and I'm amazed in talking to players who played against them both how split down the middle they are. Willie Mays is all electricity and he's east coast, New York, center field. On the other hand, playing right field, I don't think Henry ever got appreciated the same

Hank was almost like a metronome. He was there with very similar numbers every year.

way. I think a lot of people realize it's more difficult to play the angles and have to throw from there. He had great instincts. He was a great outfielder, a *great* outfielder, playing a corner position and taking balls at angles that are really more difficult than center field. He was a great base runner. He wasn't a base stealer because that wasn't the Braves game. But that doesn't mean a guy isn't a great base runner. And he had great instincts. That's not to make any comparison with Mays, because I have them both on my all-time team.

And Hank never promoted himself. He's a quiet guy. It's also unfortunate that he had to be compared with Mays. He shouldn't have had to, didn't have to share that stage. You know what I mean? But he also had the problem of the Mickey Mantle era, a white guy in New York. And Mickey Mantle was not as good a player as Henry Aaron. The tools technically might have been greater, but he wasn't a greater player. I think that Mickey Mantle is a more famous person in baseball history than Henry Aaron. I'm not saying that's an outrage, because Mickey was great . . . but he wasn't Henry Aaron.

I remember once being out to eat with Tip O'Neill, who was one of the greatest baseball fans and baseball historians I ever knew. After a couple of drinks, he was talking about his all-

time team. I said, "It's impossible, you can't compare Ty Cobb with Aaron and Mays, it's an impossibility." You can compare DiMaggio with those guys a little bit more. Ruth's got to be there. But in the end I took Aaron, Mays and Ruth in the outfield. And then I had Cobb, DiMaggio and Williams. And he said, "You know it's interesting; you're probably the only person I've ever heard put Aaron in there." And then he said, "I think you're probably right."

Take batting average, total bases, consistency, the great outfield play. I remember Hank saying to me, "You know, really, it's harder to play right field than it is center field." Henry was

I think everybody should have done more with Henry and talk about "What will it take for Mark McGwire to go after Henry Aaron?"

a great center fielder, it's just that the Braves had Billy Bruton then. I think he sometimes has felt as if he has been pushed aside in terms of history.

I was sitting at home when he hit his 715th. I live right outside of Boston, and I was covering the Red Sox at the time and I had that night off. I was really excited; I like to see records broken. On the other hand, fast forwarding to this summer, I thought maybe Henry would be pulled into this home run chase a little bit more. Now, I understand it's single season and it's Ruth and Maris, but at the same time, I would have liked to have seen the commissioner's office—all of us—do a little

bit more. ESPN—I think everybody should have done more with Henry and talk about "What will it take for Mark McGwire to go after Henry Aaron?" I did a little thing, I did a couple of them. I did one piece, one written for the paper and then one on ESPN, about what he has to do and why it's almost impossible. I think Griffey could do it.

I also think the best thing that ever happened to Maris was McGwire. And I have said many times that maybe Henry Aaron will finally get his due if Griffey starts to make a push for his record. Because you know that Griffey would be really respectful about it. But it will be hard for Griffey: it's awfully hard to keep doing it every year through injuries and inconsistency. But if it did happen, I think Hank would be afforded more glory. I think he should be afforded more respect. He is a really good man. ⬤

In the 1950s, the persistent question in New York was, "Who's better, Willie, Mickey or the Duke?" By April 8, 1974, the answer for some people was, "None of the above. It's Hank." "Willie Mays and I got so much publicity because we broke in together and played in New York," said Mantle in 1970. "Hank didn't and in my mind he is the most underrated ballplayer of my era. As far as I'm concerned, Aaron is the also the best player of my era."

he's a guy who played every day, never complained, and took great care of himself. Hank played every single game, day in and day out. He was the ideal number three batter. He was fast, he hit for average, and he hit the long ball.

—Orlando Cepeda

When I think of 755 home runs, I think of a guy who had to be consistent through the years. Every year he had to go out there and put that ball over the fence. Make contact and hit the ball over the fence. He had to be in the lineup to do that. He never did get hurt.

—Billy Williams

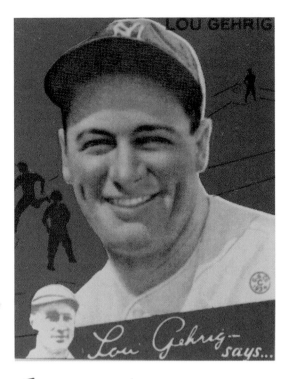

While the twin paradigms of durability were Lou Gehrig and Cal Ripken, Billy Williams was a model of constancy, too, playing in 1,117 straight games in the sixties and early seventies. Aaron's durability was also impressive. In the sixteen years from 1955 through 1970, Aaron played in 150 or more games fourteen times.

his home run total is an achievement that you have to compare to Cal Ripken's achievement, Lou Gehrig's achievement. I don't know what else you'd compare it to. Jimmy Brown playing an entire career and never missing a game. Wilt Chamberlain playing an entire career and never fouling out. As good a career as I had, I can't relate to 755 home runs. How do you compare it? You've got to go back and pick out the greatest athletes in the history of sports to compare it to anything. I probably would say that 755 home runs is probably the most recognized, most prestigious record that there is and Henry Aaron has gotten the least credit for greatness

—Reggie Jackson

hank was so good. He was so consistent, he was so durable. His record speaks not only to his incredible talent but to his durability. Boy, he could hit.

—Bud Selig

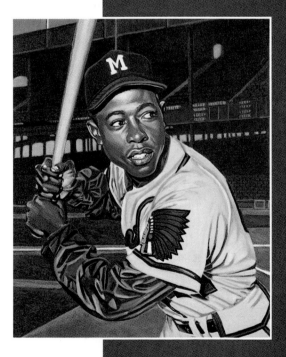

What was always so impressive to me was how Hank moved at his own pace. And how he kept focused on what he was doing out in the field, but when he was off the field he had this sense of purpose.

he just was
determined,
without making a
big deal about it,
without any fuss,
without any
whining, without
any complaining,
without any
arrogance. And
I was deeply
impressed by that.

—Tom Brokaw

If Woody Allen was right—that 80 percent of success in life is just showing up—then Hank Aaron had a huge jump on the competition. He personified an old-fashioned virtue known as constancy—an unwavering approach to his work. He hits his 600th homer off Gaylord Perry in 1971 (left) and relaxes with his first wife, Barbara Lucas, and their two children Gaile and Lary.

this sounds sort of corny, but this is a man of humble origins, who never lost sight of his roots—who maybe was never entirely comfortable in the spotlight that he was thrust into. He never really aspired to be a hero or a role model, or a celebrity. He was just such an accomplished baseball player, that all the rest kind of came to him as a byproduct. And he did the best he could. What he really wanted to do was give an honest day's work and be fair, and fulfill his promise. And to do everything he could for his family.

—Michael Tollin

teammates

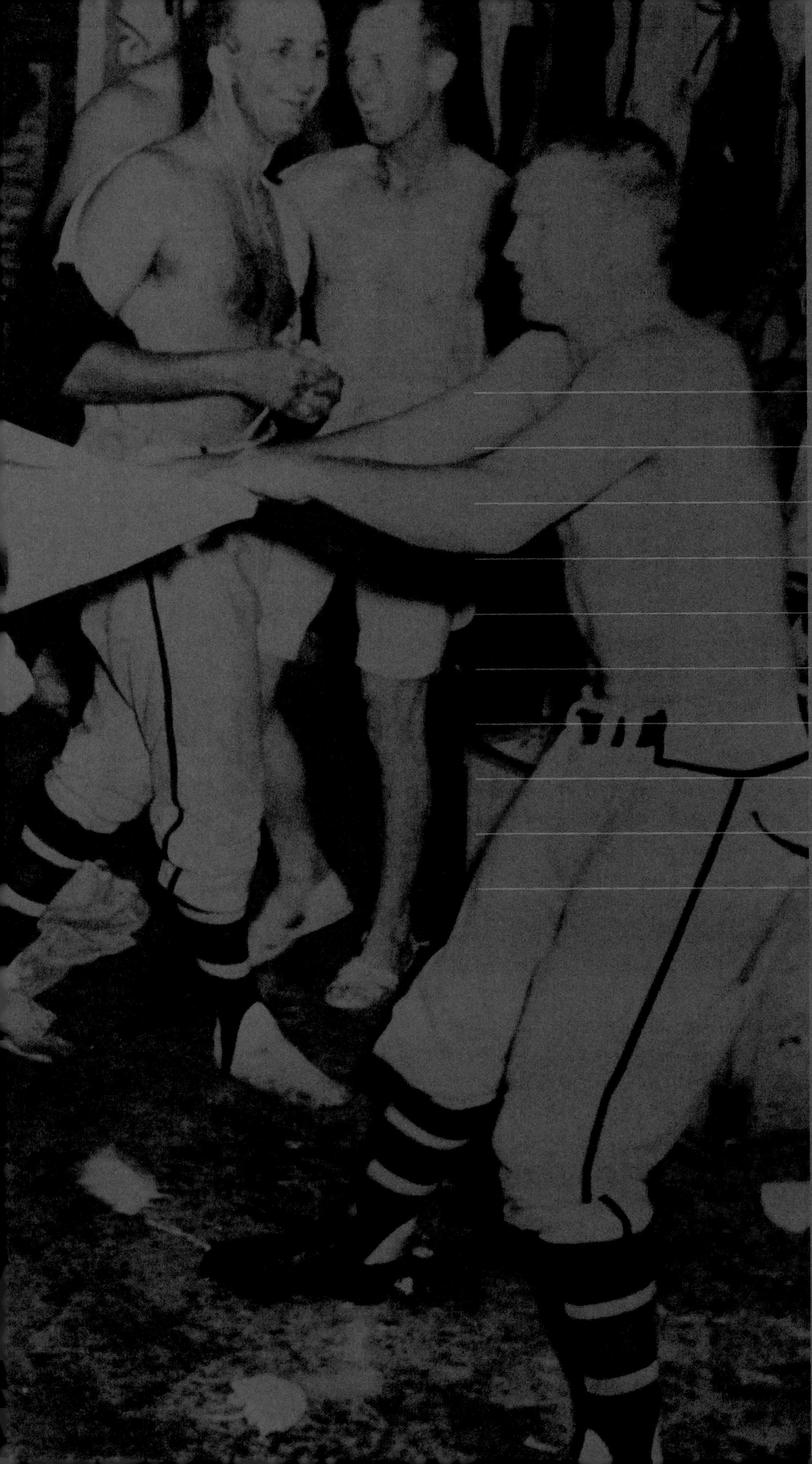

He was always
a guy who
threw the ball
to the cutoff
man. He was
a great right
fielder. He
went out
and did all
he had to do.
—Joe Torre

Preceding page: Felix Mantilla, Wes Covington, Frank Torre and Del Crandall are among a clubhouse full of Braves whooping it up after the pennant-clinching victory over St. Louis in 1957. Aaron hit the homer that clinched the flag, and he won the MVP that season.

aaron being carried off the field after his pennant-clinching home run against Billy Muffett in 1957. "I had always dreamed about a moment like Bobby Thomson had in 1951 and this was it," Aaron said.

the first time I met Hank was in 1956, when my brother Frank was playing with the Braves. I was a 16-year-old kid working out at Ebbets Field. I remember also making a trip that year to Milwaukee, and I worked out with the ball club. You knew Hank was something special. He was a diminutive guy. If you put him next to Eddie Mathews or Joe Adcock, he was a lot smaller than they were. One time when I did visit Hank during that season, I remember sitting behind the third base dugout in Milwaukee. I forget who the pitcher was on the other team, but he threw a pitch to Henry and the ball was actually to the right side of his head—in other words it was past him already from my angle—and Henry's back is to me because he's batting right-handed. He actually hit that ball over the right center field fence and the ball was already past him. There was so much talk about his great wrists and if I hadn't understood what that meant before, I did at that point in time.

Home run hitters always pull the ball. They always try to hit it to their power field. But Henry was very unorthodox in that he was more a good hitter than a home run hitter. I think what enhanced the home run situation was the fact that he played so long and he was such a good hitter, and he knew exactly what his capabilities were. I batted behind him for eight years. I batted fourth, he batted third.

I remember watching, especially with young pitchers, they'd throw strike one, strike two, and I'm saying, "Watch this. They're going to try to move him back off the plate and then go away with another pitch." But

Legend has it that Simmons gave Aaron fits with an assortment of off-speed stuff. Despite his frustration with the deceptive lefty, Aaron still rapped six homers off him.

they'd never get that third pitch inside enough. He'd hit a home run. His hands were so quick.

Of course, the comic part of Henry was trying to face Curt Simmons. Simmons used to throw that real slow change. One time in the old St. Louis ballpark, he threw one of those change-ups and Henry ran up in the box and hit a ball on the right field roof for a home run. Chris Pelekoudas was the umpire. I think Bob Uecker was the catcher and he went up to Pelekoudas and said he was out of the batter's box. Pelekoudas called him out.

Henry could do everything. He was never flashy like Willie Mays or Roberto Clemente; so he didn't capture a lot of attention with the throws on the fly to the base. He was always a guy who threw the ball to the cutoff man. He was a great right fielder. He went out and did all he had to do. Again, he never said a whole lot. He was very quiet, never flashy. I think the

Joe Torre was Hank Aaron's teammate for nine years, beginning in 1960. He later managed the Braves from 1982 through 1984.

one stat—if you ever looked it up—he hardly ever got thrown out stealing bases. But again, he never stole bases just for statistics. He stole bases to win games. On a number of occasions I was called upon to sacrifice with Henry at first base. It was the easiest job in the world because all you'd have to do is bunt it right back to the mound, because they would never even think of trying to throw him out at second. He got a great jump and he had such great body control. He'd beat out infield singles and it didn't look like he was running as fast as he actually was running, because everything was so easygoing for him.

In today's game, I hate to think of how many home runs he'd hit because of these homer-friendly ballparks and the tightly wound baseball. And the fact that you can hit the ball to center field and right field and have the ball go out as easily as pulling the ball now. Again, he didn't appear as strong as other people. I think that there were only four guys that hit home runs into the center field seats at the old Polo Grounds—Joe Adcock, Lou Brock, Willie Mays, and Hank. I remember Hank hitting a line drive off Jay Hook of the Mets. It was a line drive and I said, "Well, that's a line drive, that's going to be over the center fielder's head." And it just kept going and went into the seats. It was remarkable, the power he packed in that body of his. His swing was controlled; he didn't strike out a lot. When you look at the

home run hitters now, you have to look at 100-plus strikeouts all the time.

Day in and day out, Hank was a class guy. He never tried to tell anybody how good he was because he was a proponent of the fact that you show people on the field. You don't talk about it. The one statistic that was very important to Henry was scoring 100 runs every year. I have to believe in my mind, he was saying to himself, "I know I'm going to knock in 100." But scoring 100 was a stat that he paid a lot of attention to.

After I was traded from the Braves, I talked to him at All-Star games. I remember going up to him one time and asking him about hitting off Bill Stoneman, a pitcher with Montreal who was very tough for me. I said, "I can't find the ball, I just can't find it." He said, "Hit off his slider." In other words, go up there looking for the slider and you'll be able to find the other pitches once he throws it. You know, it did work for me. He gave those kind of little tips. Another little tip he gave me was that every at bat is a new day. This way it kept you from pressing when you were 0 for 3. It kept you from relaxing when you were 3 for 3. He was a very devoted, determined hitter and I can still remember listening on one of those Mutual broadcasts when he hit that home run in 1957 to clinch the pennant. I was just a fan. I wasn't playing yet professionally. It was because of my brother that I was a big Braves fan.

In the clubhouse he was never very outgoing. You wouldn't even know he was there, aside from the fact that you knew he was a good player and you'd always look for him. But he was the leader. I have to compare him a lot to a Paul O'Neill or a Dale Murphy, guys who lead by example and not by saying "Hey, follow me." In fact, on that ball club, Eddie Mathews was named captain because he was more of the outgoing type than Henry was.

Now that I think about it, I remember one time that Henry did show some emotion. Cincinnati pitcher Jim Maloney used to knock him down a little bit. I remember in Milwaukee he walked off Maloney. And I'm the next hitter. And Henry is screaming at him, just screaming at him. And I remember stepping out of the box, asking Henry, please calm down, because I'm the hit-

ter here and I don't want to take one in the ear either. But that was one of the few times he displayed that kind of emotion.

The number 755 is mind boggling. When you consider, first of all, the fewer teams in each league and that the pitching was tougher. As I said, the ballparks were less friendly. And again, being able to play every single day. In the days that he hit home runs, he was more a line drive hitter, but he became an established hitter before he was known for the home runs. What enabled him to hit the home runs is the fact that he stayed so durable for so long. Ⓑ

After Eddie Mathews snatched Moose Skowron's sharp one-hopper and stepped on third to record the last out of the 1957 World Series, the celebration was on. Joe's older brother Frank Torre, wearing number 14, is running to join the celebration begun by Del Crandall and Eddie Mathews.

trust me on this one, he was the best ballplayer. It was probably later on in my career when he kept beating me out in every department. I watched him over many, many years and watched him never throw to the wrong base, never miss a cutoff, never make a mistake. I saw the instincts he had. We see each other occasionally but we don't make a point to see other. We laugh about old times and everything. We are good friends.

—Eddie Mathews

It was late March 1969 when the St. Louis Cardinals traded me to the Atlanta Braves for Joe Torre. Being traded in the offseason is an adjustment of sorts. Being traded in spring training is more of a burden because it means uprooting your family on very short notice. So I admit to being less than thrilled when Bing Devine told me to pack my bags and join the Atlanta Braves in West Palm

Teammates—like Felipe Alou, Bob Oliver and Eddie Mathews, here with Aaron—soon learned that Aaron's presence in the clubhouse was a plus, just like his presence on the field.

Springs that spring. There were two good reasons for going to the Braves: one was Felipe Alou; the other was Hank Aaron. Felipe and I went back a long way and I was delighted to be reunited with him again. We had been through so much together since the days that we were friends and teammates with the Minneapolis Millers in 1957, then teammates and close friends with the San Francisco Giants for six more seasons. When I arrived in West Palm Beach, Hank welcomed me to the club immediately and instantly made me feel part of the team. He said I would like Atlanta and that I would help the Braves win the Western Division title. It was the first year of divisional play and he was right on both accounts.

—Orlando Cepeda

Trying to sneak a pitch past Hank Aaron is like trying to sneak the sunrise past a rooster.

—Joe Adcock

He got along great and I think he displayed his ability so he was very well respected. I think that he hit either third or fourth in our lineup. We had Hank, Mathews and Adcock in a row, so you couldn't pitch around any of those guys. You didn't want to pitch to Mathews by pitching around Hank. He just represented hitting for power and to all fields in the middle of our lineup. He was a guy who went about his business; he loved to play. Our ball club was one with a bunch of pranksters, a very close-knit ball club and our clubhouse was like a zoo— everybody agitated everybody, but when the game started it was one for all and all for one. Our main objective was to beat the other club and we did a pretty good job of it.

—Warren Spahn

Early on, Aaron was a quiet guy on a team of cut-ups. Here Aaron and Chuck Tanner share a laugh with Warren Spahn, the Braves chief prankster, after Tanner's homer won the Opening Day game in 1955.

Hank was the
best friend to
us. He would
chastise us
sometimes if
we were getting
out of line and
we weren't
acting right,
like not eating
right or staying
out too late
or not getting
up in the
morning to eat
breakfast.

—Dusty Baker

leading by example

i just visited Dusty out in San Francisco and we talked about our days together in Atlanta. He again told me what Hank meant to him and I knew at the time that Hank was like his father. All of our young players just watched Hank so carefully and he set such a great example in his work habits. He didn't pass up infield or outfield practice, even at the end of his career. When we took infield, he would throw from the outfield and set an example for our young outfielders because sometimes it was like they didn't want to participate. But when a person of Hank's stature does it, how can a 21- or 22-year old say, "I don't want to do it today?"

—Clyde King

i first met Hank in the summer of 1967, when I graduated from Del Campo High School, in Carmichael, California. I was a 25th round draft choice, and the Braves sent for my mom and I to come to Los Angeles and work out with the team. My mom was negotiating my contract.

I don't know how it happened, but I think my mom requested me to talk to Hank or something and so I met him. I didn't know what to do and was about to forfeit quite a few scholarships in football and basketball. My mom and dad had just gotten divorced so I was at a crossroads. I asked Hank what he would do, and he told me that if I had enough confidence in myself to be in the big leagues, then sign. And if not, then go on and go to college. But if I did sign, that I had to go to college. He wanted me to go to college in the off-season. So did my mom. My mom asked him, "If my son signs, will you take care of him as if he's your son?" Hank said "Yeah," and he kept his word.

I ended up going over to his house at least three or four days a week. His wife, Barbara, would cook for us and we knew all his kids. His kids were closer to me in age than he and I were. I think his daughter Gaile was 13 or 14, and I was 18. We were tight with Hank. Hank would tell us about our eating habits. He said, "Eat every day around one o'clock because it gives your food time to digest before a night game. If you eat late, you have got to eat light—chicken or fish, or pasta or something." During spring training, we'd always be over at Hank's room. Our job was kind of like to make Hank laugh during those days. He loved to laugh. Hank was getting all this free music from all over the country. You name it, they were sending it. I was kind of in charge of telling him what music was hip and what wasn't. I was like 18-19, and now I'm in the position that I ask my daughter what's hip. Through Hank, eventually, Ralph [Garr] and I used to go over to Jesse Jackson's house to eat. We met the Staple Singers. We met Andrew Young and Maynard Jackson. You name them, we met them through Hank.

Hank was the best friend to us. He would chastise us sometimes if we were getting out of line and we weren't

Aaron had an influential way with the younger players on the team, stressing the right eating and sleeping habits. In turn, they (with the perennially hip Sammy Davis Jr.) taught him about how to be in tune.

> Hank didn't take a lot of walks. He didn't care that you didn't protect him, he was going to swing anyway. He didn't walk a lot and he didn't strike out a lot. It's that whatever he swung at, he usually kept it fair.

acting right, like not eating right or staying out too late or not getting up in the morning to eat breakfast. For him to find out you didn't get up early enough to eat breakfast before a day game, he'd get mad. He's big on that. We lockered next to him.

By the time guys were just starting to have agents and the game was starting to change, Hank helped sort of keep the front office off us. If we had a problem, we could go to Hank. And then when Hank wasn't offered a job back with the Braves in 1975, that was the worst year of our careers, first for Ralph Garr and myself, and Darrell Evans, we didn't have anybody to go to. One time I called Hank from a pool room in West Palm Beach. I was playing pool with some Spanish guys and some white guys and when the owner found out I wasn't Latin black but American black, she threw me out. I called Hank, crying, and the next day he went to the Braves and they didn't do much really. So he called the NAACP for me. Hank would help if you had a problem with anything, anything.

And Hank was a prankster. I remember a time I wasn't feeling too good and he gave me sulfur pills. They make you urinate orange and red and stuff. I thought I had some disease or something. I'm peeing in the toilet, thinking I had some disease. I ran in Hank's room, did not know what to do, and he and Ralph Garr were falling down laughing on the floor.

I'll tell you, Hank liked to laugh. Everybody used to come over to Hank's room and we'd go out with Hank after the game. He had a lot of home-boys around the league: Willie McCovey, Billy Williams, a lot of men from Mobile, Alabama. And we'd hook up with Cleon Jones and Tommy Agee. And the only pitcher on another team I ever saw Hank associate with was Jerry Koosman.

Hank was also a leader. Most of the time he led by example. In the outfield he'd tell me where to play and sometimes I'd feel like saying, "Man, move over, dude; you're too close." But that was Hank Aaron and I didn't say that. I hit behind him in the order. And that's what kills me today when I hear guys talk about nobody protecting them in the order. Here I was, a 22-year-old, hitting behind Hank Aaron, and not once did he ever complain about it. I was more worried about it than he was. He told me, don't worry about it. He said, you hit enough singles and doubles, they'll stop walking me so much.

Hank didn't take a lot of walks. He didn't care that you didn't protect him, he was going to swing anyway. He didn't walk a lot and he didn't strike out a lot. It's that whatever he swung at, he usually kept it fair. A lot of guys walk because they foul off some pitches that they could hit and then the pitcher can't make a quality pitch two or three times. Or they'll take that pitch, thinking the pitcher's scared of them. But Hank was ready to hit all the time and he had an idea what the guy was going to do to him. He knew the umpires. I've seen him tell me, probably half a dozen times, that he was going to look for this pitch and he's going to hit it over the right center field fence. He's going to look for this one.… Or like he'll say, "Dusty, that left fielder drops his head when he fields a ball. So if I hit a single I'm going to trot halfway down and then as soon as he drops his head I'm going to put on speed and I'll be at

second base." He did it. He stole a base whenever we needed it. He did whatever was necessary to win a ballgame.

The thing I loved the most about him was that he could play in pain better than everybody I've ever seen. He taught me that one too. He was the one that did 150 games a year for 14 out of 16 years [and in those two "easy" years he played 145 and 147]. Two games off a month and that's about it. He never would take it off against the real good pitchers, never ducked the good ones. Did he play in pain? Back pain is the most that I can remember. I think he had sciatic nerve problems. He used to limp in like an old man and then go to the training room, come out of the training room, sit in his locker, look at the newspaper and not be reading. Just sit there. Ralph and I just looked at him trying to figure out what he was doing. And then he'd get up, walk outside on the field.

ank was mentally tough and easygoing and steady. Like Willie Mays, you could always write his name in the lineup. If you got in the trainer's room and lay down, the boys would walk by and say "How is she today, doc?" It was a little tougher, and more credit is due Hank for that.

—Bobby Bragan

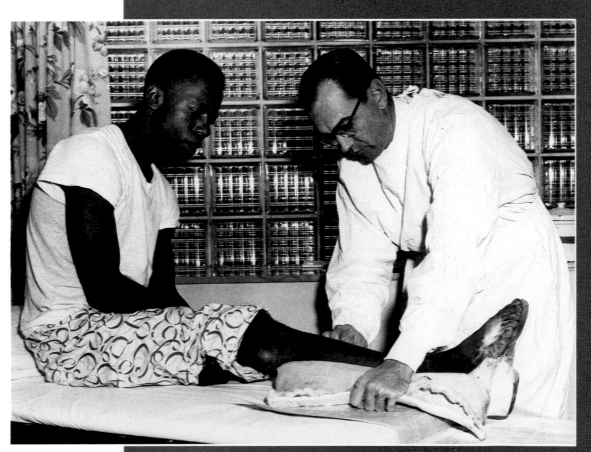

Aaron's broken ankle late in the season in 1954 may have kept him from winning Rookie of the Year. St. Louis outfielder Wally Moon won the award. Three years later, Moon would watch Aaron's pennant-clinching homer sail over his head.

You think of him as a contact hitter, a man who could win ballgames for you with singles and doubles. But the fact that he had that great longevity and was not injury prone and played a lot more games than most people— all that contributed to his amazing total of home runs.

—Ralph Kiner

Three who stood the test of time (below), Hall of Famers Roberto Clemente, Willie Stargell, and Hank. Aaron's approach to hitting might be considered an outside-in method. Rather than spend time on his own batting mechanics, he studied the tendencies of pitchers around the league, thus enabling him to predict what they would throw on a given count. Hank was a "guess hitter," but his guesses were well educated indeed.

Chasing the dream: nobody thought that young pitcher Phil Niekro threw Hall of Fame stuff, but it turned out he was the stuff Hall of Famers are made of.

h e wasn't boisterous, he wasn't real talkative, he just kind of came into the ballpark, put his uniform on, and just did his business every day.

—Phil Niekro

W ith Hank, you're not talking about going out and having a good year for the first three years and being called a superstar. Hank did this day in and day out, year after year, for 23 years. So when you talk about superstars and you try and put titles on these other guys who are not superstars, it peeves me off. These guys have potential to be superstars. But they're not superstars yet, until they can put numbers together on a consistent basis.

—Willie Stargell

i
doubt strongly if Henry's home run record will ever be broken. I doubt that very much.

Aaron, on Opening Day 1974 with Vice President Ford and baseball immortals Johnny Bench and Pete Rose. More than two decades earlier Aaron shone in Eau Claire, Wisconsin, where he was later honored with a monument.

Henry Aaron

On June 14, 1952, Henry Aaron made his professional baseball debut here at Carson Park with the Eau Claire Bears. In his first two at-bats, he hit run-scoring singles in a game against St. Cloud, Minn.

Aaron is depicted here as the Bears' 18-year-old shortstop from Mobile, Ala., wearing No. 6.

He went on to hit .336 with nine home runs for Eau Claire, a class C minor league team. He made the all-Star team and was Northern League Rookie of the Year.

Two years later, in 1954, Aaron joined the Milwaukee Braves and hit the first of his major league record 755 home runs. He retired in 1976 with the Milwaukee Brewers. In 1982, "Hammerin' Hank" was inducted into the Baseball Hall of Fame in Cooperstown, N.Y.

i
don't think today's players are going to play long enough. One thing about Henry is that he always kept himself in awfully good condition at all times. His habits were good. I think that was one of the great pluses that he had. I don't think players today who are making the kind of money the top guys make are going to want to hang around that long.

—Bill Rigney

Aaron, Mathews, and Spahn led the Braves to pennants in 1957 and 1958. Aaron always felt they should have won in 1956 and 1959, too, which would have stamped the team as a dynasty.

he was a guy who went about his business; he loved to play.
—Warren Spahn

trying times

The average citizen didn't know—at least I didn't know what he was going through. In fact, that was one of the things that really made me say "Yes, this is a story that we need to tell because we didn't know."
—Denzel Washington

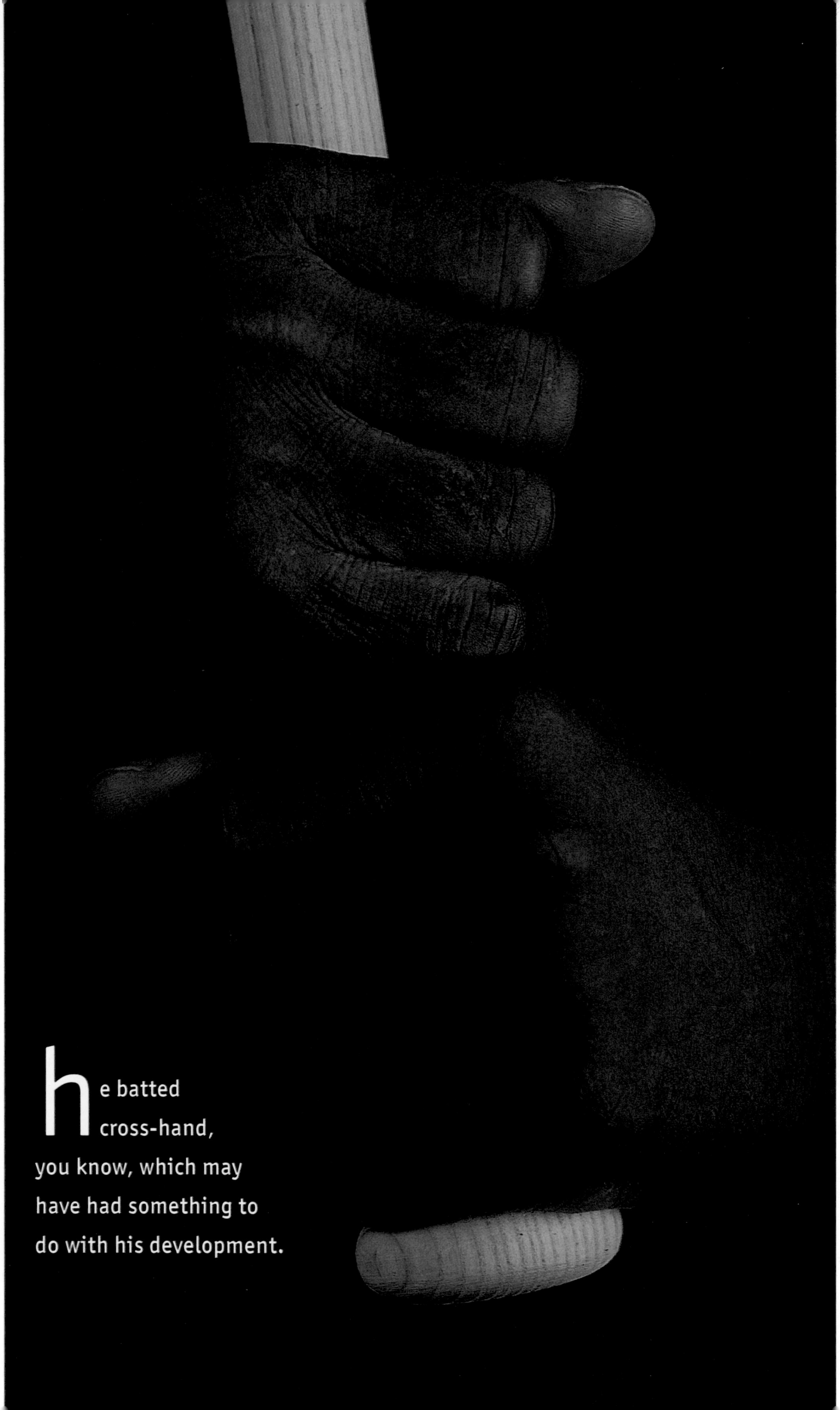

h e batted
cross-hand,
you know, which may
have had something to
do with his development.

the strongest image that comes to mind when I think of Hank Aaron—it's funny how you remember things—I remember looking at his wrists and forearms. And I was looking at how he walked. I said, this guy doesn't look that big. He's really quiet. He's just like he was, coming around second base with those fans grabbing at his hat after he hit the 715th. Just like that. Just another day, ho hum.

Hank Aaron just happened to hit more home runs than anybody else in the history of baseball. Because of the time he played in and because of where he was, he was able to sneak up on people. I really didn't get the chance to follow him a lot; in those days I followed the Yankees, and then the Giants after that because I followed Willie Mays. But we didn't get a lot of information about what was going on in the middle of the country. Maybe you'd hear a little bit about Chicago, but you sure didn't hear about Milwaukee. And Hank wasn't getting 60 home

Nothing unusual, a true American story. A hard working guy that worked his way up from the bottom. It's a great lesson.

Denzel Washington was executive producer of the documentary about Aaron's life, *Chasing the Dream*.

runs, he wasn't getting 59, he was getting 35 and 40 every year.

After a while, you knew he was going to get to 715 homer runs. I didn't know what he had gone through at that time. (Later on, I got involved in this documentary, *Chasing the Dream,* and ended up being the executive producer.) Again, it's a testament to him. He didn't complain about it, didn't make noise about it. The average citizen didn't know—at least I didn't know what he was going through. In fact, that was one of the things that really made me say "Yes, this is a story that we need to tell because we didn't know." You say "Hank Aaron," and someone says "Oh yeah, he broke Babe Ruth's record, blah blah." But do you know he got 900,000 pieces of mail one year and over 100,000 pieces of hate mail that they wanted to kill him at every stadium? He would get letters that said things like, "It may not be the first inning, it may not be the third, but I'm going to wait until you get up your third time." Or "When you come to town at 4 o'clock, that home game, I'll be there with a bullet with your name on it." Or "I'm going to get you at 711, 712. 712 is your last one!" To keep getting up there, to keep swinging, not to be gun shy—no pun intended—and then to knock the ball out of the park! Not just a single, not a foul tip, to knock the ball out of the park. I can only imagine what pressure that must have been. And, as he said too, he got a lot of that mail that came from New York, those Ruth fans.

He has strong wrists even now. He gave me a bat and signed it for me. I was like "Man, this is a heavy bat." It had an odd number on it. I forgot what it said, 41M or something weird. I have

The cover of *Sports Illustrated* needed no more information than this: 715.

it at home. Very skinny down at the handle, very skinny grip and fat down on the end. I just think about him hitting bottle caps a block and a half with a broomstick, cross-handed. He batted cross-hand, you know, which may have had something to do with his development. It's the eyes.

Because I grew up about 20 minutes from Yankee Stadium, in my younger days I was following guys like Mantle, Boyer, Pepitone and Bobby Richardson. That was the team that I followed. Whitey Ford, Ellie Howard, Yogi Berra. . . . Ballantine Beer. The only way you could follow those other teams was through the paper. And then you picked your team. I followed stats, but again, even following the stats at that younger age, I didn't see this guy coming. When I was in the ninth grade

I remember they made us read the *New York Times*.

That's when I really got into following the stats and that's when I picked. I'm talking about the wrong guy, but that's when I picked San Francisco as my team to follow because you'd hear a lot about Willie Mays. You heard more about him. It wasn't that I wasn't a fan of Hank's; but you didn't hear about Hank until it was time to challenge the record. It's interesting in our society now as it relates to the business I'm in, and to baseball players, and basketball players. If anybody has an iota of ability, they're exposed and exploited so quickly that it's almost impossible to break a record like Hank Aaron's now. Because the pressure's on a Ken Griffey Jr. from age 22, he hits 40 home runs.

Oh, is this going to be the guy? It's probably going to be some other guy that we're really not watching. You know what I mean? They're just hanging around.

It was a marathon with Hank, it wasn't a sprint. You're looking at the runners at the 20th mile. He's in the pack but you think he'll never break out. He's 20 out of 21 in the pack. He'll never make it. There's 3 miles left and now he's in 18th place, now 12th. All the big boys were one, two, three, four, five. Now there's two miles left and Hank's fourth. No way, there's no way he's gonna. . . . They're not even really looking at him because nobody has talked about him. And then all of a sudden the camera is not behind the ribbon. Wait a minute, who is that? If it happened like that, you wouldn't even know it was Hank. He'd just be cruising up there.

Then he ends the 1973 season with 713. He had to wait all that time until 1974. It took a Hank Aaron to do it. It took the smoothness of that guy coming around second base to deal with all that. And the strength. You know like they say, still waters run deep? I don't know—and I'm not knocking the other guys—I don't know if the other guys could have taken the pressure. And I'm not even naming names. *He's the guy* who could take the pressure. He didn't slow down, he kept hitting. He was unwavering.

Hank is a gentleman, a quiet man, very unassuming. Humble man. I was down in Atlanta, we went out to eat lunch. Everybody knew him. People were saying, "Hey, how you doing Hank?" Or "Hammerin' Hank, how's it going?" I almost got the feeling that he was happy that people knew him. Not

that he needed it, you know what I mean, but like it was still new to him.

He's just a solid guy. We get in the habit of looking for these $10 words, brilliant, we throw all these words around. His brilliance is his steadiness, his *consistency.* That's the word I'm looking for.

You know what is funny with Hank? The times I remember spending with him, I don't remember a big laugh. I don't remember deep sadness. I don't remember big swings in emotion. I remember a gentle smile. I just see him now waving to people that spoke to him. It's like you look at the guy and go, "Man, that's the same guy." You could tell, *this is the guy his parents raised,* to be a decent guy. He could hit the ball, but that didn't make him an egotistical nut.

Nothing unusual, a true American story. A hard working guy that worked his way up from the bottom. It's a great lesson. We need to run the thing again because it's a great lesson for everything we talked about earlier—for all these athletes who want the money first and the recognition first, all the media attention first. The ones that are first won't last. You could say he was last and became first. ①

When Hank was a boy, his parents, Estella and Herbert, provided him with everything that mattered.

he's gone through a lot, especially with the situation pertaining to race. You can imagine how Jackie Robinson felt, who preceded him by seven years. We didn't speak much about that, but he was amazed that I had his Jacksonville uniform. Actually he wore number 5 as a rookie and switched to 44.

—Barry Halper

i did know that there were racial comments at the time, that there were a lot of threats on his life, that the pressure was enormous. And he was really sad. It should have been the most joyous time of his life and he was oppressed. His mood was downtrodden. And that's tragic. That's something that I think lives with Henry to this day. The sparkle in his eye, the gleam in his teeth and the smile are not as there as they might be, because of this heartache that he endured for the better part of 18 months, and years and years afterwards. It wasn't until the last two years—and I think I'm being generous by saying two years—that he started to get from baseball this welcoming to greatness, welcoming to becoming an icon or part of the folklore, part of the fabric of the game. He has deserved this for such a long time.

—Reggie Jackson

i was right there in Brooklyn when Jackie got started in 1947. I wasn't really enamored of him. It was because I was born in Birmingham. Mr. Rickey called us in separately, one-on-one and said "Are you guys going to play any differently if he's on the team?" I said "No sir." He said, "Would you like to be traded?" I said, "I'd just as soon be traded." I signed a petition with other Dodgers saying we wouldn't play. But we played with Robinson that year. The fact that Jackie was there and I got to play with him made me identify better as a manager with Maury Wills, Tommy Davis, and Clemente and Aaron. Had I not had that experience with Jackie, I might not have been able to identify with Aaron. I became friends with him.

—Bobby Bragan

Even at the height of the celebration for home run 715, Aaron was shadowed by his bodyguard, policeman Calvin Wardlaw. Mark McGwire and Sammy Sosa had to deal with nothing like the death threats Aaron endured. Brother Tommie had played on the Braves for seven years and was Hank's roommate. But he was gone from the team after 1971 and wasn't with Hank during the tough times.

i heard a lot of rumors that he was getting threats and that a lot of things were happening to him emotionally. I think that he was able to handle that very well. He let his performance on the field overshadow what was happening off the field.

—Ferguson Jenkins

123

h e had this iron will and determination.

The figure of Ruth still looms large in baseball history, and always will. But the Babe has had to make room at the top for Hank. "Will white America accept this black hero?" the magazine cover asked. It may have been a real question in 1974; it is no longer.

BLACK SPORTS

JUNE 1974 50 CENTS

HENRY THE GREAT

"AARON'S THE COOLEST"
SAYS COOL PAPA BELL

HAITI & ZAIRE
WORLD CUP SOCCER

ESSEX & CROSS
BEST IN BASKETBALL

RAPPIN' WITH UCLA'S FRED SLAUGHTER ON ATHLETES AND ETHICS

Braves 44

WILL WHITE AMERICA ACCEPT THIS BLACK HERO?

Inside— Special Hank Aaron Section

O f course, you had the man Hank Aaron and the myth Babe Ruth, and then the commercialized image of Babe Ruth. It was just amazing, that the myth of Ruth and this home run number was a kind of white supremacy symbol for many people.

—Reverend Jesse Jackson

It was rough. I had heard about it a few times, but the letters he was getting weren't just from the South. These letters were coming from everywhere, all over. And he was getting death threats. I guess his bodyguard, Calvin, was with us every day. It was

rough, man. He had one room he slept in, another room that was a decoy room. And that was his sleep room. You didn't mess with Hammer or knock on the door when you knew what his sleep hours were. I remember one day, he got a death threat that somebody with a red coat on was going to shoot him in Atlanta. He told me and Ralph [Garr] that day we better not sit

next to him because somebody was going to shoot him and he said he wasn't moving. They didn't want him to sit in the dugout. He said, "I'm not going anywhere." Me and Ralph, we were the only ones looking around for the guy in the red coat. Me and Ralph were scared. We were like, "Hank, we're down with you man, we ain't going nowhere." But we were looking the whole time.

—Dusty Baker

Aaron's teammate in Atlanta, Dusty Baker, went on to play with the Dodgers, Giants, and the As. He is the long-time manager of the Giants.

125

PRO sports
DELL
JULY A 50¢

RATING THE POWER HITTERS

Willie Stargell Has A Right To Gripe

Will Baseball Pay Its Debt To Hank Aaron?

Nolan Ryan— Flash In The Pan, Or For Real?

The Inside Story Of Jon Matlack, The New Met Meal Ticket

i feel sorry he went through any kind of pain in setting the record. That's what I feel when I see him: a man who is just as he played—a person of great dignity. They all talk about what Maris went through and what Hank Greenberg went through, but Aaron's struggle and how baseball treated him when he got near that 714 really breaks your heart and makes you angry.

—Billy Crystal

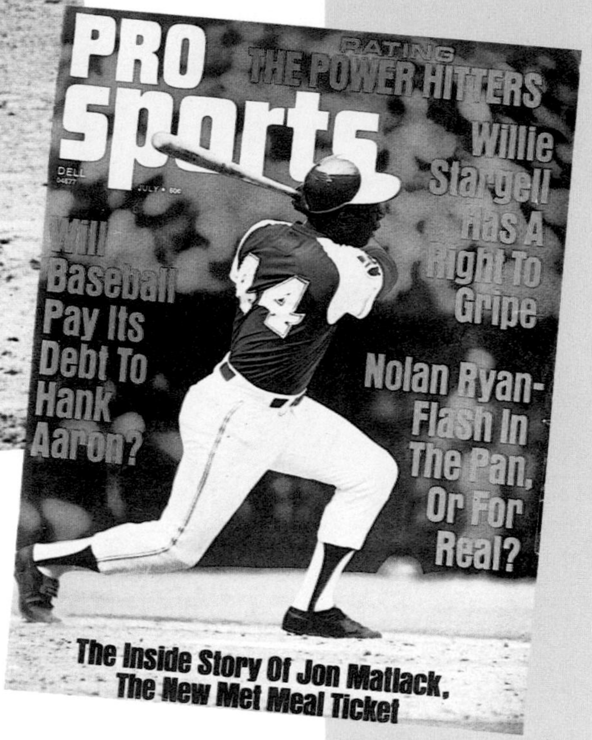

i remember just being elated that Hank broke the record and I remember being greatly disturbed by all the hate mail he was receiving. I understood, and I felt deeply for him, the pressure that was on him as he approached the record of Mr. America, Babe Ruth. It was blasphemous. And to this day I still think Hank hasn't really been given his due. Billye Aaron and I both sat on the Board of Trustees at Morehouse and [in Fall 1998] the Board met. We were talking about this whole Mark McGwire-Sammy Sosa home run race and how it would have been very natural for Hank Aaron to come into that discussion. The home run race was discussed on sports radio across the country. People have amnesia, they don't really want to remember what Hank did.

—Spike Lee

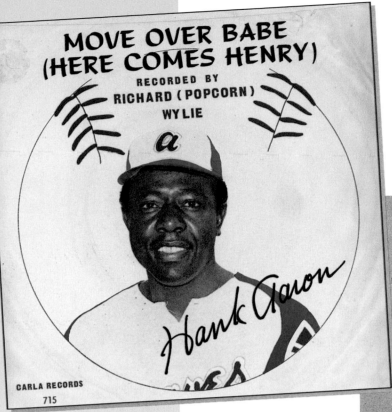

MOVE OVER BABE (HERE COMES HENRY)

RECORDED BY
RICHARD (POPCORN)
WYLIE

Hank Aaron

CARLA RECORDS
715

Here following through on his 61st home run, Roger Maris (left) was swinging not just against American League pitchers, but against legions of fans who wanted Ruth's 1927 record to remain intact. Below, Hank shares a light moment with Curtis Mayfield and Jesse Jackson.

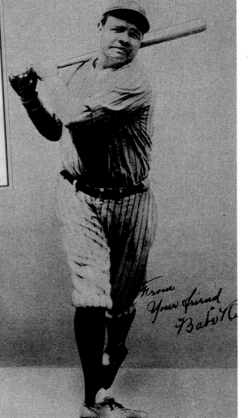

From Your friend Babe R

hank had a great enduring capacity. Twenty-three years, he was just steady. Good shape, good mental attitude, and he was always aware of the race factor. When the Braves first wanted to move from Milwaukee to Atlanta, he was reluctant to do so because of the way that Georgians responded to him and other black ballplayers.

—Reverend Jesse Jackson

i remember my excitement as Hank approached the home run record, I was certain he was going to break it. In fact, I never doubted it because he was such a superb player and determined person. Unfortunately, and much to my sorrow, I wasn't aware, until long after he broke the record, of how much trauma he experienced at the time. I couldn't imagine people attacking him, I thought the achievement was being widely celebrated as it should have been.

—Rachel Robinson

My pursuit of Lou Gehrig's consecutive games played record was 99.9 percent positive. Hank's pursuit of the record was not always positive. As a matter of fact, a lot of people didn't want him to do it.

—Cal Ripken Jr.

to play the game requires you to have a certain amount of mental stability, but his had to be above and beyond everyone else's. Despite some of the things he had to go through in the pursuit of the record—forces outside the sport— he had the ability to zone in and do it. You have to do that in a year of 162 games, but then you have to do that for a whole career. I just can't fathom what it took for him to have the mental toughness to do what he did.

—Cal Ripken Jr.

i became aware of the things he put up with later on,

through reading and being a fan of baseball history. Going through it I think we all were naive and ignorant, and being young, I only paid attention to what was right in front of me. At 13 years old I had no idea.

—Cal Ripken Jr.

Signs of racial division were omnipresent in the 1950s. Black players didn't room with their white teammates and especially down south, few hotels were integrated. Rookie Hank Aaron, Charlie White and Bill Bruton are shown during spring training in 1954 (above) with their boardinghouse landlady, who cooked for them.

The same principle of separation was a theme for promoting the team, too. Here Aaron, Bruton, White, Jim Pendleton and George Crowe are posed awkwardly in 1955, united by no obvious bond but race.

the hate mail that he got, all the black players got it. I got it. Whenever I got in the World Series and did well, I got the same thing that he got. They called you names and said if you come to Florida in spring training you're going to get shot. All kinds of crap. But that was the thing that most black players went through back in those days.

—Bob Gibson

i was the vice president of the Braves up until the end of 1973 and then I resigned. But all of 1973 I was in charge of the hate mail, the problems. A lot of that Henry didn't want to know, so I pretty well filtered it by working with his secretary. We filtered an awful lot of the calls and the mail. Some of it, the death threats, we sent on to the FBI. But most of the stuff we just kind of stuck in a corner.

—Dick Cecil

It was the dubious task of Aaron's secretary, Carla Koplin, to sort through his mail. Letters containing death threats were put aside for the FBI. By the end of 1973, Aaron had received 930,000 pieces of mail, about 100,000 of which were hate letters. It was the most mail received by any non-politician, according to US Postal Service calculations. Second was Dinah Shore with 60,000 pieces.

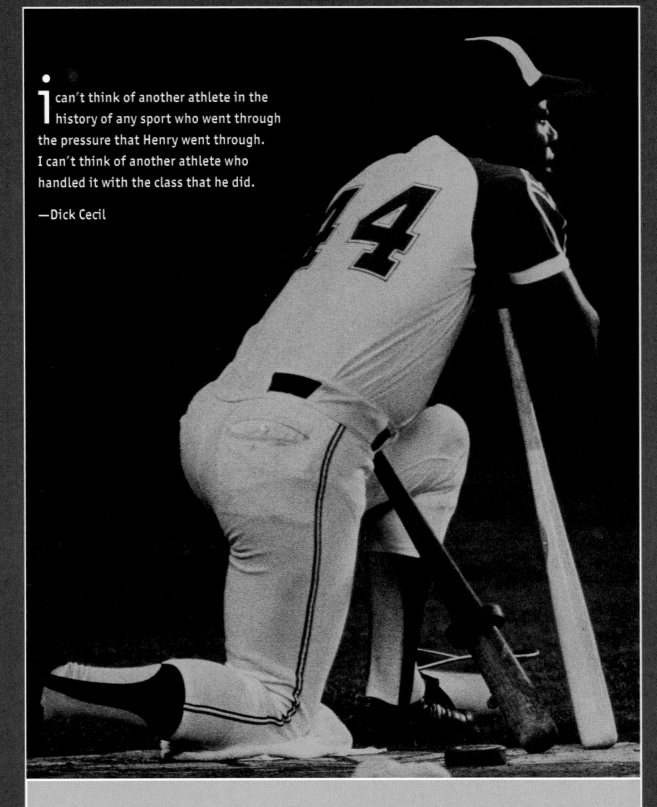

i can't think of another athlete in the history of any sport who went through the pressure that Henry went through. I can't think of another athlete who handled it with the class that he did.

—Dick Cecil

Rene Descartes wrote, "Though we cannot change the world, we can change ourselves." Aaron and other black players knew they might not be able to change people's attitudes, but they could work at the game, play it hard, play it well, so well that in time the game—and the world—would have to change.

I was at
WSYR-TV,
Channel 3
in Syracuse,
when Aaron
hit his 715th
homer. I
was 22 years
old and we
were watching
in the
newsroom of
the station.
—Bob Costas

t he adjectives used to describe Hank Aaron refer to sustained excellence, as opposed to any one thing that jumps right off the page. He never hit 50 home runs, he wasn't the most powerful, he didn't hit tape-measure home runs like Mantle, he didn't hit them as frequently as Ruth. He didn't have the flair of Willie Mays or Roberto Clemente. He didn't hit .400 like Ted Williams or in 56 straight games like Joe DiMaggio. He just did everything excellently for two decades plus and virtually never slumped but just kept on doing it, doing it, doing it. So here you have Mark McGwire, whose home runs per times at bat for any given sea-

son and for his career are much higher than Hank Aaron's. And yet he would have to hit 50 home runs for the next six years in a row to catch Henry. Which would mean that he would have to hit 50 or more for nine straight years, with a 70 thrown in, to catch what this guy did for his career.

Aaron was also an excellent fielder and a very good base runner. He hit home runs but he also hit for a high average and hit doubles and triples. He didn't strike out that often for a power hitter. He was known as a clutch hitter. Virtually every positive thing that could be said about a ballplayer could be said about Hank Aaron.

I was at WSYR-TV, Channel 3 in Syracuse, when Aaron hit his 715th homer. I was 22 years old and we were watching in the newsroom of the station. The game was on NBC and Curt Gowdy was doing the game. Everyone in the newsroom got together and signed this telegram to Aaron, which of course was one of thousands and thousands he received. We didn't expect him to really read it or see it but just wanted to add to the pile of good wishes. I was aware of what he was going through at the time. Subsequently, I read interviews where he gave greater detail. It had been documented that there had been death threats, that the FBI was around him, and some portion of the country felt that Babe Ruth's record was sacred. That notion was out there. But remember, too, that as he's pursuing this record, I'm a student at a northeastern university in the early 1970s and the sentiment is anti-racism, anti-establishment, anti-Vietnam War. So a guy like Aaron or Ali was a hero to us. Ali faced racism, but he also became a hero not

Babe Ruth led the league in home runs 12 times, posted a .690 slugging average, and a 1.399 total average. All three figures are Major League records.

Aaron's 715th homer was a memorable moment, frozen in time for everyone who witnessed it. But the meaning of that home run was no matter of a moment—it was the culmination of a career of sustained excellence.

just to black people but to a lot of young white people. Aaron was a hero, too. Lots of white kids of our generation would have said that Willie Mays or Hank Aaron or Roberto Clemente or Bob Gibson was their favorite player.

This is a discussion that I've had with Hank several times. I think he might be a little bit off in his perception of things. And you can hardly blame him because he had to live through all the threats and racism. I don't think he fully understands how a majority of white Americans liked him and really respected him. But when people do awful and hateful things, they stand out disproportionately. And I know he saved the thousands and thousands of hate letters. But at the same time, there were many, many Americans, not just black Americans, but white Americans, who may have loved Babe Ruth but also respected what Hank Aaron was doing. Just about every white baseball fan I knew thought he was just terrific. They were respectful of what he did. I wish he could have perceived more of that, although that doesn't negate the hate and the racism and small-mindedness, but it does put it in perspective. I think he gave too much proportion to the hate. I think at some level he understood what I was saying. But emotionally, the greater impact was delivered by the hate. That took the greater emotional toll. Even if it could be scientifically proven that there

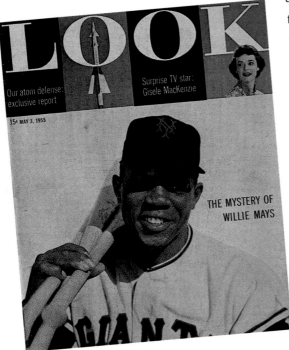

Willie Mays appeared on the cover of *Look* in the mid-sixties, when that magazine, like *Life,* mirrored universal acceptance by the American public. Aaron's broader cultural appeal came later, after he broke the record. (Right) Billye sat in on the press conference following the historic 715th.

were 100 well-wishers for every bigot, I don't know that that balances the scales.

I would describe Hank as a person who tried to see the world beyond himself, and tried to see what part he could play in standing for something that mattered, and doing what he did with some kind of dignity and respect for the game. And at the same time, he tried to speak out when he thought it was right to speak out. There was probably tremendous pressure on him from the left to be even more militant and from the baseball establishment to just be quiet and play. And he had to chart his own course and what felt right for him between those two extremes. I think he tried to do that with as much integrity as he could.

My guess is that he grew out of being shy and reserved, as he was in the early days of his career, due to a combination of things. One, as a person ages and has more experiences, his personality kind of fills out and he becomes more a man of the world, with more achievements and attention, and Hank had to learn to cope with that. What he was doing put him so front and center that he couldn't be as withdrawn as he might have been as a young player. Also, being a prominent black athlete in the 1960s especially, he couldn't have been unaware of the racial conflict going on and the civil rights issues, and he was thrust right in the center of it. He was the subject of so much hate and vilification, simply being a black man pursuing Babe Ruth's record. I know that hurt him deeply and disillusioned him. But it also probably led to wisdom and compassion as well, because he became very

sensitive to how insensitive others could be.

Has Hank gotten enough credit these 25 years later? One of the things that makes this hard to judge is that almost everything that happens now in sports is amplified because of marketing and the explosion in media coverage. So for example, Michael Jordan is the greatest basketball player of all time. But is he *that* much better than Wilt Chamberlain, or Bill Russell or Jerry West or Oscar Robertson, or even Bird or Magic, who precede him by half a generation? Is he as much better as his degree of recognition would lead you to believe? I think the answer to that is "No." But Jordan's the top guy at the time when the marketing and the television and the hype have reached unprecedented heights. If someone approaches Hank Aaron's record, Hank Aaron will have a renaissance like Roger Maris had, because of all the attention that the modern media will focus on the active player who's doing it. When Hank played, you

didn't have ESPN, CNN and countless talk shows.

My earliest memory of Hank was probably a faint recollection from the 1957 and 1958 World Series, when the Milwaukee Braves played the Yankees. I lived in New York. I was a Yankee fan. After that, it was watching him on *Home Run Derby.* What I remember about all of these guys was how stilted these guys were. Some guy hits a ball off the wall and Mark Scott says "It's a double during the regular season, but it's just a long out on *Home Run Derby!*" And Hank Aaron has to say, "That's right, Mark." ⚾

Y ou have to see Hank's achievement of 715 in a context of a sport that, until 1947, said that blacks were inferior and couldn't play this game. With that home run, Hank said that an individual could achieve greatness in America in spite of color and in spite of being born poor.

—Andrew Young

Atlanta's Fulton County stadium was rife with anticipation and pageantry on the night of April 8, 1974.

Magnavox Hank Aaron 715 CLUB

i think the 715th home run epitomized what baseball finally represented and embraced—an inclusion of all who were capable of playing our game, whether they be native-born Caucasian, or native-born African-Americans, or farm-born Cubans, or whomever. If the Good Lord gave you the talent and the special qualities, you could be great. We saw this year another remarkable accomplishment, a single season total of 70 home runs hit by one man, which is amazing on its own. But you can understand that more than you can understand somebody hitting the number of home runs that Hank hit over his career. It requires a continuity of great and sensational years. How many people have the inner drive and the toughness, not even counting the issues that were at play when Hank was trying to do what he was doing?

—John Schuerholz

the pitch wasn't higher than I wanted, it was just too much over the plate. I think that if the pitch had been a little farther away, he might have been reaching for the ball. That's when a hitter tries to hook a ball and usually you don't get a real clear connection when you try to hook a ball. You usually pull it foul or get it off the end of the bat. The thing you're dealing with is he's not a normal hitter; he's the greatest.

—Al Downing

i saw it later on television. I was playing in Cleveland at that time, so I was out at the ballpark trying to win a ball game. We knew it was going to happen. We just didn't know when.

—Gaylord Perry

If a fan had a seat in the upper right field stands, this was his view of Aaron's 715th, off Al Downing.

the year that Henry tied the Babe and then broke the record I remember well. We were doing the *Game of the Week* for NBC. We did fifteen Monday night games. I specifically recall going to opening day in Cincinnati even though we were not doing that particular game. Now it has always been said how Henry made things look so easy. He certainly did when he hit home run number 714 off Jack Billingham to tie the Babe's record. Then we did the *Game of the Week* and the first swing Henry took at home off Al Downing—I believe it was the first swing—he broke Babe Ruth's record. Wow, I'll never forget those two games. Henry's dramatics were not contrived. There was nothing flashy. He just went out and did it.

—Tony Kubek

i was just happy for him. I saw him hit his first home run, and I would have loved to have seen him hit his last one. But I wasn't in Milwaukee when he hit it, when he went back with the Brewers.

—Lew Burdette

Left fielder Bill Buckner scaled the fence but couldn't catch the ball; Atlanta reliever Tom House (above, right) snatched it in the bullpen.

Well, it was a foregone conclusion. It wasn't like it was the last day of the season and he was going to retire. It was something that was going to happen and my thoughts were, "Here's a guy who is tired of all the hubbub, disappointed with the way he's been treated, and he's going to get it over with. The next time this guy swings the bat he's going to hit number 714, then the next time it's 715 and then he may not hit any for awhile."

—Reggie Jackson

i t was big news in Japan when Hank hit home run number 715. Many fans had already been following the USA home run race, so it had everyone's attention. Japanese fans and players were excited when he hit number 715. We knew baseball history had just happened.

—Sadaharu Oh

We completely thought of him as the home run king. Later, I reached 868 home runs in Japan, where, in some places, the outfields are shorter. So Hank is still the champion.

—Sadaharu Oh

ank's breaking the record was good for the sport, I felt. To see a guy accomplish this is something that people just didn't think would happen. A guy that had kind of been in the shadow of Mays his entire career—he hadn't gotten his just due, still hasn't as far as I'm concerned. But he continually went along, did his thing, didn't complain, didn't pat himself on the back, didn't beat his own drum or try to get publicity for himself. He just did what he had to do. Day in and day out he helped his team win ballgames.

—Frank Robinson

Fifteen-year-old Frank Robinson, here getting the autograph of Phillies catcher Andy Seminick at the 1950 World Series, dreamed about one day playing baseball in the big leagues, just as Hank Aaron and Willie Mays had. The trio would go on to occupy three of the top four spots in career home runs.

i'll set it up by saying, wasn't it the previous Friday that he tied Ruth's record off Billingham? I was calling home from high school to my mother to see if he had tied the record. It was obviously inevitable that you wanted to be somehow connected to it. You can't conceive of this process in our extremely electronically wired world but I spent several dimes calling mom to find out if he had hit the home run and she was listening to the radio for news updates and then the home run itself. For 715, obviously I was sitting in front of the TV like everybody else.

—Keith Olbermann

"I never knew she could hold so tight," Hank said after being hugged by his mother Estella.

i can't forget the 715th. I was sitting between his mother and father in my box, right by the dugout. Then I was out on the field with his mother and father. I was as tickled as I can be. It was an overwhelming night.

—Bill Bartholomay

i was a huge Dodger fan and was a fan of Al Downing. I was always watching the Dodgers so I saw that highlight plenty of times. Bill Buckner was my favorite player. When I was a kid seeing it I remember how badly I wanted Buckner to catch it. Although even as a kid I realized Hank was going to break the record, I remember thinking how cool that would have been if Buckner would have come up over the wall and made that catch, sort of extended and added to the suspense. As I get older my appreciation for Hank and what he accomplished continues to grow.

—Brady Anderson

the number 715 suggests to me that it's not only a physical record that was achieved on the field, but I think of Hank's background and where he came from in terms of his growing up, his youth. It's an achievement which transcends the baseball field, really into the larger society in the sense that Hank stands for everything that we want to stand for, and certainly that we want our children to stand for. So it is an accomplishment against great odds, and one that is absolutely enduring. Just as I think his personality has been enduring, I think that record is enduring.

—Leonard Coleman

When he was 17, Aaron played Sunday home games with the Mobile Black Bears in Prichard, Alabama. He received $10 per game, though his mother forbade him to travel to the team's road games. The Mobile Whippets were another semipro team of the era.

now here is Henry Aaron.

The crowd is up all around.

The pitch to him . . . bounced it up there, ball one.
(Loud boos.) Henry Aaron in the second inning
walked and scored. He's sitting on 714. Here's the
pitch by Downing. . . . Swinging. . . . There's a drive
into left-center field. That ball is gonna beee . . .

outa here! It's gone! It's 715!

There's a new home run champion of all time!

And it's Henry Aaron! The fireworks are going!

Henry Aaron is
coming around
third! His teammates
are at home plate.
Listen to this
crowd. . . . "

—Milo Hamilton, April 8, 1974

i was proud to be out on the mound at that moment. I've been a part of a lot of historic moments in the game of baseball. Those are things you don't anticipate when you begin your career; you just anticipate having a good career. That moment is still underpublicized by the baseball community. That was a record that many people thought, because of the myth of Babe Ruth, would never be broken. So much of it was based on longevity and productivity over a long period of time. It was broken by a man who was 40 years old so he must have been a heck of a hitter. So I'm very proud to have been a part of that evening. Naturally, I wished I could have won the ballgame, but you can't have everything.

—Al Downing

Moments after he rose above all the home run hitters, he rose above his teammates, with their help.

He was just
the ideal man,
day in and
day out, the
kind of guy
you want
working for
you every day
in any
business.
He is the
professional's
professional.

—Johnny Bench

a gentleman who
played baseball

by johnny bench

m

y first impression of Hank Aaron was of how big his forearms were. I always thought and asked people, "How can a little guy like this hit the ball out of the ballpark?" I knew he had a quick bat, but I guess I started looking at the guy closely when he came up to the plate for the first time. It was like, "Wow, this is no little guy. This is a man who has got huge forearms and some of the quickest wrists."

You know Hank never had the big swing. Not like Ruth or Mantle. It was just such great timing and great ability to hit the pitch. He was just so quick and waited so long with his upper body, and then was able to use those forearms and those great wrists. I know everybody talked about his wrists, but I was always basically in awe of his forearms. We've seen more and more of the hitters today going to a lighter

Aaron slid hard and slid fair, even when an immovable object like Johnny Bench stood between him and home plate.

bat. Hank just made the bat feel light. He probably was one of the first who used a very thin handled bat, not real thin, but he had such whip and he got such great spring out of it. He was able to get the bat through the hitting area and get it out in front as well as anybody could ever do it; as well as anybody in the game has ever done it.

I would call for the pitcher to run the ball in on him. You had to move the ball around. I mean, it wasn't just one pattern. Hank could adjust to anything. You tried to keep the ball down on him. Anything inside, he was so quick, try to keep the ball down and down and away, and offspeed pitches that you could keep down and away. When the game was on the line, it was always a situation that you really tried to avoid giving him anything to hit. And that lineup of course, later on when he played down in Atlanta, even though he had a couple of guys that wound up hitting 40 home runs with him—Darrell Evans and Davey Johnson—you still keyed on that one particular guy. He became a much bigger problem for us because with men on base you had to try to find a way to pitch to him. But it never was that mammoth home run. What I liked about Aaron's style was he always seemed to get the ball just to creep over the fence or just 10-15 feet extra.

He never hit more than 50. I got a good look at 714 because I called it. Jack Billingham was pitching on opening day, 1974, and there was a question of whether Hank should be playing or should be waiting to get to Atlanta to try to break the record.

Hank hit almost all mistakes. You couldn't hang a slider. You couldn't make a mistake with a fast ball that

didn't have good velocity and good location. I caught the first game of a double header in Crosley Field when he got his 3,000th hit. He didn't get a hit in the game I caught and then I was in center field for the second game, and actually fielded the ball; it was a ground ball up the middle.

And Hank was always nice. He always said hello when he came to the plate, and was class, and played the game with respect, the way he wanted the game to be played. He was a great example for anybody that wanted to follow him. Hank sort of lived in anonymity because he would hit his 40 home runs and, so what? You expected it. That's what he was supposed to do. He stole a lot of bases early in his career, but I didn't have to worry about him stealing too many bases later on. He was solid defensively, never diving, never sliding. He was just the ideal man, day in and day out, the kind of guy you want working for you every day in any business. He is the professional's professional.

The reason he never hit 50 was that he wasn't a home run hitter. He didn't think home run. He thought of going up and making good contact, hitting .300, hitting the ball where it was pitched. A lot of times he went up the middle, went the other way, never trying to overpull, never trying to force anything. Hank always was one guy who played within himself, even on 715.

It was just the top hand rolling over those great wrists, fly ball to left field, just creeped over into the bullpen. But that's the way they seemed like they all were—never an over-swing, just great patience and great timing. You see golfers like that every now and then,

they take that same pace of swing and it's the same every time. That's the way he played. It was like "I'm going to show up, I'm going to get a pitch to hit, and I'm going to hit it." And if it's a base hit it's a base hit, if somebody catches it, somebody catches it. He had the unique ability and the tremendous talent to be able to hit the ball into the alleys and get extra base hits. Of course, as we all found out, he was also the one guy who could hit 755 homers.

We played in Chicago the night Henry hit the 715th. I was a great admirer of Hank's. Obviously for the record itself, but for the fact that he was a class act. I think in some ways we see Hank regretting that he didn't get more notoriety. But he never was flashy and played effortlessly. He was very content with what he had and didn't want to draw any attention to himself. I think he was more overlooked for that a little bit later on in his career, and even now.

Being somebody who loved to hit home runs, I thought it would be unbelievable but possible to break 60. But Ruth's 714 was out of reach, just not possible. Aaron's is just such a tremendous record, so I have great admiration and respect for him; he deserved it. He was the type of guy—if somebody deserved to do it and lived the life and acted like a professional the way he did, then it's absolutely the way it should have been, and it was right that the man to do it turned out to be Hank.

I met Hank in Milwaukee, maybe 1963. He may not remember, but I was struggling one time when we went in there and I asked him for some tips. He said you go up the middle and go the other way for a couple of days and get your timing. It made a lot of sense. That night I hit two home runs. He seemed quiet but he was comfortable around ballplayers. I thought he was just a very special person to take time out with a guy he didn't even know, and from another ball club, and extend courtesy. It was very special to me at that point. I've been in awe of Hank Aaron ever since and I'm still in awe of him. I think he is, without a doubt, the guy who has done so much and you hear about so little.

—Willie Stargell

153

He was a guy who went about his business; he loved to play. I remember he hit the ball so often for homers and one day we were agitating Hank by giving him the silent treatment so that when he hit a homer, no one would say a word to him. He'd go down the bench and go to get a drink and of course, everyone would congratulate him. It was so routine; it was kind of a game we played.

—Warren Spahn

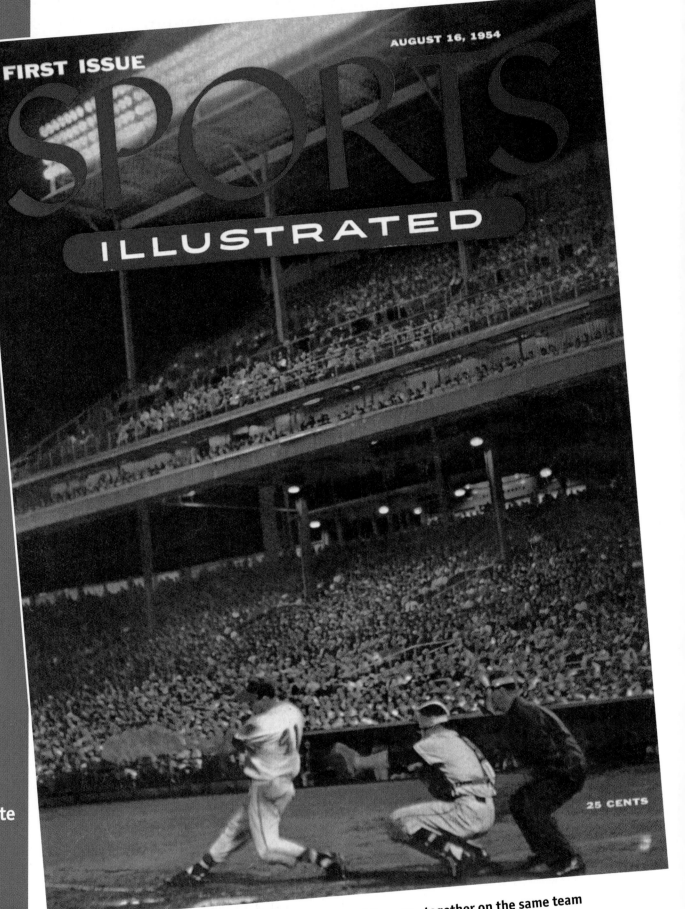

With Mathews, Aaron and Spahn—three future Hall of Famers—together on the same team for 11 years, the Braves had power, pitching and defense and were usually in contention.

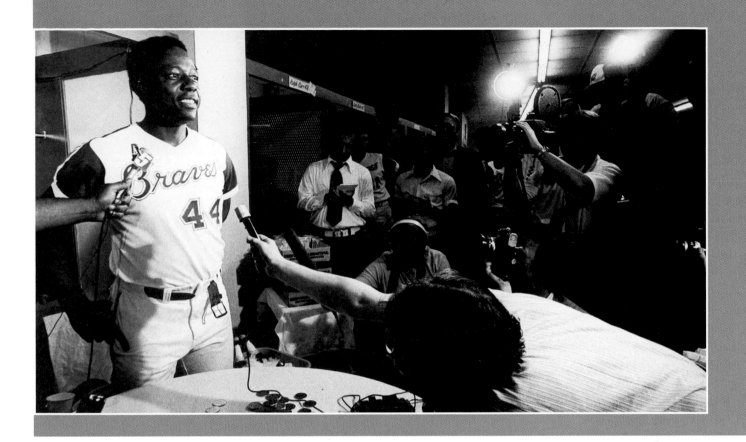

my first reaction to him, when I met him as a minor league player, was that he carried himself with honor and dignity. I guess even before I understood the word "class," I thought he was a good example of it. He was quietly confident with what he was doing and he speaks well and he handles himself very well. I remember thinking that again when I had a chance to talk to him in greater detail on my celebration night, the 6th of September, 1995. We were just talking about baseball in general, kind of philosophically viewing the game. He shared some of his experience, his pursuit of the record. But it was just general baseball talk and it really hit me again. My wife and I talked later on the same night about what great people the Aarons are. I actually saw them recently down at the Orlando Player's Choice Awards. In fact, I went right up to them and I sat at the table with them and said, "I don't know what you did to my wife, but she can't stop talking about you guys."

—Cal Ripken Jr.

a nice, polite, friendly man. No pretentious airs or anything like that.

—Kareem Abdul-Jabbar

i met him in the late sixties. He's always been one of my good friends since the very first time I met him. We hit it off real well. I was kind of an excellent athlete in sailing and in sailboat racing. So we had something in common. I didn't want him to leave Atlanta but he was getting up in years and if I were him I would have gone to Milwaukee, too. I wanted him back and so I offered him a job to be in charge of the minor leagues.

—Ted Turner

h ank is very reserved, very quiet, very bright. The decisions he makes about life are good. He's a smart man and a good businessman. He's a different sort of guy, and he has not been appreciated for the great ballplayer he is.

—Sy Berger

I met Hank at a dinner, I think in New York. We were both receiving awards for our respective sports. The first thing I thought was, what a gentleman. He was very soft spoken and seemed very modest, not one of those loud, rambunctious, outrageous athletes that we seem to come in contact with these days. When I met Pele, it was the same kind of a feeling. He was just kind of an old fashioned guy who seemed to have such a passion for his sport and at the same time, was not arrogant. I think the humbleness struck me more than anything, and also just what a gentleman he seemed to be.

—Chris Evert

As a record holder, Aaron's way became more attractive and instructive to other star athletes, including Dominique Wilkins. Young people might take note.

The one thing about Hank, as his career peaked, he was easier to communicate with. He always remained accessible to the people. And then when he came to Chicago, we gave him a Hank Aaron Day. We had a lot of the children there, and Hank promised he would hit them a home run that day, much in the Babe Ruth pointing-his-finger style. We took a lot of the kids to Wrigley Field and as he came up to the plate he gave the kids in the bleachers a high sign and they screamed. About two pitches later the ball went out on Waveland Avenue.

—Reverend Jesse Jackson

He approached the game so casually, it seemed. But he was good in all phases of the game and never brought any shame, and no disgrace, no drugs. Just a gentleman, always a gentleman. He had dignity and he didn't hit a home run to take dignity from the pitcher. He hit a home run to assert his skill.

—Reverend Jesse Jackson

hank was sensitive to the civil rights movement, he had a sense of manhood off the field. He was not so programmed in terms of being camera ready. He would take a position and ask, why aren't there more blacks in the front office of baseball? Why aren't there more black managers, he would say. Why aren't there more black sports announcers? He used his celebrity to improve life for other people in the industry.

—Reverend Jesse Jackson

hank Aaron wrote history in a way that brought great credit to the game. He is, and will remain, a national treasure. His courage both on and off the field is legendary. He is a hero to millions.

—Dr. Gene Budig

Aaron engaged in other Ruthian activities besides hitting home runs.

henry's a man's kind of man—he doesn't dress anything down or dress anything up. You know exactly where he stands at all times. He's a guy's guy.

—Paul Snyder

As part of a Flag Day observance with House Speaker Carl Albert in the background, Aaron addresses the House of Representatives on June 13, 1974. He had come a long way from the sandlots of Mobile, even from the 1961 Milwaukee Braves.

Henry Aaron has meant so much to baseball, and I'll tell you why. He's been a standup guy, and an idol, I'm sure, to every American kid— black or white—because of the way he conducted himself on and off the field. I'm just delighted that he was able to stay in the ranks of the baseball world because he is a great addition to it.

—Bill Rigney

He's not quiet to me. He's not reserved to me. As a public figure, I don't think he would be considered either quiet or reserved. I think Hank has certainly made the public know his feelings on how difficult it was for him to go through the Babe Ruth home run chase, of how he had the difficulty of being accepted because of his race.

—Reggie Jackson

i have a great reverence for Hank and what he has accomplished as a player and what he stands for as a man. So I'm happy to say that I think we have a friendship. Hank's not the kind of a guy that forces himself on situations. He's a man of quiet dignity and he doesn't need to push himself into a spotlight or into the forefront, except that he does when there are issues that are important to him.

—John Schuerholz

Here with Rachel Robinson, Aaron increasingly recognized that his celebrity could make social contributions. In 1974, Aaron exchanged a ball for a bat with Mayor Abe Beame in front of City Hall on Hank Aaron Night in New York. To Beame's left are Mrs. Lou Gehrig and Mrs. Babe Ruth. To Hank's right is his wife, Billye. Behind every great man there stands a great woman, the saying goes. "Alongside" is surely the better word.

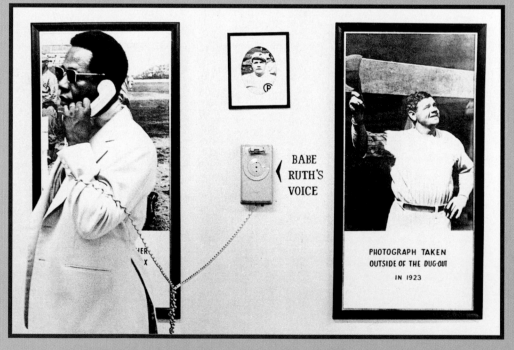

h ank stayed in his own world. The way Jack Nicklaus just won tournaments, Hank just kept on going. They're not that outgoing, Pollyannish type of person, you know, laughing and talking with everybody. They focus on what they do and they go do it.

—Ernie Banks

i 've only met him on a couple of occasions, here at Cooperstown, and at baseball functions. But nothing has changed, he's still a delightful person. He's a great ambassador for the game in my opinion.

—Don Marr

BABE RUTH'S VOICE

PHOTOGRAPH TAKEN OUTSIDE OF THE DUG-OUT IN 1923

What would the Babe say to Hank if he had the chance? Hank listens to the Bambino's voice while visiting an exhibit at the Baseball Hall of Fame. During another trip to Cooperstown, Aaron (top) enjoyed linking up with several former Negro Leaguers. Aaron had played with the Indianapolis Clowns in 1952 (top left).

i was impressed with his quietness, with his unassuming attitude. The fact that he seemed not too taken with himself or his accomplishments. And of course, the name I had known for years, just from the news, the sports part of the news. But he seemed very . . . we overuse "nice," but he seemed a very nice person. A genuinely nice person. I was also impressed with what I heard, that he was a family kind of man. And he didn't have the reputation that many in the sports arena get. So in other words, his reputation did not precede him, and I was just sort of impressed with that about him.

—Billye Aaron

When she met Hank Aaron, Billye Williams was the co-hostess of *Today in Georgia,* an Atlanta morning show. She did a series on some of the Braves players entitled "Billye at the Bat" and Hank was her first interview subject. They married late in 1973. Several years later, Hank was hired by Ted Turner to work for the Braves.

Hank Aaron,
a gentleman
who played
baseball.
—Billy Crystal

hank and I worked on an innovative project called the "World Children's Baseball Fair" [a program started by Japanese home run hitter Sadaharu Oh, designed to bring all children of the world together by teaching them baseball]. I enjoyed the extended time we spent together in Tokyo and other places. My fondest memories of Hank are those trips we took together, because I had a chance to be with him.

—Rachel Robinson

Comparisons between Jack and Hank have often occurred to me. They came from similar backgrounds and despite the odds against them became not just outstanding ballplayers, but men of determination and courage. These qualities and their resilience enabled them to endure and transcend obstacles with dignity and pride. When each of them retired from baseball they went on to become successful businessmen and civil rights advocates . . . maturing and expanding their influence as they developed.

—Rachel Robinson

I wouldn't say
Hank is shy
but he is still
modest. When
we go together
in a crowd,
Hank always
responds with
generosity to
kids who rush
up and want
to get his
autograph.
—Jimmy Carter

community

i was right there watching when Hank hit his 715th homer. I had prepared a gift for Hank. As governor, I had had our state make me an automobile tag that said HLA 715. And so the Chamber of Commerce and the people of Atlanta took up a collection and gave Hank a new Cadillac. I gave him the tag to go on it and in fact some of the pictures actually wound up in an Encyclopedia Britannica of me handing Hank the HLA 715 tag. I don't know if Hank still has it or not. But it would be a good memento to go in the Hall of Fame. I got ten times more publicity with that tag, since it was unique, than the Chamber of Commerce did with their $12,000 Cadillac. But Hank and I have joked about how I was a skinflint and gave him a $10 tag, which got all the publicity. I was right there and I

guess there have never been any sporting events that were more exciting than that particular time.

I do think the home run was one of the historic events of the sports world. And when you ask people what do they remember of an extraordinary achievement that happened in any sport, I believe that this one would be one of the few top ones. It got a lot more publicity than Roger Maris' record did. The news media kind of downplayed Roger Maris' achievement. In fact, Yankee Stadium wasn't near full, with just over 20,000 people at the park. There was such a strong feeling that Babe Ruth's record ought to stand. I never met Roger Maris but I think he felt disappointed the rest of his life that he didn't get the public accolades and rush of emotional support that Hank Aaron did after the 715th was hit. Of course, Hank went

On April 8, 1974, Jimmy Carter, then Governor of Georgia, was part of the celebration with 54,000 others. He presented Aaron with a license plate to remember.

Sitting in front of Mickey Mantle, with Yogi Berra standing, Roger Maris, like Aaron later on, could understand what it felt like to chase an American icon.

on to hit more than anyone has hit since. I think that in general, after the event took place, the negative attitudes dissipated. That was my impression, though he may have still gotten some hate mail.

I certainly found myself rooting for him to do it, no doubt about that. The Klu Klux Klan was peripherally involved. I already had the Klan demonstrating against me, because I had put Martin Luther King's portrait in the capitol. Those were kind of difficult days—to some degree for me as a political figure—but even more I think for Hank. He was struggling not only with the publicity and the constant cross-examination by reporters, but there was the racist element too, in addition to those who were genuinely loyal to the Babe Ruth record.

It was a wonderful thing for us to see the Braves come to Atlanta in 1966.

They didn't do very well for the first few seasons there. But as a state senator I had watched the Braves' stadium being built. Every morning I walked from what was the Howard Johnson's hotel then to the state capitol to work and I went by the construction site and watched them build it in the summer of 1964. Of course, I was very eager to attend all the games I could. I cannot recall my first meeting with Hank Aaron. I was governor when Ted Turner bought the Braves and Hank moved down and I met all of the team members. I went down with Ted Turner and visited in the locker room and I met Hank then and I was very excited to meet him. But I don't remember any specific details about it.

Earlier, my wife and I were very avid Yankee fans. We lived up in New London, Connecticut when television first came out and we went to a few

games, didn't have much money, but we watched the games on TV. I had seen the year when Mickey Mantle and Roger Maris struggled to overcome Babe Ruth's record and had seen the extremely negative reaction to Maris' achievement. It was of some concern to me, although I had mixed emotions, since I was also loyal to Babe Ruth's record, as I was to Ty Cobb's records, since he was from Georgia. But when Hank began to approach Babe Ruth's record of 714, I was intensely interested in it. I'm an avid baseball fan and I watch all the Braves games now, either in person or on TV. I was somewhat concerned, as a fairly moderate governor, to see the negative reaction to Maris' attack on Babe Ruth's record mirrored with Hank Aaron, with a racial overtone applied to it. This made it even more an emotional experience for many of us who really were avid fans and supporters of Hank Aaron. It wasn't as momentous as Jackie Robinson playing for the Dodgers in 1947, but it was a significant breakthrough and the end of much racial discrimination in sports.

I wouldn't say that 755 is an

unmatchable total. I would have said it maybe before this year. But I certainly think it is within the capability of someone who is physically able to play 15 or 20 years. I think it's in the realm of possibility now.

I see Hank regularly now. For the last few years Hank and I and his wife Billye have all gone skiing together out in Colorado. The Carter Center sponsors an actual ski event where we go out for four days and raise money for our humanitarian project. We take a group of 10 to 20 poor kids from a low income area and Hank has been gracious enough to go along for the last three or four years. In fact, I saw my first skis when I was 62 years old. And I think Hank began skiing about the same age. So he and I have shared experiences about how difficult it is to do downhill skiing. But almost invariably for the last couple of years, Hank and Billye and his friends and Rosalyn and I and a couple of our friends have gone out for supper together while we were out on the ski slopes. And then we share experiences. We go to Braves games and sometimes there is a fundraising event around Atlanta where they like prominent people to come and raise money for nice projects and I see Hank on those occasions.

I wouldn't say Hank is shy but he is still modest. When we go together in a crowd, Hank always responds with generosity to kids who rush up and want to get his autograph. Every year he'll sign a baseball bat or something for us to auction off to raise money for the kids in Atlanta. He is modest, self-assured, has a good and happy life with his wife and is well respected. I think Hank is perfectly at ease with what he's doing now.

One thing I observed was the first day Hank went out on the ski slopes. He was with a group of high school kids from the ghetto areas of Atlanta, which is the purpose of our ski weekend. Hank fell down a lot more than they did. They're young and athletic and resilient. That night he was extremely sore and discouraged. We had supper together. But there was never any thought in Hank's mind that "I'm not going out there any more." He stuck with it. In microcosm, that is kind of Hank's attitude, having reached the age of 60 or so, having found something new that's uncomfortable and also embarrassing. If you get up at the plate in baseball—like I did in softball, just a week or so ago—and you hit a couple of balls to the pitcher or the shortstop or you just strike out—which doesn't happen much in softball, it's like a two-out-of-three thing event with a good batter; if you get out on the ski slopes and you fall down, everybody on the darned ski slopes can see your feet go out from under you, particularly if you're a famous person like Hank. I just think he's a wonderful man. You can tell I'm full of admiration for him. I'm very proud of his friendship. ⚾

The Aaron family today, with, from left, Dorinda, Hank Jr., Ceci, Lary and Gaile.

Well, I don't know how much progress, to be honest, has been made. We've been very, very proud to see the four or five African-American managers that baseball has had. Unfortunately they keep dropping out and that is the nature of the game. You get in there and you do the best you can do, I suppose, for however long the owners let you do it, then you have to understand that you are subject to be fired the next day. Hank is very, very hopeful I am sure, that with the new commissioner of baseball, things will begin to take a better look and that the picture for African-Americans and other minorities will get much brighter. There is certainly a terrific need for that kind of approach to the whole baseball operation.

—Billye Aaron

h ank and I did spend a lot of time together when he started doing the RBI program. It started with Arby's, based in Atlanta. Len Roberts was the CEO and they decided to start a program to help out Big Brothers and Big Sisters of America. Arby's would donate $1,000 for each RBI for each league leader. Hank was the spokesperson for this program and I traveled with him back and forth.

—Roberto Clemente Jr.

i was hired the winter of 1990, my first year on board was 1991. By then Hank had already moved to the television side with TBS and has been there up until about a year ago when he came back and now has an office here at Turner Field. His last venture, which I think was a very successful one, was selling the airport network, the airport channel. You know, when you sit waiting for a plane and you're watching TV? That was Hank's project.

—John Schuerholz

Hank has always had time for children and the causes that benefit them.

Since Ted Turner hired him after his playing career ended, Aaron has succeeded in several capacities with the Braves.

Unlike so many current players who seem not to know or care about the sacrifices of African-Americans who played baseball before integration, Hank Aaron pays them homage.

he's one of the few people that I can honestly look at and say, that while he was a baseball hero 25 years ago, he is a greater hero today for what he's done after baseball. He's kind of used baseball as a stepping stone to greatness. I see him as a business person, I see him in the community and in the work that he does with young people. I see the opportunities that he creates and how he speaks out on issues which sometimes make people uncomfortable. But the point is, he has something to say and he says it. He holds his position and he genuinely means what he says. He doesn't do it to make headlines, he just does it because he has the opportunity, since people know who he is, to say what he feels. I think that's a great trait.

—Frank Belatti

hank started the Chasing the Dream Foundation, of which I'm a board member, and he has to date helped 44 children and has a goal of helping 755 children to coincide with his home runs. He spends a lot of time on that project. He speaks out on our New Age of Opportunity Program here at the company, which is designed to encourage more minority franchisee involvement, more minority supplier involvement. He goes out and he really talks to young people about career opportunities. And he gives people ownership opportunities in his businesses, which I think is really remarkable. He really tries to give some of these young people who come to work in the restaurants a chance to own something and be a responsible member of the community. He goes down and works in the restaurants and is very accessible and is very visible. He and I have become known as the Frank and Hank show. We went out and spoke on ethics in baseball and ethics in business.

—Frank Belatti

One of the things that we really saw eye to eye on is that I said to him, all my documentary projects have had beneficiaries and I'm proud to say that every one of them has contributed to a charitable cause. I'd like to extend that opportunity to you to sort of dictate what it will be on this film (Chasing the Dream). He said he wanted to help underprivileged kids. We made it a stipulation in the agreement with Turner that there would be a donation in lieu of a check going to either of us for back end rights; we asked for the

Aaron and filmmaker Spike Lee sat on the board of trustees at Morehouse College.

donation to be made to establish a foundation, which is the Chasing the Dream Foundation. At the world premiere in Atlanta, Ted Turner turned over a check for $50,000 to start this foundation. We were the grand prize winners of something called the Heartland Film Festival, and we turned over another $10,000 check to the foundation as a result of that prize, and Henry and Billye came and joined me in Indianapolis to accept that honor. There have been several other opportunities along the way where we've steered people in that direction. So I think maybe the thing we're proudest of is beyond doing a film that was an entertainment, we've actually given something back to the kids and again, I think that's what says it all about Hank Aaron, that's his cause, that's what he cares about. I think he's happier on a ball field teaching underprivileged kids how to hold a bat, than he is in a press conference talking about the strides Major League Baseball has or hasn't made integrating the game.

—Michael Tollin

174

I remember Hank Aaron from the time I covered civil rights in the South, working both on the Macon paper and college papers and others. Here was somebody on one hand that was one of America's finest athletes and demonstrated that in a spectacular way on the field, but also, he was confronting the problems of segregation and racism as he traveled. So there were two parts to his life, and for that I always admired him. He did it always with great courage and dignity, and with class. I always felt that Henry never received the type of attention or compensation, or maybe the recognition that is today bestowed on the Sosas and the McGwires, and many others of the heroes of today.

—Tom Johnson

Of Jim Pendleton, Charlie White, Billy Bruton and Hank Aaron, shown here in 1955, only the latter two were with the Braves when they won the World Championship two years later.

When I came to Atlanta I'd never really lived in a city with a large black community. And largely through Hank and Billye, and because of them, I got involved in the United Negro College Fund and the APEX Museum and the Urban League, and the NAACP. Hank and I were co-chairs of the NAACP annual fund raiser along with Nelson Mandela. That's kind of a funny story. You had Hank, Nelson Mandela and me. I get up there and say, "Now, which of us doesn't belong here?" But through them I really became accustomed to understand and be involved with a group of people that I did not know. And I really became more understanding of a community, of an ethnic group, and I give them a lot of credit for really opening my eyes. Their genuineness and their honesty allows me to do a number of things that I probably wouldn't have done.

—Frank Belatti

i remember when I ran for Governor a few years back and I was holding a press conference at the Atlanta City Hall. I remember going over to City Hall and they had this press event set up and there were a lot of people just lining the steps, three or four steps deep, holding cards that said, "Vote for Miller" or something like that. I came out of the door at the top of the steps, and all of a sudden, out of the corner of my eye, I saw down on the bottom step, over in the left-hand corner, Hank Aaron holding this posterboard sign for me. I have never felt, I have never been so touched in my life. Here was this hero of mine, that I never dreamed that I'd even get to meet, standing there, almost anonymously, in this crowd of people, there for me. It really did touch me.

—Zell Miller

The governor of Georgia, Zell Miller, is yet another Georgia governor whose company Aaron enjoys.

In Game 2 of the 1957 World Series, won by Hank's Braves, supporters of rebel Fidel Castro showered the field with leaflets urging the overthrow of the Batista regime.

Hank, Billye, and the President. As this book goes to press, President Clinton has initiated a "baseball diplomacy" overture to Cuba, with whom the U.S. has had chilled relations for four decades.

hank has been around and there is not a situation that he doesn't have a historical perspective on, which he didn't live through, which he didn't live with. It is just unimaginable that that stuff happened in our lifetime, in this country. Yet he carries himself to this day without public bitterness, with tremendous grace, wherever he is and whatever situation he is in. He continues to be a credit to himself and to his game.

—Stan Kasten

big Brother, Big Sister is a national organization in every community. Basically it's a program whereby adults mentor children. What the Big Brother, Big Sister organization does is match youngsters, typically from single-parent homes, with adult mentors. So Hank and I became mentors for two young men. Hank had his little brother and I had my little brother. At the time, Hank's little brother was about 8 years old. Mine was 10 years old. In both cases my little brother and Hank's little brother came from single-parent homes and so you want to make sure that you expose them to values in life and different experiences. I exposed my little brother to what it was to run a company. But we did things that fathers would do: play baseball, go to parks, go to the zoo. You meet twice, once a week, three or four times a month, and it's a great program. It's a big national program. It's actually gaining some steam here at the national level in every community in America because of the rise in single-parent homes. There are Big Sisters too. It was pretty good for Hank's little brother, since he got to hang around with Hank Aaron. Hank took out some valuable time, not to have a huge impact on a large audience, but took a lot of time just to have an impact on a single person. I think that says something about his character.

—Leonard Roberts

Len Roberts and Hank introduce two little brothers from the Big Brother, Big Sister program.

178

i have been chairperson of the Hank Aaron Youth Leadership Foundation in Milwaukee since 1976. In January, we were renamed The Hank Aaron Chasing the Dream Foundation and will be more like the Atlanta Foundation, looking to benefit 9- to 12-year-old children. Hank and I grew up together in Mobile. In terms of his basic personality and outlook on life, he has not changed. Even with the fame and the money, he has not changed. What you see is what you get. Years ago, people used to say he let his bat speak for him. He's a person who leads by example. The burden of saying certain things is on him now because people listen and other people ought to be saying them but they're not. It's on him now because of his perseverance and who he is.

—Joe Kennedy

Hank now speaks for himself and his causes with more than his bat.

by jerome holtzman

the way to fame

i don't want to be the guy to give up the home run," insisted Al Downing, a cunning left-hander with the Los Angeles Dodgers the day before he made his first start of the 1974 season. "No pitcher likes to give up a home run at any time. It could cost me the ball-game."

Downing giggled, a nervous little giggle: "The ideal situation would be to have a 6-0 lead in the ninth inning."

The prognosis for a Hank Aaron home run was good. Aaron batted against Downing eight times the previous season and had hit two home runs off him, numbers 674 and 696.

"If he does it," Downing said, "I wouldn't feel any disgrace, and I wouldn't feel any pride."

And the next night, April 8, before a standing-room crowd of 52,780 at Atlanta's Fulton-County Stadium, with one on and none out in the fourth, the count one ball and no strikes, Aaron lifted a Downing fastball over the left field fence for his 715th home run to

break Babe Ruth's career record. "I didn't think it would carry," Downing said later. But it did, an estimated 415 feet, far out of the reach of left fielder Bill Buckner. Atlanta reliever Tom House ran to the bullpen wall and caught the ball that had been marked with the numbers 12-12-2-2 in invisible ink.

After the game, Milo Hamiton, the Hall of Fame announcer, was startled by something he had never seen before in his nine seasons as the Braves' play-by-play man.

"As Aaron turned toward third base, his solemn face suddenly turned into a big grin," Hamilton said. "It was surprising to see, considering his usual mien. It was as if he had started doing an Irish jig coming down the base path and running for home." But Hamilton never had time to describe it; by the time he recovered, Aaron was running into the pack of players and dignitaries with others streaming from both benches and the grandstand. "It's the one image I'll particularly remember of that day. It was a scene everyone

The swing on number 715 was the same as ever. The visitors from the stands were different.

wished they could take away and store in the attic."

For Tony Kubek, of the NBC television crew, who had seen Mantle drive balls into the wild blue yonder and who batted in front of Roger Maris when he hit 61 home runs, all of that seemed obscure next to Aaron's achievement. When Aaron had fulfilled his mission, the stadium emptied. Even the ballplayers seemed to play the rest of the game in a trance, as if saying, "Let's shut down the shop and pack up and go home."

When Aaron reached the plate he was greeted by his father, Herbert, and his mother, Estella. Jimmy Carter, then the Georgia governor who was to become the President of the United States, was also there to offer his congratulations. The fans cheered. Bands were playing. Hammerin' Hank had done it!

"Thank God it's over," Aaron said.

Before the game Dodger manager Walter Alston predicted, "I know he's going to hit one out. I just hope it doesn't cost us the game." Aaron's home run tied the score at 3-3 and triggered a 7-4 Atlanta victory.

Remarkably, it was not Aaron's most memorable home run. In the *Baseball Digest* series, "The Game I'll Never Forget," Aaron told author George Vass his pennant-clinching home run, on September 23, 1957, when he was with the Milwaukee Braves, was the bigger thrill.

"The Cardinals started a skinny, red-haired pitcher named Herm Wehmeier and we had Warren Spahn, just about the best pitcher in baseball," Aaron recalled. "The game was tied at 2-2 in the bottom of the 11th. There were two outs when I came up. Johnny Logan was on base [with a single] and Billy Muffett, a chunky guy, was pitching in relief for the Cardinals. I remember looking up at the clock. It showed 11:34 and that's when I hit the home run that won for us. All the players grabbed me as I came across the plate and carried me off the field."

Aaron connected on Muffett's first pitch, a high, arching drive to dead center. It was well hit but when Wally Moon leaped for the ball at the fence it appeared he had made the catch. Moon fell to the ground. Initially, it seemed the ball had not cleared, that the side was retired. Aaron also thought it had been caught. But as Moon lay on the ground, several boys swarmed out of the bleachers in pursuit of the souvenir.

"I timed my jump right," Moon told reporters. "It was just out of my reach. I missed it by about two feet."

As Aaron circled the bases, his first thought was of Bobby Thomson's legendary home run: "That always was my idea of the most important home run. And now I'd hit one, too. People were snake-dancing in Milwaukee that night. The next morning I felt like the King of Wisconsin."

Hank Aaron, in his fourth major league season, was also the King of the National League. It was his most enjoyable year. He led the league in home runs with 44, in runs batted in with 132, in total bases and in runs scored. The Cardinals' Stan Musial had the highest batting average, depriving

Aaron of the Triple Crown. Aaron finished at .322 in a third place tie but he did win the league's Most Valuable Player Award. He also led the Braves to their World Series victory over the Yankees, hitting .393, with three home runs and seven runs batted in.

Said teammate Eddie Mathews, the Braves' Hall of Fame third baseman: "Over the years his greatest contribution was his ability to ignite the team."

Early on, Aaron had a deserved reputation as a "bad ball" hitter. He stood

the friendly competition between Aaron and Mathews, who alternated hitting third and fourth in the order, made each a better player.

A panther at
the plate,
Aaron derived
his power
from quick
hands and
wrist action,
along with
impeccable
timing. Before
he surfaced to
the majors,
he batted
cross-handed,
which was
easily
corrected.

calmly between pitches, well back from the plate, slightly slouched, and crushed the ball with a seemingly effortless swing. There was none of the tension about him that most hitters radiate. Robin Roberts, at that time one of the National League's premier pitchers, once said, in jest, "How can you fool Aaron? He falls asleep between pitches."

Whitey Lockman, a baseball lifer who had a 15-year major league playing career and after that put in four decades as a big league manager, coach and super-scout, insists he never saw Aaron look bad on a pitch, take a half swing or make an easy out. No little dribblers back to the pitcher. "He was very analytical at the plate. He studied the pitchers and was very focused. That's why he was so good."

Once, when asked to compare himself to Ted Williams, Aaron corroborated Lockman's view. Said Aaron: "Ted Williams concentrated on the things he had to do, I concentrated on the pitcher. I didn't stay up nights worrying about my weight distribution or the position of my hands or the turn of my hips. I stayed up thinking about the pitcher I was going to face the next day."

Unlike some strong hitters, including more than a few Hall of Famers, Aaron was never intimidated. He had no fear at the plate. Many times, after being knocked down, he got up and responded with a home run.

"Don Drysdale always tried to hit him in the ass, not once in a while but every time," said Paul Blair of the Baltimore Orioles who was among the best defensive center fielders of the time. "But no matter how many times Drysdale did it, the next time he threw the ball over the plate, Henry would hit a line drive."

Though victimized by of hundreds of knockdown pitches, Henry rarely complained. Appealing to the umpires, he realized, indicated weakness. I heard him complain only once. Sam "Toothpick" Jones sent him sprawling in the dirt at least a half dozen times during the 1957 September stretch when the Cardinals and Braves were challenging for the pennant. Frustrated, Aaron complained to reporters. As soon as the story hit the street, he realized his mistake. Expressing annoyance would prompt more pitchers to throw at him.

A panther at the plate, Aaron derived his power from quick hands and wrist action, along with impeccable timing. Before he surfaced to the majors, he batted cross-handed, which was easily corrected. But his swing remained unorthodox: he hit off his front foot. For the first 10 to 12 years, he was a straightaway hitter with remarkable power to right and right center field. Later, when he was swinging for home runs, he began pulling the ball to left and left center.

After watching him for a week in spring training, Hall of Famer Paul Waner, one of baseball's best "place hitters," hired by the Braves as a special batting instructor, carried a simple message to the front office. "Don't let anybody touch that swing. Leave that swing alone."

During an unparalleled 23-year big league career, particularly in its beginning, Aaron was an unassuming and stoic assassin. Even when he was beyond mid-career, baseball writers were slow to grasp that he was likely to displace Babe Ruth as baseball's all-

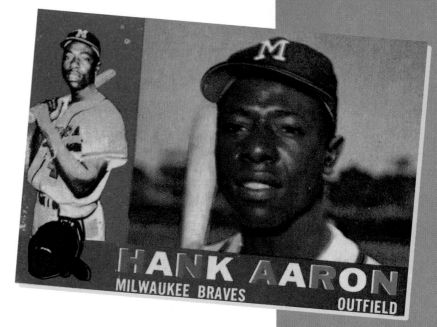

time home run champion. He was mostly a silent loner, uncomfortable with the press, performing in faraway Milwaukee, a thousand miles from the New York media hub, and never receiving the adulation of such glamorous contemporaries as Willie Mays, Mickey Mantle, and Roberto Clemente.

Aaron played without flair. Consistency was his game: seven seasons with 30 or more home runs, eight with 40 or more, with a high of 47. At the finish he'd hammered 755 home runs, a record that may never be approached. To surpass it would require an *average* of almost 40 home runs for 20 seasons. He batted .300 or higher 13 times and holds the major league career record for runs scored, runs batted in and total bases. Thirteen times he batted more than .300.

Natural hitter though he was, Aaron knew that success was the result of hard work. In a 1967 interview with the late Ken Smith of the Baseball Hall of Fame, Aaron insisted nothing came

easy to him: "To be good at anything you have to work at it. I've always had a little ability, but I always worked at my weaknesses and studied the pitchers. I knew what I could do at the plate but to get an edge I had to try and figure what the pitchers were doing to get me out."

Mickey Mantle ranked him "as the best player of my generation." "Trying to sneak a fastball by him is like smuggling a sunrise past a rooster," said pitcher Don Drysdale, the Dodgers' Hall of Fame fireballer, the victim of 17 Aaron home runs, more than any other pitcher. [The remark, with slight variations, has been attributed to several players, Joe Adcock among them.] Drysdale called him "Bad Henry." Bobby Thomson, an Aaron teammate in Milwaukee, simply said, "Magic is the only word I can use to describe him."

Born in Mobile, Alabama on February 5, 1934, Henry Aaron the beginning baseball player, has been difficult to

to this day, the difference in price between Aaron's baseball cards and Mantle's (like this 1951 Bowman worth more than $10,000), seems more a matter of geography and publicity than ability, or even race.

trace. Sports editors in Mobile gave up trying to get a consistent portrait of him as a young man. "Every time we start," one of them said, "we find a couple of things that don't add up. No one has ever been able to put the whole thing together."

What does add up, is that Aaron began playing baseball at the age of 11. One of eight children, the third oldest of four boys, he grew up in above average circumstances for an African-American in the Deep South. His father, Herbert, who had been a ballplayer in his youth, worked as a boilermaker's assistant. "There was enough money for what we needed but it was week to week," Aaron recalled. "It was always one week to the next, waiting for the pay."

His mother, Estella, said he was a quiet boy. "He never made many friends. He liked to stay in and read a lot. Mostly, he read comic books and things about sports. And he just loved to play baseball. Every time there was a game anywhere, and he could join, he'd be there. He liked to play shortstop the best."

His early baseball experience had been in a playground league. He played football and basketball at Central High School but not baseball—which had been dropped due to lack of funds the year before Henry became eligible. Instead, he played on the Central softball team. His coach, Edwin Foster, has a vivid memory of him: "Hank was with us in 1950 and '51. He was the kingpin. We only lost three games in the two seasons he was with us. He was a great player."

Aaron also played in a Sunday sandlot hardball league. In the spring of 1951, soon after he had turned 17, the Indianapolis Clowns came to town to play a Negro American League exhibition game against the Mobile Black Bears. The Bears recruited Aaron to play shortstop for them that day. According to Furman Bisher, an Atlanta sportswriter who was Aaron's first biographer, Bunny Downs, the Clowns' business manager, asked Aaron if he would like to join their club. A year later, after Henry had graduated from high school (his mother insisted on his obtaining his diploma), he signed for $200 a month, a financial windfall to the Aaron household.

Ike Brown (amazingly, in 1969) and Paul Casanova were the last players to leave the Negro Leagues to play in the Majors, though Hank was the last former Negro Leaguer when he retired after the 1976 season.

The trademark of the Clowns was entertainment, the baseball counterpart of the Harlem Globetrotters. For years the team included a midget, a juggler and a contortionist, all competent players. The last of the barnstorming teams, the Clowns were on the road for more than 40 years. Aaron was to become the team's most illustrious graduate. Some of the other alumni included the legendary Satchel Paige, who was pitching into his 60s, Choo Choo Coleman, the first Met to hit a home run, and Paul Casanova, who was among Aaron's teammates with the Atlanta Braves. The great track star, Jesse Owens, traveled with the Clowns for one season, just after his victory in the 1936 Olympic Games in Berlin.

In the biography he wrote with Lonnie Wheeler, *I Had A Hammer*, Hank recounted the day he left home, when he left Mobile to join the Clowns. "Mama was so upset she couldn't come to the train station to see me off. She made me a couple of sandwiches, stuffed two dollars in my pocket, and stood in the yard crying. My knees were banging together when I got on that train. I'd never ridden in anything bigger than a bus or faster than my daddy's old pickup truck. I never felt so alone in my life. I just sat there clutching my sandwiches, speaking to nobody, staring out the windows at towns I'd never heard of. It was the first time I had been around white people. After a while I got up the courage to walk up and down the aisle. I wanted to see what a dining car looked like, and I needed somebody to tell me where I wasn't allowed to go. Then I sat back down, listened to those wheels carrying me farther away from home, and tried to talk myself out of

getting off at the next stop and going back."

While with the Clowns, Aaron got a bitter taste of racial prejudice. On a northern trip the Clowns were rained out of a Sunday doubleheader at Griffith Stadium in Washington, D.C. Aaron was having breakfast with his teammates at a restaurant behind the ballpark. "After we finished eating," Aaron recalled, "the plates were taken into the kitchen and broken into little pieces. Here we were in the capital of freedom and supposed equality and the plates were broken because they had touched the forks that had been in the mouths of black men. If dogs had eaten off those plates they would have washed them."

Aaron first came to the attention of the Boston Braves early in the 1952 season through a postscript in a letter from Syd Pollock, owner of the Clowns, to farm director John Mullen. It was two years before the Braves moved to Milwaukee. "P.S.," Pollock wrote, "We've got an 18-year old shortstop batting cleanup for us." Mullen alerted scout Dewey Griggs.

In the beginning, Buster Haywood, the Clowns manager, wasn't impressed.

after Boston scout Dewey Griggs saw Aaron, it was just a matter of time before he would be playing in Milwaukee's County Stadium, here shown on Opening Day, 1953.

"the kid's worth $7,500 just for his swing," Dewey Griggs, the Boston scout, told John Mullen, who ran the Braves' minor league operation. "I'd make the down payment out of my own pocket. He can play anywhere, except pitch and catch. But don't do anything to him at bat. He's one of the best natural hitters I've ever seen."

Hank Aaron
M

"This kid barely talks," said Haywood. He used Aaron sparingly in the belief he didn't have much of a baseball future. Hank was a good soldier and rode the bench without complaint. Still, it was apparent he could hit. Once he fell asleep on a long bus trip and woke up hitting, adding to his reputation for nonchalance. "He didn't wake up until we got to Buffalo," a teammate marveled. "Then he got off the bus and got 10 hits in 11 times at bat."

When several of his players went down with injuries, Haywood had to put Aaron in the lineup and the hits started to fall—hard singles through the infield, line-drive doubles into the gaps and an occasional home run. It didn't take Aaron long to earn a reputation as a dangerous hitter. He also became aware that "people were noticing me."

Buck O'Neil, who later worked with the Chicago Cubs as a coach and a scout but was then managing the Kansas City Monarchs, was awestruck.

"We were playing the Clowns down in Alabama or Louisiana during the spring," O'Neill recalled. "I noticed this young boy hitting in the fourth spot and I said to Haywood, 'Buster, what about this kid?' And he said, 'Buck, he can really swing the bat.'

"I had some pretty good pitchers who had been around the block a few times, and the first time he came up I told the pitcher to throw him a good fastball. He threw a fastball and the kid hit it up against the right field fence. The next time he came up I had my best left-hander in there, and I said 'Throw this kid a good fastball.' He threw his fastball on the first pitch, and the kid hit it against the center field fence. I looked over at Buster and Buster was just laughing at me. The last

time, I had the star of my staff in there, an old pro named Hilton Smith, and I told Smith to throw curveballs. The kid hit a curveball over the left field fence.

"After the game, I told Buster, 'You and I both know that by the time you get to Kansas City to play us, this kid won't be with you anymore.' No way a hitter like that is going to stay in the Negro League."

"The kid's worth $7,500 just for his swing," Dewey Griggs, the Boston scout, told John Mullen, who ran the Braves' minor league operation. "I'd make the down payment out of my own pocket. He can play anywhere, except pitch and catch. But don't do anything to him at bat. He's one of the best natural hitters I've ever seen."

Griggs continued on Aaron's trail. The more he saw the more he was convinced. In a May 23, 1952 report to Mullen, Griggs wrote:

Scouted the doubleheader between Indianapolis and Memphis at Buffalo Sunday afternoon. Heavy morning showers left the field in a muddy condition and prevented good fielding.

Henry Aaron looked very good. In the first game he had seven chances, two fly balls back of third and five hard-hit ground balls. Started one double play from short to second to first, hit three-for-five, two line drive singles over third and short and a perfect bunt down the third base line. These hits were made off a good-looking left-hander.

In the second game he accepted five chances without an error and hit three-for-four. Off the starting left-handed pitcher he hit an outside curve ball over the right field fence, 350 feet away, and dropped down another perfect bunt. In the sixth inning he hit a low inside curve for a single over second base off a right-hander with bases loaded.

By midseason Aaron was leading the league with a .457 average. Pedro Zorilla, a scout with the New York Giants, had joined Griggs in the hunt. On Zorilla's recommendation, the Giants agreed to meet Pollock's $7,500 asking price.

The Braves topped the Giants' offer, and the deal was made. Pollock would get $2,500 down, another $500 if Aaron made a Triple A league, and the full $7,500 if he reached the big leagues. This was in the bonus-baby era, the age of the $100,000 signing price. The Braves signed Aaron for $350 a month and gave him an airplane ticket to Eau Claire, Wisconsin, where they had a farm club in the Class C Northern League.

He reported in the latter part of the season, played in only 87 games, and batted .336 with 9 home runs and

61 runs batted in. He was named the league's All-Star shortstop and Rookie of the Year. The next season Aaron was promoted to the Jacksonville Tars of the Class A Sally League (Southern Atlantic League). At the season's end there was no longer any doubt, if there had ever been, that he was en route to stardom.

Henry led the league in hitting with a .362 average, in RBI, 125; runs, 115; hits, 208; and in putouts, assists and even errors. He had 22 home runs, and was second in triples, the best indication of his speed. Better yet, he struck out only 22 times, a ratio of one K for every 26 at-bats, unusually low for a power hitter.

Ben Geraghty, his manager at Jacksonville, couldn't remember a batter who so thoroughly dominated the Sally League. Said Geraghty: "He just stood up there flicking those great wrists and simply overpowered the pitching." Henry won the Most Valuable Player Award and led the Tars to their first pennant in 41 years. For his good work, Henry was invited to the Braves' major league spring training camp in Bradenton, Florida.

By this time it was apparent he could make the big leagues as a hitter but not as an infielder. He had played second base at Eau Claire and short at Jacksonville but was not impressive at either position. It was then decided to convert him into an outfielder.

So he was dispatched to the Puerto Rican Winter League where he would be competing against other top major league prospects. He joined the Caguas club managed by Mickey Owen, a one-time big league catcher

It was Mickey Owen, Aaron's manager in the Puerto Rican Winter League, who moved Aaron from second base to the outfield.

Aaron's Eau Claire contract stated the salary of $350 a month, but it didn't mention the signing bonus: a new cardboard suitcase.

who is most remembered for dropping a third strike in the 1941 World Series. Recalled Owen: "He was just a kid but he wasn't green."

The trip to Puerto Rico was Aaron's honeymoon. Two days before departure, on October 6, 1953, he and the former Barbara Lucas were married. She had been a student at Florida A&M but was then living at home in Jacksonville, less than two blocks from the ballpark. Her father had played ball and so did one of her brothers, Bill, who several years later was also signed by the Braves. Bill failed as a player but subsequently became the Braves' respected front office boss, the first African-American to become a major league general manager.

Six months earlier, during the middle of the 1953 spring training season, because of falling attendance, the Braves moved from Boston to Milwaukee, the first change in the major league map in a half century. The Boston newspapers yelled "foul." The Braves had been in Boston for 82 years without interruption. For Henry and his bride it would be an easier life. Milwaukee was comparatively free of racial tension.

The shift to the outfield was painless. As usual, Aaron had no problem adjusting to the pitching and was among the league's leading hitters. All eyes were on him. Tom Sheehan of the New York Giants, who was in the Caribbean on a scouting mission, was unable to restrain himself and told whoever would listen, "I've seen a kid who could turn out to be a better ballplayer than Willie Mays. His name is Henry Aaron."

The next stop was the Braves' spring training camp in Bradenton,

Florida. "When I first saw him I thought he had come to deliver a telegram," recalled Charlie Grimm, the Milwaukee manager. Soon, Aaron was delivering base hits to all fields. In Sarasota one afternoon, during an exhibition against the Boston Red Sox, Ted Williams, who seldom participated in these games, heard the sound of a bat meeting the ball.

"Who the hell hit that one?" Williams asked Bob Wolf of the *Milwaukee Journal.*

"Aaron, a new kid," Wolf replied.

"Sounds like a helluva hitter," Williams said.

Aaron's sojourn in the Braves camp was a courtesy invitation. The Braves had promoted him from Jacksonville to the roster of their Toledo club in the Triple A American Association. No one expected Aaron to make the parent team. The scenario changed in the middle of spring training, on March 13 in St. Petersburg, in an exhibition against the Yankees. Bobby Thomson drove a ball into the left field corner and broke his right leg, just, above the ankle, sliding into second. It was a crushing blow.

The Braves had finished second the previous season, their first in Milwaukee, and during the off-season had acquired Thomson, who had hit the most famous home run in diamond history, the so-called "Shot Heard 'Round the World." The home run came in the ninth inning of the decisive playoff game against Brooklyn and lifted the Giants to the pennant. Thomson was expected to provide similar heroics for the Braves and help lead them to the 1954 pennant.

The next day, in a game against Cincinnati, Aaron replaced Thomson in left field and responded with three

hits—a single, triple and home run. A few days before the Braves broke camp, Grimm told him, "Kid, you're my left fielder. It's yours until somebody takes it away from you."

Phil Musick, in his wonderfully detailed Hank Aaron, *The Man Who Beat the Babe,* said Aaron was eager to take advantage of his sudden opportunity. "I kept reading the Braves had lost the pennant when Bobby Thomson broke his leg. That didn't do my confidence any good," Aaron said, "but I didn't want to open the trap door and find myself on the way back to Toledo."

The trap door never opened. He was signed to a Milwaukee contract and was in the Braves' Opening Day lineup. Aaron had the usual rookie problems of adjusting to big league pitching, particularly to off-speed breaking pitches. In his big league debut against Cincinnati he was hitless in five trips. Bud Podbielan, a slow-baller, started for the Reds and was relieved by Joe Nuxhall in the second inning. Nuxhall doesn't remember much of that game, except the pre-

game clubhouse meeting. "We thought he was a high-ball hitter," Nuxhall recalled.

But there was no precise way to pitch to him. Bob Friend, ace of Pittsburgh's staff, said Aaron's advantage was that he never committed himself early; he waited longer on the pitch than anyone in the National League.

"I've seen him hit pitches off his ear into the right field seats," Friend moaned. "And he gets more hits off bad balls than most batters get off a pitch in the middle of the plate. He swings at everything he can reach." Grimm, asked to describe Aaron's strike zone, said "Anywhere from the top of his head to the tips of his toes."

Two days before Labor Day, Aaron fractured his right ankle sliding into third base. Ironically, Thomson, who had returned in August, went in to run for him. His season was over, but Aaron had played in 122 games, had 468 at-bats, drove in 69 runs and, after going 5-for-5 on the last day, had lifted his average to .280. He was limited to 13 home runs but hit one or more in each National League park. The first of

Ford Frick, baseball's Commissioner, shot this photo from the stands at the 1955 All-Star Game, Aaron's first. Can you spot Hank?

his 755 home runs was off Vic Raschi of the Cardinals on April 23 in St. Louis.

From then on he terrorized National League pitchers: .314, with 27 home runs and 106 RBI in 1955; and .328, 26 HR and 92 RBI in 1956, when Aaron had a 25-game hitting streak from July 15 through August 8. The Braves held first place for 126 days and had a one-game lead with three games to play but lost the pennant to the Dodgers on the final day.

Henry was tuning up for one of his best seasons. He led the Braves to their first Milwaukee flag in 1957 and won the league's Most Valuable Player Award with a near-Triple Crown performance: 44 home runs, a career high 132 runs batted in, and a .322 average. Appropriately, his 44th home run, off Billy Muffett of the Cardinals, clinched the pennant and broke a 2-2, 11th inning tie.

It was a slump-proof season for The Hammer. In late July, he was leading both leagues in batting, home runs and RBI. Fred Haney, an old-school martinet, had replaced the popular Grimm as the Braves manager. Aaron had difficulty adjusting to Haney, who was overly critical and constantly pushing for perfection. In late August, after the Braves had won 17 of 19 games, Haney joined the chorus.

"He's more like Hornsby than any hitter I've seen," Haney said. "And Hornsby was the greatest right-handed hitter I ever saw. It's incredible the way he hits the ball to right field with all that power. He's more than just a natural hitter. He has the temperament and the disposition to go with it."

Other baseball veterans also watched in awe. Observed Mayo

Smith, manager of the Philadelphia Phillies, "There's no book on him. You have to pitch to him down the middle with everything you've got and then close your eyes."

An hour before the midnight June 15 trading deadline, two days before Grimm was dismissed, the Milwaukee brass consummated a deal with the Giants that helped put them across: Red Schoendienst for the aging Bobby Thomson and pitcher Ray Crone. Schoendienst was precisely what the Braves needed: a seasoned second baseman who steadied the infield. He finished third in the MVP balloting, behind Aaron and Musial.

The Braves were an enormous success at the gate. For the second year in a row they set an all-time regular-season National League attendance record, 2.2 million; then they beat the Yankees in a seven-game World Series. Aaron was the batting star. He led both teams with a .393 average, three home runs, and 7 RBI.

The next year, 1958, the Braves won their second successive pennant. After a hot second half, Aaron finished with a .326 average, 30 home runs and 95 RBI. Because of injuries to Schoendienst, pitcher Bob Buhl and outfielder Wes Covington, the Braves didn't take command until early August. Still, they won the flag by eight games, same as the previous season.

The Yankees also won again, the ninth pennant in ten years under the direction of manager Casey Stengel. The Braves won three of the first four Series games but lost in seven games, only the second time in baseball history that a team had come back from a 3-1 deficit. Aaron, now alternating between right and center field, had a

TOPS IN NL

HANK AARON • WILLIE MAYS

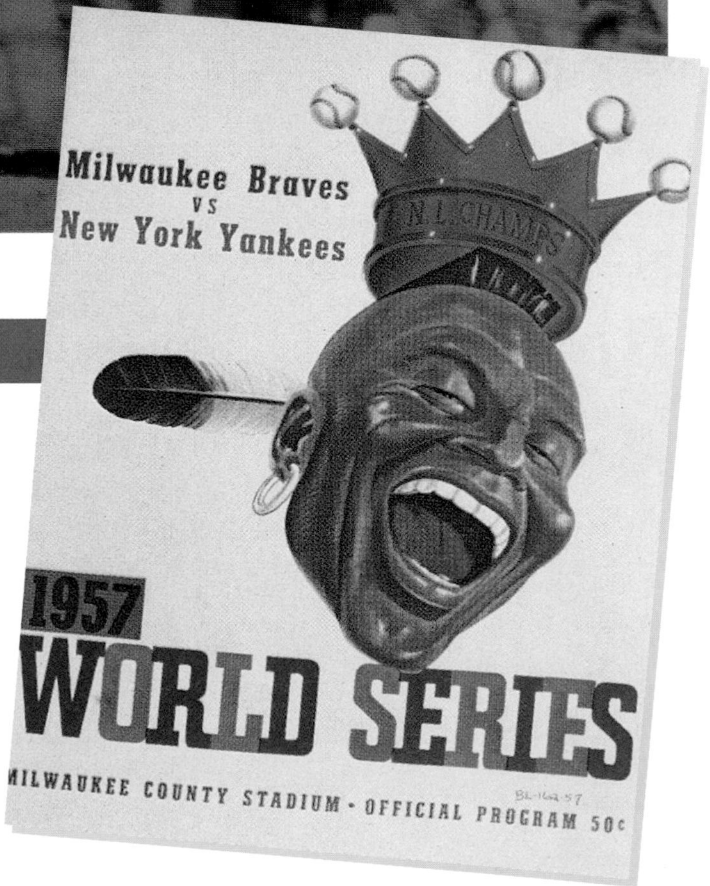

It was expected that Mickey Mantle or Aaron, perhaps Whitey Ford or Warren Spahn, might be the hero of the 1957 World Series. But Lew Burdette unexpectedly won three games and the World Series MVP.

Milwaukee Braves
vs
New York Yankees

N. L. CHAMPS

1957
WORLD SERIES

MILWAUKEE COUNTY STADIUM · OFFICIAL PROGRAM 50¢

> He has become a better hitter than ever because he's gotten more confidence. Call it poise or experience, he pays more attention to the strike zone. He hits with power to all fields and that's the test of a hitter.
>
> —Rogers Hornsby

relatively poor Series. He batted .333, but didn't hit with his usual power—no home runs and only two RBI. In 27 at-bats, he was limited to two extra-base hits, both doubles.

It was his last World Series. But the Braves continued on the pennant track and in 1959 finished in a first-place dead-heat with the Los Angeles Dodgers. Had the Braves won the play-off, it would have been their third successive league championship but they lost the first two games of a scheduled three-game playoff series. It was another strong year for The Hammer: a league-leading and career-high .355 average, with 39 home runs and 123 runs driven in.

It was also the year he flirted with .400. Off to his best start ever, Henry hit .508 in April and was whaling away at a .487 pace though games of May 14. On May 16, in a 6-0 victory against the Dodgers, he slammed two home runs but lost four points off his average. Ten days later he was at .461, all the while prompting speculation he would be the first .400 hitter since Ted Williams in 1941.

Rogers Hornsby, whose .424 in 1924 is the modern big league high, was asked to comment. Said the Rajah: "He has become a better hitter than ever because he's gotten more confidence. Call it poise or experience, he pays more attention to the strike zone. He hits with power to all fields and that's the test of a hitter."

Added Birdie Tebbetts, then managing Cincinnati, "He could win the batting title the next five or six years."

The Hammer didn't drop below .400 until June 16. In this same month, he knocked out his number 1,000 base hit, reaching this plateau at the age of

25, younger than seven of the then eight members of the 3,000 hit club. He was the first unanimous choice on the National League All-Star team (then chosen by the players) and led the league in batting, in hits (223), and in slugging percentage (.636). Barring injury, he was on the road to Cooperstown. After six years in the majors he had a cumulative .327 average along with an annual average of 30 home runs and 103 RBI.

Along the way, there were many memorable moments, including an incredible parlay at the Polo Grounds in New York in 1962 when Aaron and Lou Brock hit home runs into the distant center field bleachers on consecutive days. In the long history of the Polo Grounds there had been only one verified previous instance of a pitch hit into the remote bleachers since their remodeling in 1923. (The only previous authenticated home run into the Polo Grounds bleachers was by Joe Adcock, Aaron's future teammate, on April 29, 1953.)

Brock, then a Cubs rookie, turned the trick on June 17. He drilled a pitch by the Mets' Al Jackson an estimated 470 feet. The following night Aaron connected off New York's Jay Hook into the bleachers for a grand slam home run.

Aaron's 200th home run was off the Cardinals' Ron Kline on July 3, 1960. Number 300, off the Mets' Roger Craig, came three years later. The Phillies' Bo Belinsky was the victim of Number 400, on April 20, 1966 immediately after the Milwaukee franchise had been transferred to Atlanta. Sportswriters then began linking Aaron to Babe Ruth. The Babe and Aaron, whose birthdays were one day apart, had reached the

Aaron became the ninth player, and the first since Stan Musial 12 years earlier, to join the elite 3,000 hit club. He had hoped Number 3,000 would be a home run, but was satisfied it was a "clean hit." He clubbed a three-run home run, Number 570, in his next at-bat.

for most of his career, Willie Mays stayed ahead of Hank Aaron in home runs. When Aaron hit his 649th home run on June 10, 1972, he passed Willie Mays for good.

400 home run level at the age of 32. Two years later Aaron was ahead of Ruth's pace. It was now apparent Ruth had a worthy challenger.

There was more. On May 17, 1970, with an infield single off Cincinnati's Wayne Simpson in Crosley Field, Aaron became the ninth player, and the first since Stan Musial 12 years earlier, to join the elite 3,000 hit club. He had hoped Number 3,000 would be a home run but was satisfied it was a "clean hit." He clubbed a three-run home run, Number 570, in his next at-bat. Henry became the first player with 3,000 hits and 500 home runs (Willie Mays and Eddie Murray have since earned the same distinction).

Musial and Bill Bartholomay, the Braves' chairman, jumped over the low fence and trotted to first base to congratulate The Hammer on his 3,000th hit. Aaron thanked Musial "for coming to see me do it." It was a monumental achievement, a coupling of talent and endurance. It is baseball's finest unsung record. To collect 3,000 hits would require 20 seasons with a minimum of 150 hits. Aaron did it in his 17th season.

A blizzard of accolades hailed the achievement. Joe Torre, who had been among Aaron's Atlanta teammates and subsequently a successful big league manager, made the most telling observation: "Henry belongs in a higher league."

Ruth's record was now in sight. Aaron admitted that catching and surpassing Ruth would be a once-in-a-lifetime thrill. But he was also convinced 3,000 hits were more important because it showed consistency

"I don't know if I'll be around long enough to break Ruth's record," he said, "But I won't hang on for the sake of hanging on, picking up 12 home runs one year and 20 the next. I have too much respect for baseball to do that."

Hang around? Henry responded with 47 home runs in 1971, his single-season high. But it was a bittersweet year. After 18 years of marriage, Henry and Barbara Aaron agreed on a divorce. It was a friendly parting and Henry has an enduring relationship with their four children.

Three years later Henry married the former Billye Suber, a vibrant talk show hostess for an Atlanta television station. It was the second marriage for both. Originally from Dallas, Billye was a widow with one child. Asked how they get along, Billye said, "I do all the talking and Hank makes all the decisions."

As Aaron approached Ruth's record he became the target of a virulent hate-mail campaign which strengthened his resolve. By what right, the racists wanted to know, did he, a black man, dare to supplant the beloved Babe? Some of the letters included the threat he would not live long enough to succeed. The police were alerted. Bodyguards were hired. What was supposed to have been his finest hour had become a monstrous ordeal.

Always proud of his heritage, Aaron would shake his head in disgust and feel sorry for the demented losers who seldom signed their name. It was about this time that Henry, no longer the shy young ballplayer, began to speak out and criticize the owners not only for refusing to hire African-American field managers but also for denying them significant front office positions.

In a lengthy interview with me for *Sport Magazine,* Aaron said:

"I've been thinking about this for a long time and I'm still not certain where to start. I could manage a big league club and there are many other Negroes who also have managerial qualifications—or will have. Willie Mays could manage. So could Jackie Robinson. Bill White could manage and Billy Bruton and Junior Gilliam and Ernie Banks. You don't have to cut this list off. It can go on and on because no two managers manage the same way.

"The only thing, really, that every good manager has to do is get along with his players. That is, the players must respect him. I don't believe the manager must be chummy with his players. A manager is the boss and the boss shouldn't mix freely. But he does have to try and keep a good feeling among his players, especially among those who aren't playing."

He conceded he was describing the ideal manager-player conditions.

"People aren't perfect and the manager is dealing with people, human beings. I have yet to play for a manager who's been able to keep everybody

hank married Billye Williams (née Billye Suber) in November 1973.

happy. All ballplayers think they should be playing but the manager can only play nine guys at a time.

"That's why it's impossible for total harmony. And disharmony isn't all bad. It's a good feeling to have the reserves wanting to play. I wouldn't want a player who is content sitting on the bench. Plenty of angry and disgruntled players have helped win pennants.

"The problem will be magnified for the Negro manager. He'll get it from the whites who can accuse him of prejudice and/or from the Negroes who will call him an Uncle Tom. Negroes aren't perfect, either. They put their best interests first, too.

"I have been with Eddie Mathews for 13 years and he's never said anything out of the way. Mathews was born in Texas and grew up in California. If he were to become our manager I'd play for him. I'd be delighted. And he'd be delighted to play for me."

Even after his retirement and for many years thereafter, Aaron spoke out against racial prejudice. But he didn't allow it to affect his play.

"Hank kept almost everything to himself," recalled teammate Paul Casanova. "You couldn't read him because he wouldn't let anything show. I've never seen anyone who could control his emotions like Hank did. We had bad teams in those years, and there was a lot of pressure on him. The only one time I heard him mention Babe Ruth was one night in Montreal.

"We'd lost eight in a row and Hank came to bat in the ninth inning with two men on and us down by two runs, and he hit one that was headed way out of the park. Everybody in the dugout jumped up and started screaming because our losing streak was finally over. But all of a sudden the wind caught hold of the ball and brought it all the way back into the ballpark, and the left fielder caught it at the fence.

"We got on the bus to the airport and nobody said anything for 30 minutes. We felt terrible. Finally, Hank stood up in the back of the bus and said, 'I'll bet any amount of money that damn Babe Ruth was up there blowing it back.' It loosened everybody up, and we started playing better ball after that."

Home run number 500 was off the Giants' Mike McCormick, number 600 off Gaylord Perry, also of the Giants, number 700 off Ken Brett of the Phillies. On the last day of the '73 season he closed the gap with Number 713 off Houston's Jerry Reuss. He was now within one home run of Ruth's record.

After a winter of hibernation, Hank couldn't wait for the 1974 season. Anxious to end the quest, he tied Ruth's record on his first swing, connecting off Jack Billingham in Cincinnati. Aaron was ahead on the count, three balls and one strike. "Billingham threw a fastball and I was guessing fastball," Aaron told reporters. "I was happy to see the ball drop over the fence. I didn't watch it. I've never watched any of my homers. I let the umpires do that."

The entire country was watching, including Red Smith, the nation's premier sports columnist. "Of all the contributions Henry Aaron has made to baseball in 20 blameless seasons, of all his accomplishments as a player and his acts of graciousness, generosity and loyalty as a person, none was half so valuable as his achievement of yesterday. It isn't only that his 714th home run matched a record that for more

On the last day of the '73 season he closed the gap with Number 713 off Houston's Jerry Reuss. He was now within one home run of Ruth's record.

HANK AARON

than 40 years was considered beyond human reach, and it isn't particularly important that this courteous modest man has at last overtaken Babe Ruth's roistering ghost. What really counts is that when Henry laid the wood on Jack Billingham's fastball, he struck a blow for the integrity of the game and for public faith in the game."

"With one stroke he cancelled schemes to cheapen his pursuit of the record by avoiding a carnival attraction staged for the box office alone, and he rendered moot two months of wrangling between the money changers and the Protectors of the Faith."

Smith was referring to the firestorm of criticism directed at the Braves' management. Bill Bartholomay, the Atlanta chairman, in an early-February announcement, two months before Opening Day, revealed Henry would be held out of the opening Cincinnati series so he would have the opportunity of equaling and breaking the record before his home crowd. To his astonishment, Bartholomay was accused of trying to fatten the Braves' gate, which had been diminishing. They had been under .500 in three of the four previous seasons.

Most, but not all of the sportswrit-

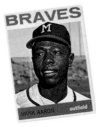

Aaron crosses the plate after air-mailing a slow curve from left-hander Jerry Reuss. The scoreboard records his tally. The home run was his 40th, on the next-to-last game of the 1973 season. He went three-for-four, without a homer, on the last day, bringing his average to .301.

Aaron showed his frustration after popping out against Houston's Don Wilson in his last at-bat of the 1973 season.

ers were enraged and pleaded that Commissioner Bowie Kuhn should order the Braves to play Aaron in Cincinnati. "C'mon, Bowie, make them play the cards the way they've been dealt," wrote David Condon in the *Chicago Tribune.*

"Baseball has gone crooked," shouted the influential Dick Young of the *New York Daily News.* "A fix by any name is a fix. There is no delicate way to put it. I would feel better if the Commissioner comes out with a blistering order that Hank Aaron play the first three games under threat of forfeit." Young also quoted Yankee president

Gabe Paul, a highly respected and long-time executive who said, "Everything you do in baseball must be predicated on winning. If you take that away, even one little bit, you are doing the game great harm."

Dave Anderson of *The New York Times* called it "brazen defiance" of baseball's integrity" and Jerry Nason of the Boston Globe described it as a "contrivance of the most blatant sort." Commented Garry Brown of the *Springfield* (Mass.) *Union:* "The Braves are off base. It would hurt the game and turn it into some kind of sideshow in which the star attraction is used only

when he can do the most good at the box office."

Ron Hudspeth of the *Atlanta Journal:* "He's the best player the Braves have and should be playing. Without him in the lineup they have a good chance of coming home 0-3. The Braves should let the record happen."

Bartholomay had some scattered support. Tom Callahan of the *Cincinnati Enquirer* insisted, "The Braves are entitled to take advantage of Aaron's drawing power at home since they are paying him $600,000 on a three-year contract."

The *Sporting News* also sided with Bartholomay and pointed out: "There is a precedent for this kind of maneuvering. The Cardinals did it in 1958 when Stan Musial was about to log his 3,000th hit. Musial was withheld from the starting lineup in Chicago. The Cardinals were to be in St. Louis the next day and tried to arrange for hit Number 3,000 to come before a home crowd. But late in the game in Chicago a pinch-hitting situation arose and manager Fred Hutchinson did not hesitate to call on Musial. Stan delivered, which helped spark a Cardinal victory. We can't conceive of Eddie Mathews, the Atlanta manager, playing it differently with Aaron if a comparable situation arose in Cincinnati.

"The Braves could have waited until the eve of the opener and manufactured a pulled muscle for Henry. If Henry said he was hurt, the self-appointed defenders of the faith would be unlikely to challenge him. But Aaron and the Braves have resorted to no phony alibis. Their integrity comes through a lot stronger than the complainants' common sense.

"Why haven't the arbiters of

uprightness blasted the practice of testing youngsters in September games? It's done often enough, always in games that have no bearing on the standings. And since when does a 'best effort' depend on the presence of a single player who is deemed essential by writer-pundits? The Braves have a right to play Aaron when and where they see fit. A 'best effort' does not hinge on a lineup made out in the press box."

Leonard Koppett, in his *Sporting News* column, also defended the Braves and asked: "If Commissioner Bowie Kuhn follows the storm of advice being heaped upon him and orders Aaron to play in Cincinnati will he also order him to hit a home run? And if Aaron plays in Cincinnati and does not hit a home run, will he then be suspected of giving less than his best?"

Jesse Outlar of the *Atlanta Constitution:* "With Aaron answering the bell annually the Braves have lost seven pennants since arriving in Atlanta by a total of 132 games. Personally, I think the Braves should have left the decision of whether to play or not play to Aaron. For the other 159 games, Hank will inform manager Eddie Mathews whether he feels like being in the lineup."

Of the hundreds of thousands of words written on the subject only Sparky Anderson, the Cincinnati manager, noted that Aaron was in the middle, a helpless pawn. "He shouldn't have to take all this stuff," Sparky said. "They've got him trapped against the wall. If he says anything he's a big shot. And of all the superstars he's never said anything to make you dislike him."

Kuhn was slow in reacting. Finally, he ruled that Aaron, barring injury, must be in the starting lineup for the entire three-game series. Aaron didn't express concern over the swirling controversy and responded with his Opening Day home run off Billingham.

When he was held out of the second game, an indignant Kuhn telephoned the Braves' office and spoke to manager Eddie Mathews.

"I asked the Commissioner two questions," Mathews said. "Is this an order? And what are the consequences?"

"This is a direct order," Kuhn replied. "I haven't decided the consequences but they will be severe."

Aaron was 0-for-3 in the third game. According to Dick Young, "Aaron never looked worse." He struck out twice on three pitches and was out on a weak roller before he was lifted for defensive purposes. "Were you trying to hit a homer?" Young asked. "People might think you are saving it for Atlanta."

"I can't help what people think," Aaron said. "It's not easy walking up there and hitting a homer. Not as easy as they think."

When the Braves returned to Atlanta, Henry hit Number 715 before a standing-room-only crowd in the Braves' home opener. During a press conference after the game Aaron was asked "Are you the greatest ballplayer?" The question embarrassed him.

"I couldn't say," Aaron replied. Then innate frankness overcame embarrassment. "I'd say I'm one of the best." He rattled off the names that flashed in his mind—Joe DiMaggio, Willie Mays, Jackie Robinson, in that order. "I wouldn't say Henry Aaron is going to be fourth. I'd say Henry Aaron is going to be second or third."

According to a Harris survey of 769 fans across the country, 77 percent were rooting for Aaron. Still, the naysayers were adamant in their criticism: When he connected for Number 714, he had had 2,890 more at-bats than Ruth. The hate mail continued pouring in but was now outnumbered by letters of good cheer and congratulations.

Dear Mr. Aaron:

We were watching as a family from Room 306 at the Morton Research Hospital in Dallas when you broke Babe Ruth's record. Our grandson died just a short time later. The little eight-year old boy kept saying, "Hank can do it tonight," and when you did, this child with needles in his right arm and couldn't move his right hand, but his little left arm saluted straight up toward the TV and he yelled, "He did it, Daddy! I knew he would!" He had been very ill for quite a while with leukemia, cancer, appendicitis and pneumonia. I'm telling you this so you will know how much joy you brought to this courageous little boy. We all love you for it. And we wish you could have seen that little fellow jump and yell, "He did it, Daddy!" The entire third floor knew about it. Thanks very much for giving him the chance to see you do it.

Dear Mr. Aaron:

I am 12 years old and I want to tell you I have read many articles about the prejudice against you. I really think it's bad. I don't care what color you are. You could be green and it wouldn't matter. These nuts who keep comparing you in every way to Ruth are dumb. You can't compare two people 30 or 40 years apart. So many things are different. It's just some people can't stand to see someone a bit different from them ruin something someone else more like them set. I've never read where you said you're better than Ruth. That's because you never said it. What do those fans want you to do? Just quit hitting?

When the Braves returned to Atlanta, Henry hit Number 715 before a standing-room-only crowd in the Braves' home opener. During a press conference after the game Aaron was asked "Are you the greatest ballplayer?" The question embarrassed him.

Hank Aaron

CELEBRITY COMICS

THE UNAUTHORIZED BIOGRAPHY

$5.95 USA
$7.25 CAN

When Aaron's story was told in a comic book, it was a sure sign that his breaking the record had made him a national celebrity.

after passing the Babe, Aaron went to Japan and defeated Sadaharu Oh (here with George Foster) in a home run contest.

At the end of the year the United States Postal Service calculated Aaron's mail at 930,000 letters and presented him with a plaque for receiving the most mail of any non-politician in the country. Some of the letter-writers didn't use an address and their letters arrived at the post office designated for "Hank Aaron" or "The Hammer."

The 1974 season wasn't all wine and roses. Aaron became embroiled in a bitter dispute triggered by Mathews' midseason firing as Braves field manager. Long-time friends, Aaron and Mathews, in September 1965, had broken the Ruth-Gehrig record for the most home runs by two teammates. When Aaron arrived at the All-Star Game the Braves were still without a manager. Many sportswriters suggested him as the logical successor despite his previous remarks he wasn't interested in managing and preferred a front office position.

As the speculation grew Aaron changed his mind. "If they offered me the job I'd almost be compelled to take it simply because there are no black managers in the majors," Aaron said.

Mathews was succeeded by Clyde King. On September 27, at the season's end, general manager Phil Segui of the Cleveland Indians hired Frank Robinson, a former superstar player. Robinson was Organized Baseball's fourth black manager but the first who would direct a major league team (the others handled minor league clubs). Among them was Tommie Aaron, Hank Aaron's younger brother.

Henry finished the season with 20 home runs, raising his career total to 733. He was in Tokyo on November 14, four hours after defeating Sadaharu Oh, Japan's top slugger, in a special home run hitting contest, when the announcement came that he had been traded to the Milwaukee Brewers. The deal startled the baseball world and was made by Allan (Bud) Selig—later Commissioner Selig—who had been campaigning for a replacement team since the Braves had abandoned Milwaukee and moved to Atlanta eight years earlier.

The new Milwaukee club, now named the Brewers, had been awarded a franchise in the American League, a league that had adopted the Designated Hitter Rule in 1972. The DH, in effect, was the 10th man: he batted for the pitcher and seldom played in the field. At the age of 41, it was the ideal situation for baseball's new Home Run King.

Aaron expressed delight that he would be returning to the city where he had played his first 12 major league seasons and had hit 398 home runs. He welcomed he DH assignment. "I'll just have to keep my legs in shape because the DH sits a lot," Aaron said. As for adjusting to American League pitching, he didn't anticipate any big problems. "I expect to hit another home run or two."

Selig was also delighted. "We are very pleased to get a player who unquestionably is the greatest player of our generation," Selig said. "It's a remarkable transaction and certainly it is our feeling that Henry is coming home. We haven't bought a piece of nostalgia. We got a productive designated hitter. We expect to have a long relationship. As far as I'm concerned we've got him in perpetuity."

Then Selig added: "This could be his second honeymoon."

It was not an uncommon deal. Because of the DH, the American League had been a haven for National League sluggers who had slowed in the field. Dick Allen, Billy Williams, Ron Santo, Tommy Davis, Frank Robinson, Orlando Cepeda, Deron Johnson, and Jim Ray Hart extended their careers in the American League. When the Cubs announced that Billy Williams was available, five of the six teams that expressed interest were in the AL.

When Aaron reported to the Brewers' Sun City, Arizona, spring training camp, many of the younger players were so thrilled to have him as their teammate they were virtually dumbstruck. "It was like having a bubble gum card come to life," recalled infielder Don Money, a seven-year big league veteran. "The first time I saw him in a Brewer uniform I couldn't stop thinking the man wearing Number 44 was the greatest home run hitter in baseball history. And that feeling filtered through the entire club. Seeing him on the field those first couple days took a little getting used to."

Aaron worked on his swing until it sounded as though a machine instead

of a man was rapping baseballs through the infield, into the outfield and often over the fence. He participated in all of the tedious activities including wind sprints, running across the outfield grass with a blue windbreaker under his jersey and over a sweatshirt. His style and dedication were evident.

Unlike other superstars, he made almost all the trips during the exhibition season, aware he had a responsibility to the team and to the fans in the other cities who wanted to see him play. He kept as low a profile as possible, always trying to avoid the spotlight, handling himself as if he were just another player trying to make the club.

But of course he wasn't just another

aaron's appearance in Milwaukee, before 48,000 spectators on Opening Day, must have brought back memories of 21 seasons before.

the way to fame is like the way to heaven, through much tribulation," he said in his induction speech. "For 23 years I never dreamed this honor would come to me, for it was not fame I sought but rather to be the best baseball player I could possibly be."

player, and before the Brewers broke camp he held a one-hour batting clinic for his teammates at the request of manager Del Crandall. "If Henry doesn't know about hitting, then nobody does," said Crandall, who was astonished to learn that the Atlanta Braves had never taken advantage of his expertise.

The entire Milwaukee team attended and also heard Aaron on the necessity of adjusting the swing according to the circumstances. When he first came up he held his hands high. As he got older he dropped his hands and brought them closer to his body. He also spoke about knowing what to expect from certain pitchers in different situations and how to protect the plate with a runner on first who has the ability to steal.

He made his American League debut in the Boston opener. It was his first game as a DH. Luis Tiant, the master of the corkscrew delivery, held him hitless in four appearances—a walk, strikeout and two groundouts. Tiant pitched him low and away. Henry said the low balls didn't bother him too much, then quipped "I'm a lowball hitter and highball drinker."

Returning home on April 13, against Cleveland (managed by Frank Robinson). Henry was welcomed by a record Opening Day crowd of 48,160. Traffic snarled. Many fans didn't get to their seats until the third or fourth inning. Scorecard vendors shouted "Program, take home a souvenir of the return of Henry Aaron!" According to Lew Chapman of the *Milwaukee Sentinel,* "a three-minute ovation almost lifted the roof." After Aaron was introduced, the fans sang to the tune of "Hello, Dolly":

Welcome home, Henry,
Welcome home, Henry.
It's so nice to have you back
Where you belong!

Batting third, ahead of George Scott, Henry broke an 0-for-8 drought with a sixth-inning single that triggered a victorious five-run rally. It was the first of his 167 hits as a DH. He appeared in 137 games, of which only nine were in the field. The next season, his last, he batted .229 in 89 games, 74 as a DH. For the two years, combined, he hit 22 home runs, all as a designated hitter. In his final game, October 3, 1976, he went 1-for-3, a single and two groundouts. Jim Gantner replaced him in the sixth inning.

At the finish Henry Aaron held more records than any player in baseball history. His lifetime totals were staggering: first in home runs, 755, and runs batted in, 2,297, records that still stand. He was also second in at-bats, 12,364, and in runs, 2,174; third in hits, 3771; and ninth in doubles, 624. He had appeared in 3,298 games. Cooperstown was next.

Aaron was inducted into the Hall of Fame in 1982, his first year of eligibility. For enshrinement a candidate must be named on 75 percent of the votes cast. He received 406 of a possible 415 votes, 97.8 percent—a percentage surpassed only by Ty Cobb's 98.2 percent in 1936.

"The way to fame is like the way to heaven, through much tribulation," he said in his induction speech. "For 23 years I never dreamed this honor would come to me, for it was not fame I sought but rather to be the best baseball player I could possibly be." ◔

t he thrill and agony of the chase behind him, Aaron appeared to enjoy the game as never before.

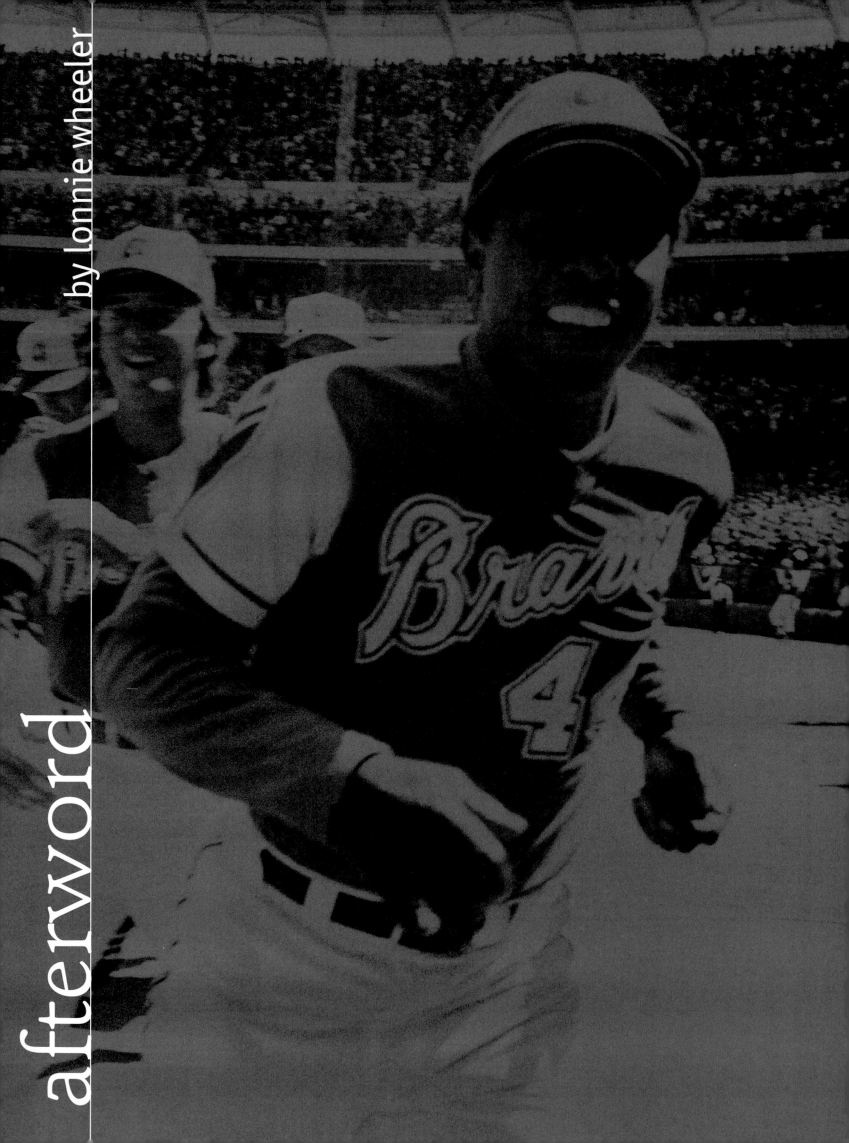

> To the
> public and
> posterity,
> he would
> be a
> famous
> ballplayer
> who hit
> more
> home
> runs than
> anybody
> else;
> nothing
> more nor
> less.
>
> —Lonnie Wheeler

history was in good form on the day it chose Hank Aaron. It could have taken the easy path, allowing Babe Ruth to hang on to the last and most sacred of his records. That would have pacified a lot of Yankee fans and traditionalists, including the white people who, taking a personal interest in the situation, suddenly realized they were one or the other.

Or it could have let the more spectacular Willie Mays do the honors. That would have brought both coasts into the loop, and in the pertinent social context, it would have been a sufficiently grand-looking stroke.

But history was more noble than that in 1974. It thought deeper and assumed more responsibility. To do the right thing, it went out on a longer, narrower limb.

Hank Aaron was an unconventional and most unlikely suspect for the distinction that ultimately befell him. Neither physically nor verbally imposing, his talent and temperament seemed best-suited for the line drives that his bat produced so methodically. As both an outfielder and a public figure, he was the anti-Ruth.

And yet, if it was Ruth who invented the home run, it was Aaron who found a use for it—a use not his, but society's. In Aaron's possession, the home run record was a public address system that gave volume to a voice nobody had ever listened to. It was an instrument of the people. It was Jesse Owens's feet, Joe Louis's fists, and Jackie Robinson's forbearance.

That's why, strange as it seemed, baseball's greatest record was meant for an unschooled, unassuming black man from Alabama. Whether they knew it or not—largely, they did not—baseball and America needed Hank Aaron to be the one.

Baseball and America needed *each other,* first of all. As the national pastime, baseball has always been the sport from which the nation takes its cues in social matters, especially those pertaining to race. But, more than a generation after Robinson had broken the major-league color line, the game seemed to think that its integration was complete. Aaron and the facts suggested otherwise.

And so the new home run king wore his royal vestments in honor of something greater than the long ball. For Aaron, it was never a question of what the record could do for him; it was what he could do for the record.

What he could do was lead. Equipped with his new amplifier, he could stand on a soapbox and attract attention. He could use every appropriate occasion to speak out on the issues that were the most important in his life, and his family's, and his people's.

There was irony in that. Owing to the circumstances of his background, Aaron had never been comfortable with language. In turn, the media, unable or unwilling to hear the message in his imperfect words, had been content to quote mostly his numbers. Fifteen years after his retirement, when I undertook to help him write his 1991 autobiography, *I Had A Hammer,* journalists warned me time and again that Aaron had very little to say.

And yet, in the course of the year and a half that I spent on his book, I found Aaron to be the most eloquent man I have ever met. His words, obviously, had taken on considerable polish

Equipped with his new amplifier, he could stand on a soapbox and attract attention. He could use every appropriate occasion to speak out on the issues that were the most important in his life, and his family's, and his people's.

in his executive years, but even so, Aaron's eloquence was not a matter of rhetoric. He spoke with his heart. He spoke, mainly, with his life.

He devoted the book, as he still devotes much of what he does, to the record—not the home run record, but baseball's record of minority hiring. Aaron would feel culpably remiss if he squandered his unique opportunity to address baseball's—and by extension, America's—racial performance. In Mobile, Jacksonville, Augusta, Savannah, Montgomery, Milwaukee, Cincinnati, Philadelphia, and Atlanta, things happened to Aaron. Things that weren't nice. Things that weren't right. The same things happened to other black ballplayers, too, and to other black citizens, but none of them turned out to be the home run king. Hank Aaron had a responsibility.

As he wrote and spoke and campaigned to meet this responsibility, a curious thing happened. Critics began complaining that Hank Aaron—the man who had nothing to say—had more to say than they wanted to hear. Knowing that I had collaborated with him, and assuming empathy in the fact that I'm white, countless people over the years have asked me, "Isn't he bitter?"

Bitter? Because he repeated the names he was called in Macon? Because he printed hate mail he received when he was chasing Ruth? Because he takes advantage of every precious chance to advance the cause of the black man in his profession and his country?

Bitter? The better question is: What would Aaron be if he didn't do and say these things? What would he be if he

didn't make use of his special opportunity?

To the public and posterity, he would be a famous ballplayer who hit more home runs than anybody else; nothing more nor less.

In his own estimation, he would be a failure, a man who misused his privileged position and let his people down. He would be a man who betrayed history.

History, though, knew him better than that. It trusted Aaron.

Inspired, it immortalized him.

home run log

HR No.	Date	Day	Gm	Nite	Tm	Lg	Pos	Ord	Pitcher	Team	Site	In	On
1	04/23/1954	Fri			MIL	NL			Vic Raschi	STL	STL	6	0
2	04/25/1954	Sun		D	MIL	NL			Stu Miller	STL	STL	5	0
3	05/21/1954	Fri		D	MIL	NL			Hal Jeffcoat	CHI	CHI	8	1
4	05/22/1954	Sat	2	D	MIL	NL			Warren Hacker	CHI	CHI	7	1
5	05/25/1954	Tue			MIL	NL			Herm Wehmeier	CIN	CIN	5	1
6	06/15/1954	Tue			MIL	NL			Russ Meyer	BRO	BRO	1	1
7	06/17/1954	Thu			MIL	NL			Johnny Podres	BRO	BRO	1	0
8	06/22/1954	Tue			MIL	NL			Johnny Antonelli	NY	NY	4	0
9	06/26/1954	Sat			MIL	NL			Robin Roberts	PHI	PHI	4	0
10	07/02/1954	Fri	1		MIL	NL			Corky Valentine	CIN	MIL	7	1
11	07/08/1954	Thu		D	MIL	NL			Warren Hacker	CHI	CHI	3	1
12	07/29/1954	Thu			MIL	NL			Johnny Hetki	PIT	PIT	10	0
13	08/10/1954	Tue			MIL	NL			Vic Raschi	STL	STL	1	1
14	04/17/1955	Sun	2	D	MIL	NL			Gerry Staley	CIN	CIN	7	0
15	04/27/1955	Wed			MIL	NL			Hoyt Wilhelm	NY	NY	8	0
16	04/30/1955	Sat			MIL	NL			Thornton Kipper	PHI	PHI	9	0
17	05/07/1955	Sat			MIL	NL			Herb Moford	STL	STL	7	0
18	05/08/1955	Sun		D	MIL	NL			Harvey Haddix	STL	STL	2	0
19	05/10/1955	Tue			MIL	NL			Max Surkont	PIT	MIL	8	2
20	05/12/1955	Thu		N	MIL	NL	LF	4	Carl Erskine	BRO	MIL	2	0
21	05/19/1955	Thu			MIL	NL			Jim Hearn	NY	MIL	2	0
22	05/28/1955	Sat		D	MIL	NL			Warren Hacker	CHI	CHI	6	0
23	06/07/1955	Tue			MIL	NL			Johnny Antonelli	NY	NY	2	1
24	06/17/1955	Fri			MIL	NL			Johnny Antonelli	NY	MIL	4	0
25	06/24/1955	Fri		N	MIL	NL	RF	4	Carl Erskine	BRO	MIL	3	2
26	06/28/1955	Tue			MIL	NL			Sam Jones	CHI	MIL	8	0
27	06/29/1955	Wed			MIL	NL			John Andre	CHI	MIL	4	1
28	06/29/1955	Wed			MIL	NL			John Andre	CHI	MIL	6	0
29	07/02/1955	Sat			MIL	NL			Jackie Collum	CIN	CIN	8	1
30	07/08/1955	Fri	2		MIL	NL			Rudy Minarcin	CIN	MIL	1	1
31	07/14/1955	Thu			MIL	NL			Bob Miller	PHI	PHI	6	0
32	07/16/1955	Sat			MIL	NL			Sal Maglie	NY	NY	8	1
33	07/21/1955	Thu			MIL	NL			Lino Donoso	PIT	PIT	2	0
34	07/22/1955	Fri		N	MIL	NL	2B	4	Roger Craig	BRO	BRO	6	0
35	07/24/1955	Sun	2	D	MIL	NL	LF	4	Ed Roebuck	BRO	BRO	8	1
36	08/07/1955	Sun	1	D	MIL	NL			Lino Donoso	PIT	MIL	8	1
37	08/09/1955	Tue			MIL	NL			Larry Jackson	STL	MIL	4	0
38	08/19/1955	Fri			MIL	NL			Warren Hacker	CHI	MIL	3	1
39	09/04/1955	Sun		D	MIL	NL			Johnny Klippstein	CIN	MIL	1	1
40	09/04/1955	Sun		D	MIL	NL			Joe Black	CIN	MIL	6	0
41	04/17/1956	Tue			MIL	NL	RF		Bob Rush	CHI	MIL	6	0
42	04/22/1956	Sun	2	D	MIL	NL	RF		Larry Jackson	STL	STL	3	0
43	05/07/1956	Mon			MIL	NL	RF		Ed Roebuck	BRO	MIL	5	0
44	05/22/1956	Tue			MIL	NL	RF		Carl Erskine	BRO	BRO	2	0
45	05/30/1956	Wed	1	D	MIL	NL	RF		Russ Meyer	CHI	CHI	1	0
46	05/30/1956	Wed	2	D	MIL	NL	RF		Warren Hacker	CHI	CHI	4	0
47	06/06/1956	Wed			MIL	NL	RF		Don Newcombe	BRO	MIL	1	1
48	06/27/1956	Wed			MIL	NL	RF		Harvey Haddix	PHI	PHI	7	0
49	07/04/1956	Wed	2		MIL	NL	RF		Herm Wehmeier	STL	MIL	8	2
50	07/06/1956	Fri			MIL	NL	RF		Don Kaiser	CHI	MIL	7	0
51	07/16/1956	Mon			MIL	NL	RF		Ron Kline	PIT	MIL	4	0
52	07/17/1956	Tue			MIL	NL	RF		Windy McCall	NY	MIL	7	2
53	07/20/1956	Fri			MIL	NL	RF		Stu Miller	PHI	MIL	1	1
54	07/22/1956	Sun	1	D	MIL	NL	RF		Ben Flowers	PHI	MIL	8	0
55	07/26/1956	Thu			MIL	NL	RF		Johnny Antonelli	NY	NY	1	1
56	07/30/1956	Mon			MIL	NL	RF		Ed Roebuck	BRO	BRO	1	1
57	08/05/1956	Sun	1	D	MIL	NL	RF		Ron Kline	PIT	PIT	3	2
58	08/19/1956	Sun		D	MIL	NL	RF		Tom Acker	CIN	CIN	8	1
59	08/23/1956	Thu			MIL	NL	RF		Curt Simmons	PHI	MIL	5	0
60	08/26/1956	Sun		D	MIL	NL	RF		Roger Craig	BRO	MIL	3	1
61	09/01/1956	Sat			MIL	NL	RF		Wilmer Mizell	STL	MIL	4	0
62	09/03/1956	Mon	1		MIL	NL	RF		Johnny Klippstein	CIN	MIL	4	0
63	09/03/1956	Mon	1		MIL	NL	RF		Johnny Klippstein	CIN	MIL	7	0
64	09/03/1956	Mon	2		MIL	NL	RF		Brooks Lawrence	CIN	MIL	8	0
65	09/13/1956	Thu	2		MIL	NL	RF		Robin Roberts	PHI	PHI	11	0
66	09/15/1956	Sat			MIL	NL	RF		Bob Miller	PHI	PHI	7	2
67	04/18/1957	Thu			MIL	NL			Hal Jeffcoat	CIN	MIL	6	0
68	04/22/1957	Mon			MIL	NL			Bob Rush	CHI	MIL	2	0
69	04/24/1957	Wed			MIL	NL			Herm Wehmeier	STL	MIL	3	2
70	04/27/1957	Sat			MIL	NL			Warren Hacker	CIN	CIN	1	0
71	05/03/1957	Fri			MIL	NL			Bob Friend	PIT	PIT	6	2
72	05/05/1957	Sun		D	MIL	NL			Don Bessent	BRO	BRO	4	2
73	05/11/1957	Sat			MIL	NL			Willard Schmidt	STL	STL	7	0
74	05/12/1957	Sun	1	D	MIL	NL			Murry Dickson	STL	STL	4	1
75	05/12/1957	Sun	2	D	MIL	NL			Herm Wehmeier	STL	STL	3	1
76	05/18/1957	Sat			MIL	NL			Vern Law	PIT	MIL	3	0
77	05/18/1957	Sat			MIL	NL			Bob Smith	PIT	MIL	4	2
78	05/27/1957	Mon			MIL	NL			Johnny Klippstein	CIN	MIL	8	1
79	06/04/1957	Tue			MIL	NL			Stu Miller	NY	NY	3	1
80	06/09/1957	Sun	1	D	MIL	NL			Bob Friend	PIT	PIT	7	0
81	06/09/1957	Sun	2	D	MIL	NL			Ron Kline	PIT	PIT	7	0
82	06/12/1957	Wed			MIL	NL			Ed Roebuck	BRO	BRO	9	0
83	06/14/1957	Fri			MIL	NL			Don Cardwell	PHI	PHI	6	2
84	06/15/1957	Sat			MIL	NL			Harvey Haddix	PHI	PHI	2	0
85	06/19/1957	Wed			MIL	NL			Ruben Gomez	NY	MIL	3	0
86	06/26/1957	Wed			MIL	NL			Don Newcombe	BRO	MIL	5	0
87	06/29/1957	Sat			MIL	NL			Johnny O'Brien	PIT	MIL	6	2
88	06/30/1957	Sun	1	D	MIL	NL			Vern Law	PIT	MIL	1	0
89	06/30/1957	Sun	2	D	MIL	NL			Joe Trimble	PIT	MIL	4	0
90	07/01/1957	Mon			MIL	NL			Murry Dickson	STL	STL	5	0
91	07/03/1957	Wed			MIL	NL			Hal Jeffcoat	CIN	CIN	1	1
92	07/04/1957	Thu			MIL	NL			Don Gross	CIN	CIN	7	1
93	07/05/1957	Fri			MIL	NL			Don Elston	CHI	MIL	9	0
94	07/12/1957	Fri			MIL	NL			Vern Law	PIT	PIT	6	0
95	07/16/1957	Tue			MIL	NL			Harvey Haddix	PHI	PHI	1	1
96	07/25/1957	Thu			MIL	NL			Robin Roberts	PHI	MIL	5	0
97	08/04/1957	Sun		D	MIL	NL			Carl Erskine	BRO	MIL	6	2
98	08/09/1957	Fri			MIL	NL			Lindy McDaniel	STL	STL	3	1
99	08/15/1957	Thu			MIL	NL			Hal Jeffcoat	CIN	CIN	1	2
100	08/15/1957	Thu			MIL	NL			Don Gross	CIN	CIN	7	1
101	08/22/1957	Thu			MIL	NL			Sal Maglie	BRO	BRO	1	2
102	08/23/1957	Fri			MIL	NL			Sandy Koufax	BRO	BRO	4	0
103	08/24/1957	Sat			MIL	NL			Johnny Podres	BRO	BRO	4	0
104	08/31/1957	Sat			MIL	NL			Joe Nuxhall	CIN	CIN	1	1
105	09/03/1957	Tue		D	MIL	NL			Dick Littlefield	CHI	CHI	8	2
106	09/10/1957	Tue		N	MIL	NL	CF	2	Whammy Douglas	PIT	MIL	4	0
107	09/17/1957	Tue			MIL	NL			Curt Barclay	NY	MIL	8	0
108	09/22/1957	Sun		D	MIL	NL			Dick Drott	CHI	CHI	4	0
109	09/23/1957	Mon			MIL	NL			Billy Muffett	STL	MIL	11	1
110	09/24/1957	Tue			MIL	NL			Sam Jones	STL	MIL	1	3
111	04/20/1958	Sun		D	MIL	NL			Robin Roberts	PHI	PHI	7	0
112	04/22/1958	Tue			MIL	NL			Ron Kline	PIT	PIT	4	2
113	04/24/1958	Thu			MIL	NL			Brooks Lawrence	CIN	CIN	3	0
114	04/24/1958	Thu			MIL	NL			Charlie Rabe	CIN	CIN	5	0
115	05/13/1958	Tue			MIL	NL			Robin Roberts	PHI	PHI	4	0
116	05/31/1958	Sat			MIL	NL			Ron Kline	PIT	PIT	1	0
117	06/03/1958	Tue		N	MIL	NL	RF	2	Ruben Gomez	SF	SF	5	0
118	06/03/1958	Tue		N	MIL	NL	RF	2	Marv Grissom	SF	SF	9	0
119	06/08/1958	Sun		D	MIL	NL			Johnny Podres	LA	LA	5	0
120	06/10/1958	Tue		D	MIL	NL			Dick Drott	CHI	CHI	3	2
121	06/20/1958	Fri			MIL	NL			Billy Muffett	STL	MIL	8	3
122	06/27/1958	Fri			MIL	NL			Sandy Koufax	LA	MIL	4	0
123	06/28/1958	Sat			MIL	NL			Carl Erskine	LA	MIL	7	0
124	06/29/1958	Sun		D	MIL	NL			Don Drysdale	LA	MIL	6	3
125	07/12/1958	Sat		D	MIL	NL	RF	4	Johnny Antonelli	SF	SF	6	1
126	07/15/1958	Tue			MIL	NL			Sal Maglie	STL	STL	2	0
127	07/15/1958	Tue			MIL	NL			Sal Maglie	STL	STL	4	0
128	07/16/1958	Wed			MIL	NL			Chuck Stobbs	STL	STL	5	0

HR No.	Date	Day	Gm	Day Nite	Tm	Lg	Pos	Ord	Pitcher	Team	Site	In	On
129	07/18/1958	Fri		D	MIL	NL			John Briggs	CHI	CHI	6	0
130	07/19/1958	Sat		D	MIL	NL			Moe Drabowsky	CHI	CHI	1	1
131	07/25/1958	Fri	2		MIL	NL			Don Elston	CHI	MIL	7	0
132	07/27/1958	Sun		D	MIL	NL	RF	4	Dave Hillman	CHI	MIL	1	1
133	07/31/1958	Thu			MIL	NL			Johnny Podres	LA	MIL	4	0
134	08/02/1958	Sat		D	MIL	NL	RF	4	Ramon Monzant	SF	MIL	7	0
135	08/06/1958	Wed			MIL	NL			Vern Law	PIT	MIL	1	1
136	08/19/1958	Tue	2		MIL	NL			Johnny Podres	LA	LA	7	1
137	08/21/1958	Thu			MIL	NL			Sandy Koufax	LA	LA	4	0
138	08/24/1958	Sun		D	MIL	NL	RF	4	Al Worthington	SF	SF	10	1
139	09/12/1958	Fri			MIL	NL			Bob Mabe	STL	MIL	3	2
140	09/21/1958	Sun		D	MIL	NL			Tom Acker	CIN	CIN	7	1
141	04/11/1959	Sat			MIL	NL			Vern Law	PIT	PIT	3	0
142	04/18/1959	Sat			MIL	NL			Vern Law	PIT	MIL	7	2
143	04/23/1959	Thu			MIL	NL			Ray Semproch	PHI	PHI	9	0
144	04/26/1959	Sun		D	MIL	NL	RF		Hal Jeffcoat	CIN	CIN	4	1
145	04/29/1959	Wed			MIL	NL			Gary Blaylock	STL	MIL	6	0
146	04/30/1959	Thu			MIL	NL	RF	3	Alex Kellner	STL	MIL	4	0
147	05/03/1959	Sun		D	MIL	NL			Johnny Antonelli	SF	MIL	1	0
148	05/03/1959	Sun		D	MIL	NL			Johnny Antonelli	SF	MIL	4	0
149	05/16/1959	Sat			MIL	NL			Danny McDevitt	LA	LA	3	2
150	05/16/1959	Sat			MIL	NL			Sandy Koufax	LA	LA	9	0
151	05/17/1959	Sun		D	MIL	NL			Don Drysdale	LA	LA	5	1
152	05/20/1959	Wed			MIL	NL			Mike McCormick	SF	SF	6	0
153	05/22/1959	Fri			MIL	NL			Robin Roberts	PHI	PHI	1	1
154	05/30/1959	Sat			MIL	NL			Don Cardwell	PHI	MIL	6	0
155	06/03/1959	Wed			MIL	NL			Al Worthington	SF	MIL	7	0
156	06/10/1959	Wed			MIL	NL			Alex Kellner	STL	STL	1	0
157	06/21/1959	Sun		D	MIL	NL			Johnny Antonelli	SF	SF	1	1
158	06/21/1959	Sun		D	MIL	NL			Stu Miller	SF	SF	6	1
159	06/21/1959	Sun		D	MIL	NL			Gordon Jones	SF	SF	7	1
160	06/24/1959	Wed			MIL	NL			Dick Ricketts	STL	MIL	1	2
161	06/25/1959	Thu			MIL	NL			Wilmer Mizell	STL	MIL	3	1
162	07/03/1959	Fri			MIL	NL			Red Witt	PIT	PIT	8	1
163	07/11/1959	Sat			MIL	NL			Don Drysdale	LA	MIL	7	0
164	07/14/1959	Tue		D	MIL	NL			Bill Henry	CHI	CHI	6	0
165	07/29/1959	Wed			MIL	NL			Dave Hillman	CHI	MIL	1	1
166	07/29/1959	Wed			MIL	NL			Dave Hillman	CHI	MIL	3	0
167	07/30/1959	Thu			MIL	NL			Art Ceccarelli	CHI	MIL	3	0
168	07/31/1959	Fri			MIL	NL			Hal Jeffcoat	STL	MIL	8	0
169	08/01/1959	Sat			MIL	NL			Ernie Broglio	STL	MIL	6	0
170	08/12/1959	Wed			MIL	NL			Jim O'Toole	CIN	CIN	5	0
171	08/17/1959	Mon	1		MIL	NL			Clem Labine	LA	MIL	8	0
172	08/18/1959	Tue			MIL	NL			Don Drysdale	LA	MIL	6	0
173	08/18/1959	Tue			MIL	NL			Don Drysdale	LA	MIL	11	0
174	08/28/1959	Fri		D	MIL	NL			John Buzhardt	CHI	CHI	4	0
175	08/29/1959	Sat		D	MIL	NL			Bill Henry	CHI	CHI	4	0
176	08/29/1959	Sat		D	MIL	NL			Don Elston	CHI	CHI	9	0
177	09/02/1959	Wed			MIL	NL			Robin Roberts	PHI	MIL	6	1
178	09/07/1959	Mon	1		MIL	NL			Bob Friend	PIT	MIL	1	1
179	09/20/1959	Sun		D	MIL	NL			Robin Roberts	PHI	PHI	1	0
180	04/14/1960	Thu			MIL	NL			Curt Simmons	PHI	PHI	1	1
181	04/16/1960	Sat			MIL	NL			Ruben Gomez	PHI	PHI	6	2
182	04/22/1960	Fri			MIL	NL			Bob Friend	PIT	PIT	3	0
183	04/27/1960	Wed			MIL	NL			Jay Hook	CIN	CIN	5	0
184	05/05/1960	Thu			MIL	NL			Johnny Podres	LA	LA	6	0
185	05/13/1960	Fri			MIL	NL			Bob Friend	PIT	MIL	4	0
186	05/15/1960	Sun	1	D	MIL	NL			Harvey Haddix	PIT	MIL	7	0
187	05/15/1960	Sun	2	D	MIL	NL			Bennie Daniels	PIT	MIL	1	2
188	05/17/1960	Tue			MIL	NL			Don Drysdale	LA	MIL	2	0
189	06/02/1960	Thu			MIL	NL			Ruben Gomez	PHI	PHI	4	0
190	06/03/1960	Fri			MIL	NL			Jay Hook	CIN	MIL	2	0
191	06/04/1960	Sat			MIL	NL			Don Newcombe	CIN	MIL	5	0
192	06/12/1960	Sun		D	MIL	NL	RF	4	Bud Byerly	SF	SF	9	0
193	06/20/1960	Mon			MIL	NL			Don Drysdale	LA	MIL	2	0
194	06/20/1960	Mon			MIL	NL			Don Drysdale	LA	MIL	6	0
195	06/21/1960	Tue	1	N	MIL	NL	RF	4	Mike McCormick	SF	MIL	4	1
196	06/24/1960	Fri			MIL	NL			Sandy Koufax	LA	MIL	1	1
197	06/29/1960	Wed	2	D	MIL	NL			Bob Anderson	CHI	CHI	2	0
198	07/01/1960	Fri			MIL	NL			Curt Simmons	STL	STL	8	2
199	07/03/1960	Sun		D	MIL	NL			Ron Kline	STL	STL	4	0
200	07/03/1960	Sun		D	MIL	NL			Ron Kline	STL	STL	7	0
201	07/04/1960	Mon	1		MIL	NL			Bob Friend	PIT	MIL	7	1
202	07/07/1960	Thu			MIL	NL			Chris Short	PHI	MIL	6	0
203	07/08/1960	Fri			MIL	NL			Jay Hook	CIN	MIL	3	0
204	07/19/1960	Tue			MIL	NL			Ron Kline	STL	MIL	8	1
205	07/20/1960	Wed			MIL	NL			Ernie Broglio	STL	MIL	4	0
206	07/22/1960	Fri		D	MIL	NL			Don Elston	CHI	CHI	8	1
207	07/23/1960	Sat		D	MIL	NL			Don Cardwell	CHI	CHI	9	0
208	08/04/1960	Thu			MIL	NL			Ray Sadecki	STL	STL	9	0
209	08/05/1960	Fri			MIL	NL			Seth Morehead	CHI	MIL	8	0
210	08/16/1960	Tue			MIL	NL			Jay Hook	CIN	CIN	4	0
211	08/17/1960	Wed			MIL	NL			Marshall Bridges	CIN	CIN	8	1
212	08/23/1960	Tue			MIL	NL			Ed Roebuck	LA	LA	5	0
213	08/30/1960	Tue			MIL	NL			Ed Bauta	STL	MIL	8	2
214	09/08/1960	Thu		N	MIL	NL	RF	4	Mike McCormick	SF	MIL	1	0
215	09/09/1960	Fri			MIL	NL			Stan Williams	LA	MIL	4	1
216	09/10/1960	Sat			MIL	NL			Roger Craig	LA	MIL	1	2
217	09/21/1960	Wed			MIL	NL			Jim O'Toole	CIN	MIL	6	0
218	09/30/1960	Fri			MIL	NL			Vern Law	PIT	PIT	1	1
219	09/30/1960	Fri			MIL	NL			Diomedes Olivo	PIT	PIT	8	1
220	04/14/1961	Fri		D	MIL	NL	RF	4	Bob Anderson	CHI	CHI	7	0
221	04/30/1961	Sun		D	MIL	NL	CF	4	Billy Loes	SF	MIL	1	2
222	04/30/1961	Sun		D	MIL	NL	CF	4	Billy Loes	SF	MIL	6	0
223	05/12/1961	Fri		N	MIL	NL	CF	4	Sam Jones	SF	SF	1	1
224	05/13/1961	Sat		D	MIL	NL	CF	4	Juan Marichal	SF	SF	1	2
225	05/21/1961	Sun	2	D	MIL	NL	CF	4	Jim Maloney	CIN	CIN	4	1
226	05/26/1961	Fri		N	MIL	NL	CF	4	Turk Farrell	LA	MIL	8	0
227	05/28/1961	Sun		D	MIL	NL	CF	4	Roger Craig	LA	MIL	3	1
228	05/31/1961	Wed		N	MIL	NL	CF	4	Joe Gibbon	PIT	PIT	8	0
229	06/08/1961	Thu		D	MIL	NL	CF	4	Jim Maloney	CIN	CIN	7	0
230	06/18/1961	Sun		D	MIL	NL	RF	4	Don Drysdale	LA	LA	3	1
231	06/20/1961	Tue		N	MIL	NL	RF	4	Mike McCormick	SF	MIL	6	0
232	06/22/1961	Thu		N	MIL	NL	RF	4	Juan Marichal	SF	MIL	2	0
233	06/23/1961	Fri		N	MIL	NL	RF	4	Jack Curtis	CHI	MIL	4	0
234	07/01/1961	Sat		D	MIL	NL	RF	4	Jay Hook	CIN	MIL	6	0
235	07/02/1961	Sun	1	D	MIL	NL	RF	4	Jim O'Toole	CIN	MIL	3	1
236	07/04/1961	Tue		D	MIL	NL	RF	4	Turk Farrell	LA	MIL	7	0
237	07/05/1961	Wed	1	N	MIL	NL	RF	4	Art Mahaffey	PHI	MIL	1	1
238	07/07/1961	Fri		N	MIL	NL	RF	4	Harvey Haddix	PIT	MIL	1	2
239	07/07/1961	Fri		N	MIL	NL	RF	4	Harvey Haddix	PIT	MIL	3	1
240	07/21/1961	Fri		N	MIL	NL	RF	4	Bob Friend	PIT	PIT	1	1
241	07/21/1961	Fri		N	MIL	NL	RF	4	Bob Friend	PIT	PIT	6	0
242	07/23/1961	Sun	1	D	MIL	NL	RF	4	Harvey Haddix	PIT	PIT	6	0
243	07/25/1961	Tue		N	MIL	NL	RF	4	Ken Hunt	CIN	MIL	4	0
244	07/26/1961	Wed		N	MIL	NL	RF	4	Ken Johnson	CIN	MIL	6	0
245	07/28/1961	Fri		N	MIL	NL	RF	4	Larry Jackson	STL	MIL	2	0
246	08/02/1961	Wed	2	D	MIL	NL	RF	4	Bob Anderson	CHI	CHI	7	3
247	08/04/1961	Fri		N	MIL	NL	RF	4	Mike McCormick	SF	SF	7	0
248	08/04/1961	Fri		N	MIL	NL	RF	4	Mike McCormick	SF	SF	9	0
249	08/12/1961	Sat		D	MIL	NL	CF	4	Don Cardwell	CHI	MIL	6	1
250	08/15/1961	Tue		N	MIL	NL	RF	4	Joe Gibbon	PIT	MIL	6	1
251	08/25/1961	Fri	1	N	MIL	NL	CF	4	John Buzhardt	PHI	PHI	4	1
252	09/03/1961	Sun	2	D	MIL	NL	CF	4	Dick Ellsworth	CHI	CHI	3	0
253	09/25/1961	Mon		N	MIL	NL	CF	3	Ray Washburn	STL	MIL	1	0
254	04/15/1962	Sun		D	MIL	NL			Sandy Koufax	LA	LA	7	0
255	04/18/1962	Wed		D	MIL	NL	CF	3	Jack Sanford	SF	MIL	1	0
256	05/03/1962	Thu			MIL	NL			Art Mahaffey	PHI	PHI	1	0

HR No.	Date	Day	Gm	Nite	Tm	Lg	Pos	Ord	Pitcher	Team	Site	In	On
257	05/03/1962	Thu			MIL	NL	·		Jack Baldschun	PHI	PHI	9	1
258	05/12/1962	Sat	2		MIL	NL			Bob Moorhead	NY	NY	5	1
259	05/18/1962	Fri			MIL	NL			Roger Craig	NY	MIL	2	0
260	05/25/1962	Fri			MIL	NL			Curt Simmons	STL	STL	4	0
261	05/25/1962	Fri			MIL	NL			Ray Washburn	STL	STL	7	2
262	05/28/1962	Mon		D	MIL	NL			Glen Hobbie	CHI	CHI	9	0
263	05/31/1962	Thu			MIL	NL			Bob Purkey	CIN	MIL	6	1
264	06/12/1962	Tue		N	MIL	NL	CF	4	Phil Ortega	LA	MIL	2	0
265	06/14/1962	Thu			MIL	NL			Stan Williams	LA	MIL	1	1
266	06/15/1962	Fri			MIL	NL			Diomedes Olivo	PIT	PIT	7	3
267	06/18/1962	Mon			MIL	NL			Jay Hook	NY	NY	3	3
268	06/20/1962	Wed	2		MIL	NL			Willard Hunter	NY	NY	3	1
269	06/20/1962	Wed	2		MIL	NL			Willard Hunter	NY	NY	6	0
270	06/28/1962	Thu			MIL	NL			Joe Moeller	LA	LA	6	1
271	06/30/1962	Sat			MIL	NL			Dick Ellsworth	CHI	MIL	1	1
272	07/03/1962	Tue	2		MIL	NL			Bob Gibson	STL	STL	4	1
273	07/06/1962	Fri		D	MIL	NL			Don Cardwell	CHI	CHI	4	0
274	07/08/1962	Sun	1	D	MIL	NL	PH		Dick Ellsworth	CHI	CHI	9	2
275	07/12/1962	Thu			MIL	NL			Lindy McDaniel	STL	MIL	9	3
276	07/17/1962	Tue		N	MIL	NL	RF	4	Billy O'Dell	SF	MIL	4	1
277	07/19/1962	Thu		D	MIL	NL	RF	4	Mike McCormick	SF	MIL	2	0
278	07/20/1962	Fri	2		MIL	NL			Art Mahaffey	PHI	PHI	2	0
279	07/22/1962	Sun	1	D	MIL	NL			Bill Smith	PHI	PHI	2	0
280	07/26/1962	Thu			MIL	NL			Craig Anderson	NY	MIL	2	0
281	07/29/1962	Sun	1	D	MIL	NL			Bob Purkey	CIN	CIN	4	1
282	07/29/1962	Sun	1	D	MIL	NL			Bob Purkey	CIN	CIN	6	1
283	08/07/1962	Tue		N	MIL	NL	CF	4	Cal Koonce	CHI	MIL	3	1
284	08/14/1962	Tue			MIL	NL			Ted Wills	CIN	CIN	7	0
285	08/19/1962	Sun		D	MIL	NL	RF	4	Billy O'Dell	SF	MIL	2	0
286	08/19/1962	Sun		D	MIL	NL	RF	4	Billy O'Dell	SF	MIL	3	1
287	08/24/1962	Fri		D	MIL	NL	RF	4	Bob Buhl	CHI	CHI	2	0
288	08/25/1962	Sat		D	MIL	NL	RF	4	Don Cardwell	CHI	CHI	4	1
289	08/29/1962	Wed		D	MIL	NL	RF	4	Billy O'Dell	SF	SF	3	0
290	09/07/1962	Fri			MIL	NL			Dennis Bennett	PHI	MIL	4	0
291	09/09/1962	Sun		D	MIL	NL			Chris Short	PHI	MIL	6	0
292	09/10/1962	Mon			MIL	NL			Bob Miller	NY	NY	7	0
293	09/18/1962	Tue			MIL	NL			Johnny Podres	LA	MIL	3	0
294	09/22/1962	Sat			MIL	NL			Tommie Sisk	PIT	PIT	8	1
295	09/23/1962	Sun		D	MIL	NL			Bob Friend	PIT	PIT	1	0
296	09/23/1962	Sun		D	MIL	NL			Bob Friend	PIT	PIT	4	2
297	09/25/1962	Tue			MIL	NL			Jay Hook	NY	MIL	3	2
298	09/26/1962	Wed			MIL	NL			Roger Craig	NY	MIL	3	2
299	04/11/1963	Thu			MIL	NL	RF		Don Rowe	NY	MIL	7	0
300	04/19/1963	Fri			MIL	NL	RF		Roger Craig	NY	NY	8	1
301	04/21/1963	Sun	1	D	MIL	NL	RF		Jay Hook	NY	NY	1	0
302	04/22/1963	Mon			MIL	NL	RF		Don Drysdale	LA	LA	5	0
303	04/23/1963	Tue			MIL	NL	RF		Ron Perranoski	LA	LA	9	0
304	04/26/1963	Fri		N	MIL	NL	RF	3	Al Stanek	SF	SF	6	1
305	04/28/1963	Sun		D	MIL	NL	RF	3	Don Larsen	SF	SF	9	0
306	05/02/1963	Thu			MIL	NL	RF		Joey Jay	CIN	CIN	5	1
307	05/03/1963	Fri			MIL	NL	RF		Bob Buhl	CHI	MIL	5	2
308	05/07/1963	Tue		N	MIL	NL	RF	3	Juan Marichal	SF	MIL	4	0
309	05/11/1963	Sat			MIL	NL	RF		Art Mahaffey	PHI	PHI	6	0
310	05/18/1963	Sat		D	MIL	NL	RF		Lindy McDaniel	CHI	CHI	7	3
311	05/19/1963	Sun	1	D	MIL	NL	RF		Dick Ellsworth	CHI	CHI	8	1
312	05/24/1963	Fri			MIL	NL	RF		Bob Friend	PIT	MIL	1	0
313	05/30/1963	Thu			MIL	NL	RF		Don Drysdale	LA	MIL	5	0
314	05/31/1963	Fri			MIL	NL	RF		Ken Johnson	HOU	MIL	6	1
315	06/07/1963	Fri			MIL	NL	RF		Tommie Sisk	PIT	PIT	9	1
316	06/12/1963	Wed			MIL	NL	RF		Galen Cisco	NY	MIL	4	2
317	06/17/1963	Mon			MIL	NL	RF		Don Cardwell	PIT	MIL	1	1
318	06/19/1963	Wed			MIL	NL	RF		Earl Francis	PIT	MIL	3	0
319	06/23/1963	Sun		D	MIL	NL	RF	3	Jack Sanford	SF	MIL	3	0
320	06/30/1963	Sun			MIL	NL	RF		Nick Willhite	LA	LA	1	0
321	07/03/1963	Wed		D	MIL	NL	RF	3	Jack Sanford	SF	SF	6	1
322	07/04/1963	Thu		D	MIL	NL	RF	3	Jack Fisher	SF	SF	5	1
323	07/11/1963	Thu	1		MIL	NL	RF		Ernie Broglio	STL	STL	3	1
324	07/13/1963	Sat			MIL	NL	RF		Curt Simmons	STL	STL	1	2
325	07/19/1963	Fri			MIL	NL	RF		Don Drysdale	LA	MIL	7	0
326	07/21/1963	Sun	1		MIL	NL	RF		Ed Roebuck	LA	MIL	7	0
327	07/28/1963	Sun	1		MIL	NL	RF		Jim Maloney	CIN	MIL	4	1
328	07/29/1963	Mon			MIL	NL	RF		John Tsitouris	CIN	MIL	1	1
329	08/02/1963	Fri			MIL	NL	RF		Al Jackson	NY	MIL	5	2
330	08/14/1963	Wed			MIL	NL	RF		Don Drysdale	LA	MIL	7	3
331	08/23/1963	Fri			MIL	NL	RF		Larry Sherry	LA	LA	9	1
332	08/26/1963	Mon			MIL	NL	RF		Hal Brown	HOU	HOU	9	1
333	08/27/1963	Tue			MIL	NL	RF		Don Nottebart	HOU	HOU	4	1
334	09/02/1963	Mon			MIL	NL	RF		Cal McLish	PHI	MIL	3	0
335	09/06/1963	Fri			MIL	NL	RF		Cal McLish	PHI	PHI	3	0
336	09/07/1963	Sat			MIL	NL	RF		Ray Culp	PHI	PHI	3	0
337	09/09/1963	Mon	2		MIL	NL	RF		Joey Jay	CIN	CIN	7	1
338	09/10/1963	Tue			MIL	NL	RF		John Tsitouris	CIN	CIN	3	0
339	09/10/1963	Tue			MIL	NL	RF		John Tsitouris	CIN	CIN	7	0
340	09/15/1963	Sun	1		MIL	NL	RF		Lew Burdette	STL	STL	7	1
341	09/25/1963	Wed			MIL	NL	RF		Jim O'Toole	CIN	MIL	3	1
342	09/29/1963	Sun			MIL	NL	RF		Bob Buhl	CHI	MIL	1	0
343	04/16/1964	Thu			MIL	NL			Jim Owens	HOU	HOU	3	2
344	05/10/1964	Sun	1		MIL	NL			Bob Friend	PIT	PIT	7	0
345	05/23/1964	Sat			MIL	NL			Ron Taylor	STL	MIL	8	0
346	05/24/1964	Sun	2		MIL	NL			Bobby Shantz	STL	MIL	8	0
347	05/30/1964	Sat	1	D	MIL	NL			Bob Buhl	CHI	CHI	4	1
348	06/07/1964	Sun			MIL	NL			Bob Buhl	CHI	MIL	5	1
349	06/08/1964	Mon			MIL	NL			Hal Brown	HOU	HOU	1	1
350	06/14/1964	Sun	1	D	MIL	NL	RF	3	Ron Perranoski	LA	LA	9	1
351	06/22/1964	Mon		N	MIL	NL	RF	3	Phil Ortega	LA	MIL	5	0
352	06/27/1964	Sat		D	MIL	NL	RF	3	Carl Willey	NY	MIL	2	1
353	06/28/1964	Sun	2	D	MIL	NL	RF	3	Frank Lary	NY	MIL	5	2
354	06/30/1964	Tue			MIL	NL			Roger Craig	STL	STL	5	1
355	07/16/1964	Thu		D	MIL	NL	RF	3	Gaylord Perry	SF	MIL	1	0
356	07/26/1964	Sun	1	D	MIL	NL	RF	3	Al Jackson	NY	NY	1	0
357	07/26/1964	Sun	2	D	MIL	NL	RF	3	Willard Hunter	NY	NY	9	2
358	07/31/1964	Fri		D	MIL	NL			Lindy McDaniel	CHI	CHI	9	2
359	08/01/1964	Sat		D	MIL	NL			Lew Burdette	CHI	CHI	8	0
360	08/06/1964	Thu			MIL	NL			Joey Jay	CIN	CIN	6	2
361	08/11/1964	Tue			MIL	NL			Ken Johnson	HOU	MIL	3	1
362	08/11/1964	Tue			MIL	NL			Hal Woodeshick	HOU	MIL	6	2
363	08/15/1964	Sat		D	MIL	NL	RF	3	Jim Duffalo	SF	SF	4	1
364	08/24/1964	Mon		N	MIL	NL	RF	3	Dennis Bennett	PHI	MIL	4	0
365	08/30/1964	Sun	2	D	MIL	NL	RF	3	Ron Herbel	SF	MIL	8	2
366	09/03/1964	Thu			MIL	NL			Roger Craig	STL	STL	4	0
367	04/29/1965	Thu			MIL	NL	RF		Ron Taylor	STL	MIL	8	0
368	05/02/1965	Sun	2		MIL	NL	RF		Bo Belinsky	PHI	MIL	5	0
369	05/04/1965	Tue			MIL	NL	RF		Larry Dierker	HOU	MIL	6	0
370	05/04/1965	Tue			MIL	NL	RF		Danny Coombs	HOU	MIL	8	0
371	05/16/1965	Sun			MIL	NL	RF		Chris Short	PHI	PHI	3	1
372	05/30/1965	Sun			MIL	NL	RF		Larry Dierker	HOU	HOU	5	1
373	06/01/1965	Tue			MIL	NL	RF		Hal Woodeshick	HOU	HOU	8	0
374	06/08/1965	Tue		D	MIL	NL	RF	3	Bob Hendley	CHI	CHI	10	1
375	06/10/1965	Thu		D	MIL	NL	RF		Larry Jackson	CHI	CHI	3	1
376	06/12/1965	Sat			MIL	NL	RF		Bob Gibson	STL	STL	1	0
377	06/19/1965	Sat			MIL	NL	RF		Ray Sadecki	STL	MIL	5	1
378	06/20/1965	Sun			MIL	NL	RF		Bob Purkey	STL	MIL	6	0
379	06/29/1965	Tue		N	MIL	NL	RF	3	Tug McGraw	NY	NY	9	0
380	07/05/1965	Mon			MIL	NL	RF		Turk Farrell	HOU	MIL	8	0
381	07/07/1965	Wed			MIL	NL	RF		Ron Taylor	HOU	MIL	7	0
382	07/08/1965	Thu			MIL	NL	RF		Don Nottebart	HOU	MIL	1	0
383	07/11/1965	Sun			MIL	NL	RF		Sammy Ellis	CIN	CIN	7	1
384	07/19/1965	Mon		N	MIL	NL	RF	3	Jack Fisher	NY	MIL	1	0

HR No.	Date	Day	Gm	Nite	Tm	Lg	Pos	Ord	Pitcher	Team	Site	In	On
385	07/20/1965	Tue		D	MIL	NL	RF	3	Larry Miller	NY	MIL	7	2
386	07/21/1965	Wed			MIL	NL	RF		Claude Osteen	LA	LA	1	1
387	07/22/1965	Thu			MIL	NL	RF		Bob Miller	LA	LA	1	2
388	08/04/1965	Wed	1		MIL	NL	RF		Don Drysdale	LA	MIL	1	0
389	08/04/1965	Wed	2		MIL	NL	RF		Claude Osteen	LA	MIL	7	0
390	08/11/1965	Wed			MIL	NL	RF		Ray Washburn	STL	MIL	3	0
391	08/11/1965	Wed			MIL	NL	RF		Ray Washburn	STL	MIL	5	2
392	08/15/1965	Sun		D	MIL	NL	RF		Larry Jackson	CHI	CHI	1	0
393	08/17/1965	Tue			MIL	NL	RF		Tracy Stallard	STL	STL	5	1
394	08/31/1965	Tue			MIL	NL	RF		Joey Jay	CIN	CIN	3	0
395	09/08/1965	Wed			MIL	NL	RF		Ray Culp	PHI	MIL	6	0
396	09/17/1965	Fri		N	MIL	NL	RF	3	Juan Marichal	SF	MIL	1	0
397	09/17/1965	Fri		N	MIL	NL	RF	3	Juan Marichal	SF	MIL	3	1
398	09/20/1965	Mon			MIL	NL	RF		Ray Culp	PHI	MIL	6	0
399	04/20/1966	Wed			ATL	NL			Ray Culp	PHI	PHI	1	1
400	04/20/1966	Wed			ATL	NL			Bo Belinsky	PHI	PHI	9	0
401	04/25/1966	Mon		D	ATL	NL	RF	3	Bob Priddy	SF	SF	5	1
402	04/26/1966	Tue		N	ATL	NL	RF	3	Bobby Bolin	SF	SF	3	1
403	04/27/1966	Wed			ATL	NL			Don Sutton	LA	LA	9	0
404	04/28/1966	Thu			ATL	NL			Don Drysdale	LA	LA	6	0
405	04/29/1966	Fri			ATL	NL			Carroll Sembera	HOU	ATL	9	0
406	05/01/1966	Sun			ATL	NL			Mike Cuellar	HOU	ATL	9	0
407	05/08/1966	Sun			ATL	NL			Mike Cuellar	HOU	HOU	1	0
408	05/11/1966	Wed			ATL	NL			Sammy Ellis	CIN	ATL	1	1
409	05/11/1966	Wed			ATL	NL			Sammy Ellis	CIN	ATL	5	2
410	05/17/1966	Tue			ATL	NL	RF		Bob Veale	PIT	PIT	5	0
411	05/18/1966	Wed			ATL	NL			Vern Law	PIT	PIT	6	1
412	05/20/1966	Fri		N	ATL	NL	RF	3	Bill Faul	CHI	ATL	2	2
413	05/21/1966	Sat		D	ATL	NL	PH	3	Billy Hoeft	CHI	ATL	7	0
414	05/27/1966	Fri		D	ATL	NL			Ernie Broglio	CHI	CHI	5	0
415	06/01/1966	Wed		N	ATL	NL	RF	3	Ron Herbel	SF	ATL	6	1
416	06/03/1966	Fri			ATL	NL			Bob Gibson	STL	ATL	9	0
417	06/08/1966	Wed			ATL	NL	RF	3	Jack Fisher	NY	NY	1	0
418	06/08/1966	Wed		N	ATL	NL	RF	3	Jack Fisher	NY	NY	3	3
419	06/14/1966	Tue			ATL	NL			Roger Craig	PHI	PHI	7	1
420	06/18/1966	Sat			ATL	NL			Vern Law	PIT	ATL	8	1
421	06/19/1966	Sun			ATL	NL			Bob Veale	PIT	ATL	8	0
422	06/21/1966	Tue			ATL	NL			Larry Jackson	PHI	ATL	3	0
423	07/03/1966	Sun		D	ATL	NL	RF	3	Ray Sadecki	SF	SF	5	0
424	07/09/1966	Sat			ATL	NL			Sandy Koufax	LA	LA	6	0
425	07/17/1966	Sun			ATL	NL	RF	3	Don Nottebart	CIN	ATL	7	1
426	07/21/1966	Thu			ATL	NL			Al Jackson	STL	STL	7	0
427	07/24/1966	Sun	2		ATL	NL			Sammy Ellis	CIN	CIN	6	0
428	07/26/1966	Tue			ATL	NL			Al Jackson	STL	ATL	7	0
429	08/02/1966	Tue		D	ATL	NL	RF	3	Robin Roberts	CHI	CHI	5	0
430	08/13/1966	Sat	2		ATL	NL			Ray Culp	PHI	ATL	9	0
431	08/14/1966	Sun			ATL	NL			Bob Buhl	PHI	ATL	2	2
432	08/22/1966	Mon			ATL	NL			Don Drysdale	LA	LA	6	1
433	08/26/1966	Fri		N	ATL	NL	RF	3	Tug McGraw	NY	ATL	6	1
434	08/30/1966	Tue		N	ATL	NL	RF	3	Ken Holtzman	CHI	ATL	7	2
435	09/05/1966	Mon	2		ATL	NL			Don Cardwell	PIT	PIT	5	1
436	09/13/1966	Tue		D	ATL	NL	RF	3	Ken Holtzman	CHI	CHI	1	1
437	09/13/1966	Tue		D	ATL	NL	RF	3	Ken Holtzman	CHI	CHI	2	0
438	09/22/1966	Thu			ATL	NL			Don Cardwell	PIT	ATL	4	2
439	09/25/1966	Sun			ATL	NL			Tommie Sisk	PIT	ATL	4	0
440	09/25/1966	Sun			ATL	NL			Al McBean	PIT	ATL	8	0
441	09/27/1966	Tue		N	ATL	NL	RF	3	Ray Sadecki	SF	ATL	4	2
442	10/01/1966	Sat	2		ATL	NL			Jim O'Toole	CIN	CIN	8	1
443	04/19/1967	Wed			ATL	NL			Dave Giusti	HOU	ATL	1	0
444	04/19/1967	Wed			ATL	NL			Dave Giusti	HOU	ATL	4	0
445	04/28/1967	Fri			ATL	NL			Dick Ellsworth	PHI	ATL	5	2
446	04/30/1967	Sun	2		ATL	NL			Bob Buhl	PHI	ATL	6	0
447	05/05/1967	Fri			ATL	NL			Sammy Ellis	CIN	ATL	5	1
448	05/10/1967	Wed	1		ATL	NL			Jim Bunning	PHI	PHI	8	0
449	05/10/1967	Wed	2		ATL	NL			Larry Jackson	PHI	PHI	3	1
450	05/14/1967	Sun			ATL	NL			Dennis Ribant	PIT	PIT	6	0
451	05/17/1967	Wed		N	ATL	NL	RF	3	Tom Seaver	NY	ATL	6	1
452	05/21/1967	Sun			ATL	NL			Steve Blass	PIT	ATL	2	1
453	05/21/1967	Sun			ATL	NL			Pete Mikkelsen	PIT	ATL	8	1
454	06/01/1967	Thu			ATL	NL			Ray Washburn	STL	STL	1	0
455	06/02/1967	Fri			ATL	NL			Sammy Ellis	CIN	CIN	9	1
456	06/03/1967	Sat			ATL	NL			Billy McCool	CIN	CIN	1	0
457	06/04/1967	Sun			ATL	NL			Jim Maloney	CIN	CIN	7	0
458	06/12/1967	Mon			ATL	NL			Dick Ellsworth	PHI	PHI	1	2
459	06/14/1967	Wed			ATL	NL			Dallas Green	PHI	PHI	6	2
460	06/22/1967	Thu	2	D	ATL	NL	RF	3	Frank Linzy	SF	SF	8	1
461	06/27/1967	Tue			ATL	NL	RF	3	Wade Blasingame	HOU	ATL	3	3
462	06/27/1967	Tue			ATL	NL	RF	3	Dan Schneider	HOU	ATL	8	1
463	07/05/1967	Wed			ATL	NL			Chuck Hartenstein	CHI	ATL	7	2
464	07/09/1967	Sun		D	ATL	NL	RF	3	Jack Fisher	NY	NY	8	0
465	07/14/1967	Fri			ATL	NL			Rick Wise	PHI	ATL	6	0
466	07/21/1967	Fri			ATL	NL			Nelson Briles	STL	STL	4	1
467	07/22/1967	Sat			ATL	NL			Dick Hughes	STL	STL	8	1
468	07/27/1967	Thu			ATL	NL			Sammy Ellis	CIN	ATL	1	1
469	08/03/1967	Thu		D	ATL	NL			Curt Simmons	CHI	CHI	3	0
470	08/12/1967	Sat	2	N	ATL	NL			Mike Cuellar	HOU	ATL	8	0
471	08/13/1967	Sun			ATL	NL			Carroll Sembera	HOU	ATL	7	1
472	08/16/1967	Wed		N	ATL	NL	CF	3	Bobby Bolin	SF	ATL	3	2
473	08/19/1967	Sat			ATL	NL			Claude Osteen	LA	LA	5	1
474	08/29/1967	Tue			ATL	NL			Tommie Sisk	PIT	ATL	1	0
475	08/31/1967	Thu			ATL	NL	RF		Claude Osteen	LA	ATL	8	0
476	09/03/1967	Sun			ATL	NL			Don Drysdale	LA	ATL	7	1
477	09/04/1967	Mon	1		ATL	NL			Rick Wise	PHI	ATL	1	1
478	09/12/1967	Tue		N	ATL	NL	RF	3	Jack Fisher	NY	ATL	3	0
479	09/14/1967	Thu		N	ATL	NL	RF	3	Danny Frisella	NY	ATL	4	1
480	09/20/1967	Wed			ATL	NL			Milt Pappas	CIN	ATL	5	1
481	09/26/1967	Tue			ATL	NL			Milt Pappas	CIN	CIN	6	2
482	04/15/1968	Mon			ATL	NL			Bob Gibson	STL	ATL	7	1
483	04/17/1968	Wed			ATL	NL			Bill Hands	CHI	ATL	7	0
484	04/19/1968	Fri			ATL	NL			John Tsitouris	CIN	CIN	3	1
485	04/21/1968	Sun			ATL	NL			Milt Pappas	CIN	CIN	1	0
486	04/23/1968	Tue		D	ATL	NL			Joe Niekro	CHI	CHI	1	0
487	04/28/1968	Sun			ATL	NL			Rick Wise	PHI	ATL	9	1
488	05/11/1968	Sat			ATL	NL			Claude Osteen	LA	ATL	1	0
489	05/11/1968	Sat			ATL	NL			Claude Osteen	LA	ATL	3	2
490	05/14/1968	Tue			ATL	NL			Larry Jackson	PHI	PHI	5	1
491	06/09/1968	Sun	2	D	ATL	NL			Bill Hands	CHI	CHI	1	1
492	06/12/1968	Wed			ATL	NL			Nelson Briles	STL	ATL	3	1
493	06/17/1968	Mon			ATL	NL			Jim Maloney	CIN	ATL	4	0
494	06/21/1968	Fri			ATL	NL			Ron Willis	STL	STL	8	0
495	06/27/1968	Thu			ATL	NL			Chris Short	PHI	ATL	1	0
496	06/28/1968	Fri			ATL	NL			Mike Kekich	LA	LA	8	0
497	07/05/1968	Fri			ATL	NL			Mike Cuellar	HOU	ATL	3	1
498	07/07/1968	Sun			ATL	NL	RF	3	Larry Dierker	HOU	ATL	4	0
499	07/07/1968	Sun			ATL	NL	RF	3	Larry Dierker	HOU	ATL	5	1
500	07/14/1968	Sun			ATL	NL			Mike McCormick	SF	ATL	3	2
501	07/26/1968	Fri	1		ATL	NL			Grant Jackson	PHI	PHI	9	2
502	08/06/1968	Tue			ATL	NL			Joe Niekro	CHI	ATL	4	0
503	08/21/1968	Wed	2	D	ATL	NL			Rich Nye	CHI	CHI	3	1
504	08/23/1968	Fri			ATL	NL			Rick Wise	PHI	ATL	5	2
505	08/25/1968	Sun			ATL	NL			Larry Jackson	PHI	ATL	4	0
506	08/28/1968	Wed	2		ATL	NL	1B		Jerry Johnson	PHI	PHI	6	0
507	08/29/1968	Thu			ATL	NL			Larry Jackson	PHI	PHI	1	0
508	09/11/1968	Wed			ATL	NL	1B		Juan Marichal	SF	ATL	3	1
509	09/22/1968	Sun			ATL	NL			Bobby Bolin	SF	SF	1	0
510	09/29/1968	Sun			ATL	NL	1B		Bill Singer	LA	ATL	6	1
511	04/12/1969	Sat			ATL	NL			Gary Nolan	CIN	ATL	4	0
512	04/16/1969	Wed			ATL	NL			Denny Lemaster	HOU	HOU	1	1

HR No.	Date	Day	Gm	Nite	Tm	Lg	Pos	Ord	Pitcher	Team	Site	In	On
513	04/28/1969	Mon			ATL	NL			Larry Dierker	HOU	ATL	3	2
514	05/02/1969	Fri			ATL	NL			Claude Osteen	LA	ATL	3	1
515	05/13/1969	Tue		N	ATL	NL	RF	3	Gary Gentry	NY	NY	1	0
516	05/15/1969	Thu		D	ATL	NL	RF	3	Don Cardwell	NY	NY	3	0
517	05/15/1969	Thu		D	ATL	NL	RF	3	Cal Koonce	NY	NY	7	0
518	05/18/1969	Sun			ATL	NL	RF	3	Roy Face	MON	MON	7	0
519	05/22/1969	Thu		N	ATL	NL	RF	3	Tug McGraw	NY	ATL	1	1
520	05/31/1969	Sat		D	ATL	NL			Ferguson Jenkins	CHI	CHI	1	0
521	06/01/1969	Sun		D	ATL	NL			Ken Holtzman	CHI	CHI	5	1
522	06/02/1969	Mon			ATL	NL			Gary Waslewski	STL	STL	8	0
523	06/03/1969	Tue			ATL	NL			Steve Carlton	STL	STL	6	0
524	06/06/1969	Fri			ATL	NL			Dock Ellis	PIT	ATL	4	0
525	06/08/1969	Sun	1		ATL	NL			Chuck Hartenstein	PIT	ATL	8	0
526	06/11/1969	Wed			ATL	NL			Rich Nye	CHI	ATL	5	0
527	06/12/1969	Thu			ATL	NL			Dick Selma	CHI	ATL	8	2
528	06/17/1969	Tue			ATL	NL			Jack Billingham	HOU	ATL	9	0
529	06/25/1969	Wed			ATL	NL			Claude Osteen	LA	ATL	8	0
530	06/27/1969	Fri			ATL	NL			Denny Lemaster	HOU	HOU	5	1
531	06/30/1969	Mon			ATL	NL			Tony Cloninger	CIN	ATL	3	2
532	07/07/1969	Mon			ATL	NL			Alan Foster	LA	LA	3	1
533	07/08/1969	Tue	1		ATL	NL			Claude Osteen	LA	LA	1	0
534	07/15/1969	Tue	1		ATL	NL			Clay Carroll	CIN	CIN	6	0
535	07/24/1969	Thu			ATL	NL	RF	3	Dick Radatz	MON	ATL	7	1
536	07/25/1969	Fri			ATL	NL	RF	3	Howie Reed	MON	ATL	7	0
537	07/30/1969	Wed	1		ATL	NL			Grant Jackson	PHI	PHI	3	0
538	07/31/1969	Thu	1		ATL	NL			Lowell Palmer	PHI	PHI	6	0
539	08/09/1969	Sat		N	ATL	NL	RF	3	Tom Seaver	NY	ATL	3	0
540	08/13/1969	Wed	1		ATL	NL			John Boozer	PHI	ATL	3	1
541	08/13/1969	Wed	1		ATL	NL			John Boozer	PHI	ATL	5	0
542	08/17/1969	Sun			ATL	NL			Steve Carlton	STL	ATL	6	0
543	08/21/1969	Thu		D	ATL	NL			Bill Hands	CHI	CHI	6	0
544	08/24/1969	Sun			ATL	NL			Jim Grant	STL	STL	14	2
545	08/28/1969	Thu			ATL	NL			Steve Blass	PIT	PIT	1	1
546	08/28/1969	Thu			ATL	NL			Bruce Dal Canton	PIT	PIT	7	3
547	08/30/1969	Sat			ATL	NL			Ken Johnson	CHI	ATL	7	0
548	09/05/1969	Fri			ATL	NL			Jim Merritt	CIN	CIN	3	1
549	09/07/1969	Sun			ATL	NL			Dennis Ribant	CIN	CIN	7	0
550	09/10/1969	Wed		N	ATL	NL	RF	3	Ron Bryant	SF	ATL	4	0
551	09/11/1969	Thu		N	ATL	NL	RF	3	Mike McCormick	SF	ATL	4	0
552	09/17/1969	Wed			ATL	NL			Ray Lamb	LA	LA	12	0
553	09/21/1969	Sun			ATL	NL			Tom Dukes	SD	SD	7	2
554	09/26/1969	Fri			ATL	NL			Mike Corkins	SD	ATL	4	0
555	04/09/1970	Thu			ATL	NL			Clay Kirby	SD	SD	1	1
556	04/10/1970	Fri			ATL	NL			Tom Griffin	HOU	HOU	3	3
557	04/13/1970	Mon		N	ATL	NL	RF	3	Frank Reberger	SF	ATL	1	1
558	04/14/1970	Tue		N	ATL	NL	RF	3	Frank Reberger	SF	ATL	3	1
559	04/18/1970	Sat			ATL	NL			Don Sutton	LA	ATL	4	1
560	04/23/1970	Thu		N	ATL	NL	RF	3	Luke Walker	PIT	PIT	5	0
561	04/28/1970	Tue			ATL	NL			Mike Torrez	STL	STL	1	0
562	04/30/1970	Thu			ATL	NL		3	Jim Cosman	CHI	ATL	8	0
563	05/01/1970	Fri			ATL	NL			Joe Decker	CHI	ATL	1	0
564	05/05/1970	Tue		N	ATL	NL	RF	3	Bob Moose	PIT	ATL	2	1
565	05/06/1970	Wed		N	ATL	NL	RF	3	Dock Ellis	PIT	ATL	1	1
566	05/08/1970	Fri			ATL	NL			Bob Gibson	STL	ATL	6	2
567	05/09/1970	Sat			ATL	NL			George Culver	STL	ATL	5	1
568	05/11/1970	Mon		D	ATL	NL			Archie Reynolds	CHI	CHI	10	0
569	05/15/1970	Fri			ATL	NL			Gary Nolan	CIN	CIN	8	1
570	05/17/1970	Sun	2		ATL	NL	RF	3	Wayne Simpson	CIN	CIN	3	1
571	06/02/1970	Tue		N	ATL	NL	RF	3	Gary Gentry	NY	ATL	7	1
572	06/18/1970	Thu			ATL	NL			Steve Renko	MON	MON	5	1
573	06/19/1970	Fri	2		ATL	NL			Denny Lemaster	HOU	ATL	5	1
574	06/20/1970	Sat			ATL	NL			Tom Griffin	HOU	ATL	4	0
575	06/21/1970	Sun			ATL	NL			Larry Dierker	HOU	ATL	1	1
576	06/21/1970	Sun			ATL	NL			Larry Dierker	HOU	ATL	4	1
577	06/30/1970	Tue			ATL	NL			Jim McGlothlin	CIN	CIN	1	1
578	07/03/1970	Fri	2		ATL	NL			Pat Dobson	SD	ATL	2	1
579	07/17/1970	Fri			ATL	NL			Nelson Briles	STL	STL	8	2
580	07/25/1970	Sat		D	ATL	NL			Ferguson Jenkins	CHI	CHI	6	1
581	07/29/1970	Wed			ATL	NL			Mike Torrez	STL	ATL	3	1
582	07/29/1970	Wed			ATL	NL			Frank Linzy	STL	ATL	7	2
583	08/01/1970	Sat			ATL	NL	RF	3	Bruce Dal Canton	PIT	ATL	1	1
584	08/01/1970	Sat			ATL	NL	RF	3	Orlando Pena	PIT	ATL	7	1
585	08/02/1970	Sun		D	ATL	NL	RF	3	Dock Ellis	PIT	ATL	5	2
586	08/07/1970	Fri	1		ATL	NL			Dave Roberts	SD	SD	6	1
587	08/09/1970	Sun			ATL	NL			Pat Dobson	SD	SD	8	0
588	08/12/1970	Wed			ATL	NL			Bill Stoneman	MON	ATL	2	1
589	08/26/1970	Wed		N	ATL	NL	RF	3	Gary Gentry	NY	NY	9	1
590	09/03/1970	Thu			ATL	NL			Alan Foster	LA	ATL	3	2
591	09/05/1970	Sat	2	N	ATL	NL	1B	3	Rich Robertson	SF	ATL	8	1
592	10/01/1970	Thu			ATL	NL			Ray Washburn	CIN	CIN	4	0
593	04/07/1971	Wed			ATL	NL			Jim McGlothlin	CIN	CIN	7	0
594	04/10/1971	Sat		N	ATL	NL	RF	3	Steve Blass	PIT	ATL	9	1
595	04/13/1971	Tue			ATL	NL			Don Gullett	CIN	ATL	6	0
596	04/14/1971	Wed			ATL	NL			Tony Cloninger	CIN	ATL	1	1
597	04/14/1971	Wed			ATL	NL			Tony Cloninger	CIN	ATL	4	0
598	04/20/1971	Tue		N	ATL	NL	RF	3	Bob Moose	PIT	PIT	1	1
599	04/25/1971	Sun	1		ATL	NL			Dave Roberts	SD	ATL	9	0
600	04/27/1971	Tue		N	ATL	NL	RF	3	Gaylord Perry	SF	ATL	3	0
601	05/01/1971	Sat			ATL	NL			Claude Osteen	LA	ATL	1	1
602	05/01/1971	Sat			ATL	NL			Pete Mikkelsen	LA	ATL	8	1
603	05/02/1971	Sun			ATL	NL			Jim Brewer	LA	ATL	8	0
604	05/08/1971	Sat		D	ATL	NL	RF	3	Jerry Johnson	SF	SF	8	2
605	05/18/1971	Tue		N	ATL	NL	RF	3	Jim McAndrew	NY	ATL	1	1
606	05/21/1971	Fri		N	ATL	NL	RF	3	Nolan Ryan	NY	NY	6	0
607	05/27/1971	Thu			ATL	NL			Ernie McAnally	MON	MON	6	0
608	06/01/1971	Tue			ATL	NL			Wade Blasingame	HOU	ATL	1	1
609	06/06/1971	Sun			ATL	NL			Bill Hands	CHI	ATL	9	0
610	06/08/1971	Tue			ATL	NL			Steve Carlton	STL	ATL	1	1
611	06/12/1971	Sat			ATL	NL			Don Wilson	HOU	HOU	3	0
612	06/21/1971	Mon	1		ATL	NL			Claude Raymond	MON	ATL	8	1
613	06/27/1971	Sun			ATL	NL			Gary Nolan	CIN	ATL	7	1
614	06/27/1971	Sun			ATL	NL			Wayne Granger	CIN	ATL	9	1
615	07/04/1971	Sun			ATL	NL			Tom Seaver	NY	NY	4	0
616	07/10/1971	Sat		D	ATL	NL	1B	3	Steve Blass	PIT	PIT	7	0
617	07/17/1971	Sat			ATL	NL			Doyle Alexander	LA	ATL	3	0
618	07/20/1971	Tue			ATL	NL			Dave Roberts	SD	ATL	9	1
619	07/21/1971	Wed			ATL	NL			Steve Arlin	SD	ATL	1	1
620	07/21/1971	Wed			ATL	NL			Steve Arlin	SD	ATL	3	0
621	07/24/1971	Sat			ATL	NL			Claude Osteen	LA	LA	6	0
622	07/31/1971	Sat			ATL	NL			Fred Norman	SD	SD	8	0
623	08/03/1971	Tue			ATL	NL			Chris Short	PHI	PHI	7	0
624	08/15/1971	Sun			ATL	NL			Ken Forsch	HOU	ATL	6	0
625	08/20/1971	Fri			ATL	NL			Reggie Cleveland	STL	ATL	1	0
626	08/21/1971	Sat			ATL	NL			Steve Carlton	STL	ATL	6	1
627	08/21/1971	Sat			ATL	NL			Steve Carlton	STL	ATL	8	2
628	08/23/1971	Mon	1	N	ATL	NL	1B	3	Steve Blass	PIT	ATL	6	0
629	08/24/1971	Tue		N	ATL	NL	1B	3	Bob Veale	PIT	ATL	4	0
630	08/25/1971	Wed		N	ATL	NL	1B	3	Bruce Kison	PIT	ATL	1	1
631	08/29/1971	Sun		D	ATL	NL			Juan Pizarro	CHI	CHI	1	1
632	09/10/1971	Fri		N	ATL	NL	1B	3	Jerry Johnson	SF	ATL	11	2
633	09/11/1971	Sat		N	ATL	NL	1B	3	Don Carrithers	SF	ATL	1	1
634	09/14/1971	Tue			ATL	NL			Don Gullett	CIN	CIN	1	2
635	09/14/1971	Tue			ATL	NL			Don Gullett	CIN	CIN	5	1
636	09/15/1971	Wed			ATL	NL			Jack Billingham	HOU	HOU	5	0
637	09/17/1971	Fri			ATL	NL			Claude Osteen	LA	LA	8	0
638	09/21/1971	Tue			ATL	NL			Jay Franklin	SD	ATL	1	0
639	09/26/1971	Sun			ATL	NL			Claude Osteen	LA	ATL	6	0
640	04/22/1972	Sat			ATL	NL			Don Gullett	CIN	ATL	3	2

HR No.	Date	Day	Gm	Nite	Tm	Lg	Pos	Ord	Pitcher	Team	Site	In	On
641	04/23/1972	Sun			ATL	NL			Jack Billingham	CIN	ATL	8	0
642	04/25/1972	Tue			ATL	NL			Bob Gibson	STL	ATL	2	1
643	04/26/1972	Wed			ATL	NL			Rick Wise	STL	ATL	1	0
644	05/05/1972	Fri			ATL	NL			Bob Gibson	STL	STL	1	1
645	05/06/1972	Sat			ATL	NL			Rick Wise	STL	STL	8	0
646	05/26/1972	Fri			ATL	NL			Juan Marichal	SF	ATL	4	2
647	05/28/1972	Sun	2		ATL	NL			Ron Bryant	SF	ATL	6	0
648	05/31/1972	Wed			ATL	NL			Fred Norman	SD	ATL	1	0
649	06/10/1972	Sat			ATL	NL	1B		Wayne Twitchell	PHI	PHI	6	3
650	06/13/1972	Tue		N	ATL	NL	1B	3	Danny Frisella	NY	ATL	10	0
651	06/14/1972	Wed		N	ATL	NL	1B	3	Jon Matlack	NY	ATL	4	0
652	06/24/1972		2	N	ATL	NL	RF	3	Jim Brewer	LA	LA	8	0
653	06/28/1972	Wed	1		ATL	NL			Mike Corkins	SD	SD	9	1
654	06/29/1972	Thu			ATL	NL			Mike Caldwell	SD	SD	8	0
655	07/02/1972	Sun			ATL	NL			Dave Roberts	HOU	HOU	1	1
656	07/03/1972	Mon			ATL	NL			Jim York	HOU	HOU	7	2
657	07/09/1972	Sun	D		ATL	NL	1B	3	Nelson Briles	PIT	ATL	4	0
658	07/11/1972	Tue			ATL	NL			Al Santorini	STL	STL	7	2
659	07/19/1972	Wed		N	ATL	NL	1B	3	Nelson Briles	PIT	PIT	1	0
660	08/06/1972	Sun			ATL	NL			Wayne Simpson	CIN	CIN	4	0
661	08/06/1972	Sun			ATL	NL			Don Gullett	CIN	CIN	10	0
662	08/09/1972	Wed			ATL	NL			Jerry Reuss	HOU	ATL	1	1
663	08/13/1972	Sun			ATL	NL			Tom Hall	CIN	ATL	3	1
664	08/16/1972	Wed		N	ATL	NL	1B	3	Gary Gentry	NY	NY	8	0
665	08/29/1972	Tue			ATL	NL			Balor Moore	MON	ATL	5	0
666	09/02/1972	Sat	1		ATL	NL			Bucky Brandon	PHI	ATL	1	1
667	09/02/1972	Sat	1		ATL	NL			Guerrand Scarce	PHI	ATL	7	0
668	09/13/1972	Wed			ATL	NL			Tom Hall	CIN	ATL	7	0
669	09/13/1972	Wed			ATL	NL			Tom Hall	CIN	ATL	9	0
670	09/17/1972	Sun			ATL	NL			Ron Bryant	SF	ATL	3	1
671	09/26/1972	Tue			ATL	NL			Don Gullett	CIN	CIN	1	0
672	09/27/1972	Wed			ATL	NL			Ross Grimsley	CIN	CIN	1	0
673	10/03/1972	Tue		N	ATL		1B	3	Don Sutton	LA	ATL	9	1
674	04/11/1973	Wed			ATL	NL	RF	3	Rich Troedson	SD	SD	6	2
675	04/12/1973	Thu			ATL	NL	RF	3	Fred Norman	SD	SD	6	0
676	04/15/1973	Sun			ATL	NL	RF	3	Al Downing	LA	LA	9	0
677	04/20/1973	Fri		N	ATL	NL	RF	4	Don Gullett	CIN	CIN	3	1
678	04/27/1973	Fri		N	ATL	NL	RF	3	Tom Seaver	NY	ATL	4	0
679	05/01/1973	Tue			ATL	NL	RF	2	Balor Moore	MON	ATL	3	1
680	05/01/1973	Tue			ATL	NL	RF	2	John Strohmayer	MON	ATL	7	0
681	05/05/1973	Sat		N	ATL	NL	LF	3	Steve Carlton	PHI	PHI	1	0
682	05/13/1973	Sun	1		ATL	NL	PH		Bill Greif	SD	ATL	9	1
683	05/13/1973	Sun	2		ATL	NL	LF	4	Fred Norman	SD	ATL	3	0
684	05/16/1973	Wed			ATL	NL	LF	4	Jerry Reuss	HOU	HOU	6	0
685	05/22/1973	Tue		N	ATL	NL	LF	4	Juan Marichal	SF	ATL	6	0
686	05/27/1973	Sun	D		ATL	NL	LF	4	Reggie Cleveland	STL	STL	1	1
687	06/09/1973	Sat			ATL	NL	LF	4	Scipio Spinks	STL	ATL	3	0
688	06/09/1973	Sat			ATL	NL	LF	4	John Andrews	STL	ATL	5	0
689	06/11/1973	Mon		N	ATL	NL	LF	4	Jim Rooker	PIT	ATL	4	2
690	06/15/1973	Fri		N	ATL	NL	LF	4	Bill Bonham	CHI	ATL	4	0
691	06/16/1973	Sat		N	ATL	NL	LF	4	Rick Reuschel	CHI	ATL	6	0
692	06/22/1973	Fri			ATL	NL	LF	4	Randy Jones	SD	SD	2	0
693	06/29/1973	Fri			ATL	NL	LF	3	Al Downing	LA	ATL	6	1
694	07/02/1973	Mon		N	ATL	NL	LF	4	Jim Barr	SF	ATL	6	1
695	07/08/1973	Sun	D		ATL	NL	LF	4	George Stone	NY	NY	4	0
696	07/08/1973	Sun	D		ATL	NL	LF	4	George Stone	NY	NY	6	1
697	07/13/1973	Fri	1		ATL	NL	LF		Bill Stoneman	MON	ATL	5	2
698	07/17/1973	Tue		N	ATL	NL	LF	4	Tug McGraw	NY	ATL	6	0
699	07/20/1973	Fri		N	ATL	NL	LF	4	Wayne Twitchell	PHI	ATL	7	2
700	07/21/1973	Sat		D	ATL	NL	LF	4	Ken Brett	PHI	ATL	3	1
701	07/31/1973	Tue	1	N	ATL	NL	LF	4	Pedro Borbon	CIN	ATL	9	0
702	08/16/1973	Thu		D	ATL	NL	LF	4	Jack Aker	CHI	CHI	8	2
703	08/17/1973	Fri			ATL	NL	LF		Steve Renko	MON	MON	6	0
704	08/18/1973	Sat			ATL	NL	LF	4	Steve Rogers	MON	MON	8	0
705	08/22/1973	Wed			ATL	NL	LF	4	Reggie Cleveland	STL	ATL	6	0
706	08/28/1973	Tue			ATL	NL	LF	4	Milt Pappas	CHI	ATL	1	2
707	09/03/1973	Mon			ATL	NL	LF	4	Clay Kirby	SD	SD	3	1
708	09/03/1973	Mon			ATL	NL	LF	4	Vicente Romo	SD	SD	5	0
709	09/08/1973	Sat			ATL	NL	LF	4	Jack Billingham	CIN	ATL	7	0
710	09/10/1973	Mon		N	ATL	NL	LF	4	Don Carrithers	SF	ATL	3	1
711	09/17/1973	Mon			ATL	NL	LF	4	Gary Ross	SD	ATL	8	0
712	09/22/1973	Sat			ATL	NL	LF	4	Dave Roberts	HOU	HOU	6	2
713	09/29/1973	Sat			ATL	NL	LF	4	Jerry Reuss	HOU	ATL	5	2
714	04/04/1974	Thu			ATL	NL	LF	4	Jack Billingham	CIN	CIN	1	2
715	04/08/1974	Mon		N	ATL	NL	LF	4	Al Downing	LA	ATL	4	1
716	04/11/1974	Thu		N	ATL	NL	LF	4	Charlie Hough	LA	ATL	7	0
717	04/21/1974	Sun			ATL	NL	LF	4	Tom Griffin	HOU	HOU	7	1
718	04/25/1974	Thu		N	ATL	NL	LF	4	Jerry Reuss	PIT	ATL	7	1
719	04/26/1974	Fri		N	ATL	NL	LF	4	Ray Burris	CHI	ATL	7	3
720	04/30/1974	Tue		N	ATL	NL	LF	4	Lynn McGlothen	STL	STL	7	0
721	05/12/1974	Sun	1	D	ATL	NL	LF	4	Charlie Williams	SF	ATL	7	0
722	05/28/1974	Tue		N	ATL	NL	LF	4	Jim Lonborg	PHI	ATL	10	0
723	06/04/1974	Tue		N	ATL	NL	LF	4	Eddie Watt	PHI	PHI	7	3
724	06/14/1974	Fri		N	ATL	NL	LF	4	Bob Gibson	STL	ATL	2	0
725	07/07/1974	Sun	D		ATL	NL	LF		Rick Reuschel	CHI	CHI	4	0
726	07/27/1974	Sat		N	ATL	NL	LF	4	Rex Hudson	LA	ATL	7	2
727	08/06/1974	Tue		N	ATL	NL	LF	4	Bill Greif	SD	SD	3	2
728	08/06/1974	Tue		N	ATL	NL	LF	4	Bill Greif	SD	SD	6	0
729	08/14/1974	Wed		N	ATL	NL	LF	4	Chuck Taylor	MON	ATL	7	1
730	08/19/1974	Mon		N	ATL	NL	LF	4	Claude Osteen	STL	ATL	3	1
731	09/14/1974	Sat		N	ATL	NL	LF	1	Dave Freisleben	SD	SD	5	0
732	09/18/1974	Wed		D	ATL	NL	LF	4	John Montefusco	SF	SF	2	0
733	10/02/1974	Wed		D	ATL	NL	LF	4	Rawly Eastwick	CIN	ATL	7	0
734	04/18/1975	Fri		D	MIL	AL	DH	3	Gaylord Perry	CLE	CLE	6	0
735	04/26/1975	Sat		D	MIL	AL	DH	5	Pat Dobson	NY	NY	7	0
736	05/09/1975	Fri			MIL	AL	DH	5	Al Fitzmorris	KC	KC	7	0
737	05/15/1975	Thu		N	MIL	AL	DH	5	Steve Hargan	TEX	TEX	5	2
738	05/17/1975	Sat			MIL	AL	DH	5	Ray Corbin	MIN	MIN	5	1
739	06/12/1975	Thu			MIL	AL	DH	4	Vida Blue	OAK	MIL	5	0
740	06/14/1975	Sat		D	MIL	AL	DH	4	Nolan Ryan	CAL	MIL	3	0
741	07/03/1975	Thu		N	MIL	AL	DH	4	Rogelio Moret	BOS	MIL	4	0
742	07/05/1975	Sat			MIL	AL	DH		Vern Ruhle	DET	DET	4	0
743	07/24/1975	Thu		N	MIL	AL	DH	4	Dyar Miller	BAL	MIL	9	0
744	08/11/1975	Mon			MIL	AL	DH	4	Tom Johnson	MIN	MIN	3	0
745	09/14/1975	Sun			MIL	AL	DH		Bill Lee	BOS	BOS	4	0
746	05/04/1976	Tue		N	MIL	AL	DH	4	Nelson Briles	TEX	MIL	4	0
747	05/19/1976	Wed		N	MIL	AL	DH	4	Mike Cuellar	BAL	BAL	6	0
748	06/14/1976	Mon		D	MIL	AL	DH	4	Frank Tanana	CAL	MIL	3	2
749	06/16/1976	Wed		N	MIL	AL	DH	4	Paul Hartzell	CAL	CAL	9	1
750	06/18/1976	Fri			MIL	AL	DH	4	Jim Todd	OAK	OAK	9	0
751	06/19/1976	Sat			MIL	AL	DH	4	Glenn Abbott	OAK	OAK	6	0
752	06/22/1976	Tue			MIL	AL	DH	5	Dave Roberts	DET	MIL	4	0
753	07/09/1976	Fri		N	MIL	AL	DH	4	Jim Umbarger	TEX	MIL	2	0
754	07/11/1976	Sun	2	D	MIL	AL	DH	4	Steve Foucault	TEX	MIL	10	0
755	07/20/1976	Tue		N	MIL	AL	DH	4	Dick Drago	CAL	MIL	7	0

Billye Aaron, who married Hank in November 1973, is involved in The Hank Aaron Chasing the Dream Foundation.

Kareem Abdul-Jabbar is the all-time leading scorer in NBA history with 38,387 points and holds the record with six MVPs. He recently wrote *Black Profiles in Courage.*

Brady Anderson, a Baltimore outfielder, became the 14th player to hit 50 homers in a season when he turned the trick in 1996.

Dusty Baker, the manger of the San Francisco Giants, was Aaron's teammate from 1968 through 1974.

Ernie Banks still possesses a sunny disposition. He is one of 15 members of the 500-home run club, hitting 512 in his 19 years with the Cubs.

Bill Bartholomay is Chairman of the Board for the Atlanta Braves.

Frank Belatti is the Chairman and CEO of AFC Enterprises in Atlanta.

Albert Belle hit 50 homers in 1995 and had the highest slugging average in the American League in 1998 (.655). He just signed with the Baltimore Orioles.

Johnny Bench has been a member of Baseball's Hall of Fame since 1989. He is a co-host on the Reds Radio Network. As a golfer, he also participates in the Celebrity Players Tours.

Sy Berger is the Senior Advisor to The Topps Company, Inc.

Yogi Berra, a mainstay of the New York Yankees dynasty of the 1950s, played in 13 World Series and on the winning team 10 times (both are records). The Yogi Berra Museum recently opened on the campus of Montclair State College in Little Falls, New Jersey.

Bobby Bonds, one of the great all-around players a generation ago, hit 30 homers and stole 30 bases in the same season five times.

Bobby Bragan played seven seasons for the Phillies and Dodgers in the 1940s and managed the Braves in 1966, their first year in Atlanta.

Tom Brokaw, the anchor for NBC News, traveled with and interviewed Hank in August 1973, when he had just passed 700 home runs. His recent bestseller is *The Greatest Generation.*

Dr. Gene Budig is the President of the American League.

Lew Burdette, a teammate of Hank's from 1954 to 1963, was the Braves' ace in the 1957 World Series, winning three games and walking off with MVP honors.

President Jimmy Carter, the 39th president of the United States, recently wrote the book, *The Virtues of Aging.* One of the Carter Center humanitarian programs involves taking underprivileged children on ski outings. For the last four years Hank and Billye Aaron have accompanied Roslyn Carter and the former president on this outing.

Dick Cecil runs Dick Cecil Associates, a consulting firm in Atlanta.

Orlando Cepada came to the Braves in 1969, after 11 years with the Giants and Cardinals, including an MVP season in 1967. He teamed with Aaron until 1972.

Roberto Clemente Jr. is the son of the late Pittsburgh Hall of Fame outfielder. He works as a broadcaster with MSG, which covers the New York Yankees.

Leonard Coleman is the President of the National League.

Bob Costas, NBC's play-by-play man, was a student at Syracuse University in 1974 when Hank hit home run number 715. He and others at WSYR signed a telegram to Hank.

Bobby Cox is the manager of the Atlanta Braves.

Billy Crystal wished to be described simply as "a baseball fan."

Al Downing enjoyed a 17-year career, which included leading the league in strikeouts as a Yankee and shutouts for the Dodgers. He surrendered Hank Aaron's 715th home run. After working as a broadcaster for many years with CBS Radio Network, he is now looking for broadcast work.

Chris Evert, a tennis analyst for NBC, won 18 Grand Slam events in her career.

Cecil Fielder hit 51 homers in 1990 and passed 300 home runs in 1997.

Whitey Ford owns the highest winning percentage (.690) of any 200-game winner in baseball history. He pitched against Hank in both the 1957 and 1958 World Series.

George Foster became the first player in 12 years to hit 50 homers when he clubbed 52 in 1977.

Peter Gammons is the chief baseball analyst for ESPN.

Bob Gibson, a member of Baseball's Hall of Fame since 1981, won seven games in the three World Series in which he appeared.

Barry Halper amassed the world's largest collection of baseball memorabilia and remains a passionate student of the game.

Reverend Jesse Jackson is the host of CNN's Both Sides with Jesse Jackson.

Reggie Jackson's 563 home runs rank sixth best on the all-time list. Known as "Mr. October," he played on six pennant winners and five World Series winners for the Oakland A's and New York Yankees.

Ferguson Jenkins won 284 games, including 20 or more six years in a row, for the Chicago Cubs and other teams. He was inducted into the Hall of Fame in 1991.

Davey Johnson, Dodgers manager, played two years with Aaron, including the 1973 season when Johnson, Darrell Evans and Aaron became the first trio in baseball history to hit forty home runs for the same team.

Tom Johnson is the Chairman and CEO of CNN.

Stan Kasten is the President of the Atlanta Braves.

Joe Kennedy is the Milwaukee Chairman of The Hank Aaron Chasing the Dream Foundation.

Harmon Killebrew hit 573 home runs, putting him in fifth place on the all-time list. Killebrew assists Hank with the World Children's Fair in Japan, which brings children of the world together by teaching them baseball.

Ralph Kiner, a Hall of Famer since 1975, led the National League in home runs for seven consecutive years, from 1946 through 1952.

Clyde King was a pitcher for the Brooklyn Dodgers in the 1940s. A long-time pitching coach, he managed the Braves for part of the 1974 season.

Tony Kubek, a Rookie of the Year with the Yankees in 1957, was working the game for NBC in which Hank Aaron hit his 715th home run.

Spike Lee is involved with Hank Aaron in several public service roles. His most recent film was *He Got Game.*

Don Marr served for many years as president of the National Baseball Hall of Fame.

Eddie Mathews hit 512 home runs and was elected to the Hall of Fame in 1978. Teaming with Hank Aaron from 1954 through 1966, the pair hit a record 863 homers together.

Willie Mays finished with 660 home runs. He was inducted into the Hall of Fame in 1979.

Tim McCarver played against Hank for 17 years, from 1959 to 1975. He is now a baseball analyst for Fox.

Willie McCovey clubbed 521 home runs. He won MVP honors in 1969. Like Aaron, "Stretch" grew up in Mobile, Alabama.

Mark McGwire owns the all-time record for home runs in a season with 70 and home runs per at bat with one every 11.23 at bats. His 180 homers in the past three seasons is the best such run in baseball history.

Zell Miller is the former governor of Georgia and now a teacher at Young Harris College in Georgia.

Minnie Minoso has been called "the Cuban Jackie Robinson" for being the first Hispanic of color to be a force in the big leagues. He batted over .300 eight times.

Joe Morgan was a two-time MVP with the Cincinnati Reds and was elected to the Hall of Fame in 1990. He is a baseball analyst for ESPN and NBC.

Phil Niekro won 318 games, which ranks him 14th all-time. He was elected to the Hall of Fame in 1997.

Sadaharu Oh, who works with Hank for the World Baseball Fair, is the international home run champion with 868.

Keith Olbermann is an anchor at Fox Sports News.

Buck O'Neil was first baseman and manager of the Kansas City Monarchs dynasty. He later became Major League Baseball's first African-American coach.

Jim Palmer won 20 games eight times in a nine-year period. He was also the youngest pitcher ever to win a World Series game and played on two World Champion teams with the Baltimore Orioles.

Gaylord Perry was elected to the Hall of Fame in 1991. A five-time twenty-game winner, Perry won 314 games in 22 seasons.

Charlie Pride, a recording artist, was a pitcher and outfielder with the Memphis Red Sox of the Negro Leagues.

Cal Ripken Jr. broke Lou Gehrig's record of 2,130 games on September 6, 1995. He ended his streak in 1998 after 2,632 straight games. A two-time MVP, he is the only shortstop in Major League history to have more than 2,800 hits, 350 home runs and 1,500 RBI.

Bill Rigney was an infielder for eight years with the New York Giants and later managed five different teams over 18 seasons.

Leonard Roberts is the president and CEO of Tandy Corp and Radio Shack.

Frank Robinson hit 586 home runs, fourth place on the all-time list, a position he has occupied for 23 years. In 1975 he became Major League Baseball's first black manager.

Rachel Robinson is the founder of the Jackie Robinson Foundation in New York. She is the widow of Jackie Robinson, who integrated baseball in 1947.

Nolan Ryan is the game's all-time strikeout leader with 5,714 and was elected to the Baseball Hall of Fame in 1999.

John Schuerholz is the general manager of the Atlanta Braves.

Mike Schmidt hit 548 home runs, more than any third baseman in the game's history. Eight times he led the National League in home runs. He also won three MVPs and ten Gold Gloves.

Bud Selig is the Commissioner of Major League Baseball.

Paul Snyder is the director of scouting and player development for the Atlanta Braves.

Warren Spahn won more games, 363, than any left-handed pitcher in baseball history. He was Hank's teammate for 11 years in Milwaukee.

Willie Stargell, elected to the Hall of Fame in 1988, hit 475 home runs. He led the 1979 Pirates to a World Championship.

Michael Tollin wrote, directed and produced *Chasing the Dream,* the 1995 documentary about Hank's life.

Joe Torre has managed the Yankees to two world championships. He was Hank's teammate from his rookie season in 1960 through 1968. Torre won the National League batting title with a .363 average in 1971.

Ted Turner is vice chairman of Time Warner, Inc. Turner Broadcasting co-produced *Chasing the Dream.*

Denzel Washington was executive producer for the documentary *Chasing the Dream.* His latest film is *Lazarus and the Hurricane.*

George F. Will is a *Washington Post* syndicated columnist, contributing editor for *Newsweek* and news analyst for ABC News. Will has written two baseball books, *Men at Work* and *Bunts,* and contributed to Ken Burns's PBS documentary, *Baseball.*

Billy Williams hails from Whistler, Alabama, close to Mobile where Hank grew up. He was as regular as the ivy at Wrigley Field, playing in 1,117 consecutive games for the Cubs. He was elected to the Hall of Fame in 1987.

Ted Williams is baseball's last .400 hitter, batting .406 in 1941. His .634 slugging average is second only to Babe Ruth's .690. He now presides over The Ted Williams Museum and Hitter's Hall of Fame in Hernando, Florida.

Andrew Young is the former mayor of Atlanta and currently chairman of GoodWorks International in Atlanta.

Hank Aaron Collection: pp. 21, 28–29, 31, 36, 50–51, 71, 74–75, 119, 131, 137, 140, 142, 143, 157, 158 (2), 159, 161, 163 (2), 165, 171, 172 (2), 174, 177, 178

Hank Aaron: vii (Carl Davaz), 22 (Bob Johnson), 88–89 (Bob Johnson), 109 (Bob Davidoff Studios), 112 (Bob Johnson), 114 (Ray Boeh), 121 (Ken Regan), 127 (Perry Riddle, *Chicago Daily News*), 147 (Blue Light Studios #2), 152 (Bud Skinner), 155 (Ken Regan), 159 (*News Sentinel*), 162 (Jerome Liebling), 166 (*News Sentinel*), 166–167 (*News Sentinel*), 176 (Phyllis B. Kandul), 179 (*News Sentinel*), 198 (Roy O'Brien), 207 (Carl Davaz)

Associated Press/Wide World: front end paper, back end paper, pp. i, vi, vii, x, 8, 42, 61, 62, 64, 67, 71, 77, 82, 87, 101, 105, 106–107, 123, 128, 130, 132–133, 138, 141, 148, 149, 160, 165, 169, 180–181, 182, 184, 201, 205, 208

Courtesy of the Atlanta Historical Society: p. 113

David Chasey Photography: p. iv

Corbis/Bettman/UPI: pp. ii–iii, 7, 11, 26–27, 41, 54, 56, 58, 60, 63, 92, 116–117, 122, 123, 125, 130, 141, 145, 150–151, 161, 168, 169, 183, 219

Detroit Tigers: p. 68

Stephen Green: pp. vii, 25, 53, 77, 118, 120, 146

Courtesy of Andy Jurinko: pp. 95, 153

Mark Kaufman/*Sports Illustrated*: p.154

Niels Lauritzen/*Sport Magazine*: p. 65

Neil Leifer/*Sports Illustrated*: p. 120

Minnesota Historical Society: p. 64 (2)

National Baseball Library: pp. vi, 7, 18, 35, 37, 38–39, 40 (2), 43, 52, 55 (3), 66, 72, 73, 79, 80, 85, 86, 102, 103, 115, 124, 135, 139, 142, 144, 156, 162, 165, 170, 173, 177, 189, 191, 193, 204, 221

National Baseball Library: vii (Louise Wilson), 43 (*Mansfield News Journal*), 96 (*Louise Wilson*)

Noirtech Research/Larry Lester: p. 162

Perez-Steele Galleries: pp. 24, 57, 94

Photo File: pp. vi–vii, 1, 12, 36, 48, 56, 57, 70, 83, 96, 144, 128, 218

Herb Scharfman/*Sports Illustrated*: pp. vi, 65, 108

Steven Schwab: p. 15

Don Sparks/*Sport Magazine*: p. 34

Brian Spurlock: pp. 14, 17, 170

David Sutton: p. 68

Topps: (All images are courtesy of Transcendental Graphics unless otherwise noted.) pp. v, 4 (courtesy of Weston Minissali), 5, 6 (courtesy of Ken Shouler), 11, 15, 23, 31, 46, 52, 61, 76, 84 (courtesy of Weston Minissali), 90, 110, 149, 155, 156, 160, 162, 169, 179, 184, 186, 187, 188 (2) (courtesy of Mark Thorn), 189 (courtesy of Weston Minissali), 190 (courtesy of Weston Minissali), 190, 191, 193, 194, 199, 200, 201, 202, 203, 217

John Thorn: pp. 13, 19, 40, 69 (Ron Lewis), 95, 137, 195

Transcendental Graphics: pp. vi, vii, viii, 2–3, 5, 22, 30, 33, 43, 44 (2), 45, 46 (2), 47, 48 (2), 49, 55, 56, 58, 58–59, 59, 60, 72, 78, 81 (2), 84, 91, 92, 93, 97, 98–99, 100, 104, 105, 111, 112, 124, 126 (2), 127 (2), 129 (2), 134, 136, 138, 160, 164, 175, 185, 187, 191, 195, 197 (2), 200, 204, 211, 220

Courtesy of Donald Wagner: p. 114